MEDITERRANEAN GARDENING

MEDITERRANEAN GARDENING
A Practical Handbook

Yve Menzies

JOHN MURRAY

Text © Yve Menzies 1991
Line drawings © Maggie Redfern 1991

First published in 1991
by John Murray (Publishers) Ltd
50 Albemarle Street, London W1X 4BD

British Library Cataloguing in Publication Data

Menzies, Y. M. (Yvonne Marie)
   Mediterranean gardening.
   1. Mediterranean region. Gardening
   I. Title
   635.091822

ISBN 0-7195-4798-9

Photoset by Rowland Phototypesetting Ltd
Bury St Edmunds, Suffolk

Printed in Great Britain at
The University Press, Cambridge

Contents

Acknowledgements

I owe an immense debt of gratitude to many more people than I can hope to mention for their help, advice and encouragement in writing this book, not least to my husband who did a great deal of the gardening I would normally do myself had I not decided to write about it instead. Whilst I enjoy gardening he does not, so it was doubly noble of him to take on such a task.

I am most grateful to Dr Kaufmann of Ciba-Geigy in Basle for arranging Italian and Spanish translations of the many pests and diseases of a Mediterranean garden and for explaining, in impeccable English, the various generic pesticides and fungicides, and their uses.

My thanks are due to Pamela Carson Ortega, who not only grows eating and oil olives but also runs an olive hybridization programme, for her explanation of the various types of olives and their different uses.

Lastly I would like to thank my editor, Patrick Taylor, who guided me through this book with great kindness, patience and good humour.

Introduction

It is to the German geographer, Theobald Fischer, that we owe the modern concept of a Mediterranean region. Northern Europeans tend to visualize it as a warm, sunny paradise of olive groves, vineyards and orange-tree lined streets. Bougainvillea, an introduction from Brazil, romping over expensive seaside villas of dubious architectural merit is one of the first visions brought to mind. Moreover, this landscape seems to have become petrified in season and is nearly always seen by dreamers in late April or early May when the Mediterranean flora is at its best. Occasionally in this dreamy vision late September or early October get a turn, for the *vendange*, but much less often.

There is such a diversity of climate in the Mediterranean Basin due to the various mountain ranges which have a significant effect on the rainfall and, therefore, on the flora. The most dramatic example of this is in the Adriatic where the effect of the Dinaric Alps and Black Mountains produces the highest rainfall in Europe!

The Garden Centre, the horticultural equivalent of the clothing industry's ready to wear, is springing up all over Europe and container-grown plants, often in flower, have encouraged many first-time gardeners to try something a little more adventurous than scarlet geraniums, *Senecio bicolor* or Dusty Miller and trailing lobelia. The main problem is that often these Garden Centres stock only the most popular and easiest plants and shrubs and compared with many British and American nurseries their lists are small and unimaginative. A large Garden Centre on the Italian Riviera *boasts* that it has over eighty items on sale! As this number includes fruit trees, roses and flowering shrubs, the more common annuals and a few hardy perennials, it can be seen that the choice is not great.

I

Mediterranean Gardening

The rich have always had gardens but a national interest in gardening is a sign of a long and well-established middle class. Thus France has more amateur gardeners than Spain and Spain more than Italy. The more orientated towards agriculture a country is the less pleasure gardens there are. Few people working on the land all day have any inclination to till the soil in their spare time except to provide food for the family. Much of the Mediterranean population lives in flats but the acquisition of weekend and holiday properties is on the increase and although these gardens must, of necessity, be simple and easy to maintain they can, and frequently are, planned with great care and imagination.

The diversity of climate throughout the Mediterranean Basin, particularly regarding rainfall, means that certain plants will grow well in one part and not thrive at all in another. Those who are lucky enough to have the choice should be careful where they buy a house. For instance, if you really detest wind, even for a few days a year, do not choose to have a house on the coast between the Toulon/Marseilles region to about Barcelona. The *mistral* or the *tramontana* wind can blow for up to one third of the year. The whole of western Greece, whilst having just as much sunshine as elsewhere in the country, has up to 1m/40in of rain annually, some of it falling in summer, and rarely has drought problems, whilst both eastern Greece and the Aegean islands can have very serious water problems. The northern islands of the Aegean are very subject to wind; cold in winter from the continental landmass to the north and the hot *livas* in summer which blows from Thessaly. On top of all this there is a constant drought problem. From this it will be seen that, from a gardening point of view, it is infinitely preferable to have a house on the island of Zanthe (Zakinthos) than on Skiathos or Limnos. Indeed, it can be said that any Ionian island is better for the gardener than one in the Aegean.

In both Spain and southern Italy water, or rather lack of it, is the main problem. There is a water shortage in northern Italy also but this is largely due to poor organisation of resources rather than anything else. On the eve of the twenty-first century the sixteenth-century water cart is still far too common a sight in Spain and her Balearic Islands. Gardeners new to Andalusia or with new properties, will not have, and never will have, access to the various water sources available to farmers and fruit growers since Moorish times. Things are better on the Costa Brava down to Valencia since, from an agricultural point of view, this is probably the most highly evolved area of Spain. As one journeys farther south towards Murcia and the

2

southern coast things get worse and worse. It is easy to understand why gardening with pots is so popular in this part of the world.

It is often said that Italian gardens are unimaginative and indeed, from a botanical point of view, they usually are but they are marvellously functional when one considers the climate, particularly that of central and southern Italy. Shade in the Mediterranean is at a premium. A typical Italian garden is made up of clipped hedges, formal walks and much – good, bad or indifferent – statuary. Statues are as expensive in Italy as anywhere else so base copies in fibro-cement are common. These are the garden gnomes of Italy and it is quite difficult to persuade an Italian that a garden does not need them. Worse still, the Italian garden is often on terraced or on very hilly land and such terrain demands skilful garden design to achieve anything other than serried rows of mixed shrubs and borders. Large stretches of open, flattish land are comparatively rare in Italy except on the Po Plain and in the Veneto and where they do occur someone, other than a gardener, has usually planted a vineyard or worse a factory or bottling plant right in the middle. Tuscany is full of this sort of thing.

The mark of the property developer on the Mediterranean part of France becomes more and more apparent as the years go by, particularly in the Alpes-Maritimes where *lotissements* or housing estates have become very common due to rocketting land prices. Until the 1860s Nice and the land to the east belonged to Italy and there are still Italianate gardens to be seen in and around Nice. However, so called exotic or Mexican gardens appear to be the current fashion since they require next to no upkeep, deter intruders (both animal and human) and demand no change of soil. Many succulents and cacti will grow in builders' rubble which is good news for a property developer.

However, in spite of the foregoing, France is still the richest country in the Mediterranean as far as gardens and gardening are concerned. It is often thought that foreigners (particularly British) are mainly responsible for the best gardens on the Côte d'Azur but this is simply not so. The French have a long gardening tradition and for every famous foreign garden there are at least two, if not more, equally famous French gardens on the coast. The gardens made by the Vicomte de Noailles in this region; the garden in Cannes made by Marino Vagliano which now belongs to a lucky block of flats; and Gustave Thuret's Botanical Garden in Antibes, are typical examples of the French flair for planting and designing gardens.

Not to be forgotten are the false *bastides* of the Marseilles bourgeoisie built during the nineteenth century in the surrounding countryside.

Originally it was a movement against northern ideas about gardening. Even today, books on gardening tend to use Paris as a yardstick which is dangerous in a country with as many climates as France and many of the plants on sale throughout Provence and the Côte d'Azur have been raised north of the River Loire. Later, French administrators and merchants returning from Indo-China, Central Africa, Algeria, Morocco or the Antilles started to build their own *bastides* which, with the introduction of both cold and heated greenhouses took on the aspect of a private botanical garden. The Parc Borély in Marseilles itself is one such example. The exotic garden of the nineteenth century was infinitely more interesting than today's counterpart on the Côte d'Azur though, of course, considerably more expensive to create and maintain.

Finally those forced to garden in the south Mediterranean should not lose heart since it quite possible to make an acceptable garden in desert conditions and the chapter on drought resistant plants is written with just such gardeners in mind.

It will be seen that there are some plants included in this book which originate from the Cape Province of South Africa which enjoys a similar climate to the northern Mediterranean as well as from Australia and New Zealand. Most of the Australian plants mentioned stand up well to drought. A very few plants from South America are included, either because they are so beautiful they are worth the extra trouble needed to grow them successfully or because they are already well established in the region – jacaranda and bougainvillea being two which immediately spring to mind.

Plants from all these places are readily obtainable in many areas of the region and certainly in England from specialist growers. With the coming of 1992 and the opening of the E.E.C. frontiers the possibility of importing plants and trees from elsewhere should be easier. In principle, we should be able to bring plants from Madeira (as part of E.E.C. Portugal) to France or Greece and purchase unusual plants in London for use in Italian gardens. However, a mere two years before this magic date Italy still forbids the importation of oranges and bananas, as fruit, on the grounds of possible insect infestation and each E.E.C. country demands a phyto-sanitary certificate for virtually everything except seeds.

Obviously there will always be certain shrubs and trees which will be denied passage across frontiers, such as prunus, pyracantha, cotoneaster and certain members of the rose family which are all subject to fire blight. No importations will be allowed from any

4

country, E.E.C. or not, where San Jose Scale is known to exist and it is wise to ask the Customs in your country of residence for a list of forbidden plants before embarking on expensive purchases abroad.

In any event, unless you are really in the back of beyond, it is often surprising what a local nurseryman, when asked, can produce as a result of enquiring through the trade. What is available from a Florentine nursery selling to a discerning clientele has probably never been heard of in Amalfi but that does not mean you cannot track it down and grow it. The same goes for Spain – Barcelona is far more interesting, horticulturally, than Marbella.

1

Geography and Climate

The Mediterranean is an inter-continental sea, washing the shores of Europe, Asia and Africa. It stretches from Longitude 5°W to 30°E and from Latitude 46°N to 31°N. Its maximum width from the Straits of Gibraltar to Iskerdun in Turkey is over 3680km/2300m and from Trieste to Marsa Susa in Libya is about 1450km/900m.

The sea is scarcely tidal even at its western end and therein lies one of its greatest problems. The western Mediterranean including much of the Adriatic Sea, is terribly polluted and assuming no more pollution occurs, which is unthinkable, it will still take over eighty years to cleanse the sea of its accumulated filth. The salinity, which increases as one travels eastwards, is high at around 37–38%, and perhaps this is a help in keeping it from smelling really foul most of the time. It certainly accounts for the sea looking clearer and cleaner in the Greek Islands and around Turkey than it does in the south of France in spite of the fact that France is much more pollution conscious than Greece or Turkey.

The area is one of immense topographical variety – mountains, deserts, deeply indented coastlines – and there are as a result many different climates. Also the eastern basin of the Mediterranean is further south in latitude than the western and is, therefore, even more subject to climatic variations.

It is interesting to note that almost all the areas which enjoy the so-called classic Mediterranean climate appear to have a land configuration of nearby mountains and deserts. In Chile there are the Andes and the nearby Atacama Desert; in the Cape Province of South Africa there is the Great Escarpment made up of several smaller ranges of mountains and the Great Karoo desert; in California the northern

7

and southern Sierras and the Mojave Desert; and in Western Australia the Darling Range and the desert-like outback. In the true Mediterranean the important deserts are the Sahara, the Libyan, the Syrian and the desert-like Anatolian plateau.

It is important not to confuse weather and climate. Weather is made up of meteorological differences from day to day whereas climate is a record of weather over a given period (usually of years). Climate is also often applied to a region in relation to its prevailing weather pattern whence the portmanteau term Mediterranean climate. This particular climate is loosely defined as having frost free winters, warm springs when much of the vegetation of the area is at its peak, long hot summers with as much as twelve hours sunshine a day, followed by a rainy autumn. Depending on the area, the majority of rain falls between mid-October and the end of March.

In fact there is no typical Mediterranean climate. Temperature and rainfall in Beirut and Montpellier are dramatically different but both have a Mediterranean climate. Nearer to each other but still dissimilar, particularly in winter, are Genoa and Malaga. Sardinia and Corsica are separated by only 12km/7½m yet Corsica has mild and rainy winters while Sardinia has hardly any rain at all and the locals would hardly call the winter mild. The poverty of this island is almost entirely due to drought and the drying wind, the *maestrale*, a sinister cousin of the Provençal *mistral*.

Large areas of the region are subject to the drying effects of gap winds which are often very violent. These winds frequently have rather romantic names, perhaps to soften the truth of their violence. They are all, without exception, deadly to plant life and any gardener living in an area known to be subject to such winds should take evasive action against their destructive powers. The easiest method is to put up cane or wattle screens or erect hedges (which in their infancy need screen protection) or even build walls, though this latter can give rise to a disadvantageous micro-climate and even frost pockets in the garden. Hedges should be made of shrubs where the wood ripens quickly and easily and, where the wind is particularly violent, should preferably be evergreen. Genista, cytisus, virtually all the berberis family, hornbeam, escallonia, *Euonymus japonica*, pyracantha and much of the prunus family make excellent windbreaks. If behind them you can plant a single line, or better still, a staggered double row of conifers, large shrubs or trees, the protection factor will be tripled. Such treatment, which is expensive, need only be undertaken where the winds are frequent and of long duration. If local vineyards and market gardens are protected in this fashion accept this warning and free advice and act upon it.

Although hedges and windbreaks may vary in many ways such as whether they are evergreen or deciduous, high or low, certain rules apply to *all* such plantings. These are in order of importance:-

1. Choose small plants because they will 'take' better and establish themselves more strongly. Do this in spite of starting with a hedge as low as 40cm/15in. Your patience will be generously rewarded.

2. Mulch the plantation for at least two years. Although it is rather ugly, black plastic is one of the finest mulches; chopped bark is excellent also, but rather costly. Straw should not be used as it is a fire hazard.

3. Plant hedges which are either native to the area or which you know are absolute winners. Looking at what grows wild is an excellent indicator. Contrary to popular belief, Leyland cypress (*Cupressocyparis leylandii*), is not very good at standing up to the mistral. It may grow very fast and be excellent by the sea and on chalk but four hours of cold gap wind can dry the life out of it. In any event Leyland cypress should be outlawed from any but the biggest of gardens. It needs far too much room when fully grown and often becomes totally inaccessible for cutting purposes. Furthermore, your neighbour may well end up complaining about its size.

4. Try to avoid planting a single row of anything – a staggered row not only looks better and thicker, it is considerably more efficient as a windbreak. This does not apply to normal hedges in gardens or on land which has a mild, non-windy climate. There, you are better off conforming to the modern theory of planting hedges in single lines.

The Mediterranean is in the westerly wind system. In winter the sea temperature is frequently warmer than land temperature whereas in summer the reverse is true. Although some of the winds such as the scirocco come from the north African deserts, they pick up a great deal of moisture coming across the sea and bring to the northern Mediterranean hot, muggy weather and sometimes rain. This rain is sometimes loaded with fine sand particles which coat everything in sight and it can be quite difficult to remove from vegetation. Plants are suffocated if it is not washed off. This same wind in the southern and central Mediterranean is oppressively hot and dry. In any of its forms it is bad news. It usually blows in March, April and May but recently we had a three-day bout of this wind in August and it often blows for long periods of up to a month.

The two best known Mediterranean winds are the *mistral* and the *bora*. The *tramontana* is a north-easterly wind in Italy and becomes the *tramontane* in the Languedoc-Roussillon. As its name suggests it comes from the mountains and usually from the north or north east.

The *mistral* blows down the Rhône valley and cools and dries out much of Provence. It is one of the things that stops Provence being a paradise. It is interesting to note that on average Marseilles has no less than one hundred days when the *mistral* blows and Nice only four. Taken overall the *mistral* is probably less violent than the *tramontane* which is said to be capable of driving a man crazy. The cloudless summer skies of the north Mediterranean are frequently accompanied by a wind which makes it impossible to leave the house let alone go on the beach or into the garden.

The *bora* is quite different. For a start it is a dialect word for the Italian *borea*. The word *bora* appears in practically every dictionary except an Italian one. It is usually confined to the northern part of the Adriatic blowing from the north east but can involve the whole of the area. By extension the word *bora* has come to be used for almost any coastal wind in the Mediterranean. However, strictly speaking, the *bora* blows as a result of cold air from the snow-covered Alps meeting the comparatively warm Adriatic. It is a cold wind and can be exceptionally violent. The whole of the northern Adriatic is surrounded by mountains, the Alps to the north, the Dinaric Alps to the east, the Italian Apennines to the west. Only the Po Plain and the Venetian lagoons offer any change from this pattern and they are often less than 80km/50m from the mountains which, in geographical and meteorological terms, is nothing. There are geographers who believe this land/sea configuration accounts for the violence of the storms in the Adriatic. France also has a sea wind, called the *marinade*, but it is warm and humid and not really violent at all.

There are many different names in the Mediterranean for the same wind. The scirocco becomes the *khamsin* in Malta and in Egypt (possibly from the Arabic *khamsun* meaning fifty since it lasts a long time); *leveche* or *leste* in Spain and North Africa; *simoon* in the more easterly part of North Africa, the *shilok* in Greece and in Italy the local name for winds seem to change every fifty kilometres or so. The *maestrale* and *maestro* seem to the outsider to be interchangeable but probably are not. The *bora* is called *la borrasca* in Spanish and I once heard a cool breeze in southern Spain described as *un siberiano!*

For those living in Spain and France the Ministry of Agriculture or their offshoots (Servicio de Publicaciones de Extension Agraria in Madrid and I.N.R.A. in Paris) publish a great deal of data on regional climates complete with graphs which are for sale to the public. Alas, Italy and Greece have such figures but do not publish them.

Frost in the Mediterranean Basin can be a very real problem as many a citrus farmer will confirm. Very often the better quality citrus grow in an area which is only just possible for their culture. Hence the use of extremely sophisticated methods of air and soil heating in many citrus plantations. The olive is another crop which does better in similar circumstances. Olive trees in Liguria and Tuscany frequently suffer quite a bit of frost, albeit usually of short duration. Indeed for two years running in the 1980s they tolerated several days of settled snow yet continue to produce some of the finest olive oil in the world. What the olive will not tolerate is cold combined with damp.

Unless in a very high or a very sheltered area, frost in the Mediterranean countries is not likely to lie around and by ten o'clock has usually melted. However, if a garden is found to be subject to frost it is as well to plant fruit trees facing north so that they will not bloom early and then have their blossom damaged by the first sharp frost. In fact this could be suggested for other plants such as camellias which, though they will tolerate frost, do not like to be fried by early morning sun as well which burns the flowers. It goes without saying that in eastern Spain, France, northern Italy, the Adriatic Coast and in parts of Greece, land over 400m/1300ft is almost certain to be subject to frost. Very often these frosts occur only in January and February but in many places they start in October and go on to the end of April. One of the best protections against frost is the new perforated plastic film under which seedlings and small plants enjoy a semi greenhouse atmosphere and now there are struts available to raise the film 10cm/4in off the ground.

Hail as a concomitant of thunderstorms can do serious damage and the Mediterranean region is not spared this phenomenon. Corsica and Sardinia, due to the juxtaposition of the mountains and sea, are particularly liable to suffer from hailstorms and locals are happy to regale newcomers with stories of hailstones the size of pigeons' eggs. Although hailstorms can occur almost anywhere in the region, they are not sufficiently frequent to constitute a significant hazard except to large horticultural establishments. The French are in the forefront of nations researching methods of preventing and inhibiting hailstorms and in south-western France experiments are conducted every year.

I do not like to talk of the sun as a problem, particularly as a great number of people envy us our many hours of sunshine, but I think it should be taken into consideration almost as seriously as water. Very often the hardiness or otherwise of a plant is of less importance than its ability to stand up to a constant twelve hours' baking every day, often for more than ninety days on end, even with watering. Many plants which farther north in Europe relish full sun, require dappled shade in the Mediterranean region. This baking has its good points. Often it hardens the wood of a shrub or tree sufficiently to prevent die back or even death in a cold winter. Nevertheless, this is of little consolation if the shrub is killed by excessive heat. It should be remembered that the Mediterranean coast of France is never less than thirty days and often is as much as sixty days in advance of the Paris region. Flowering and fruiting times, incidentally, in books and catalogues usually refer to the Paris region. Southern Spain is in advance of Barcelona by thirty days and a similar difference can be counted between Genoa and Naples. It should also be remembered that in both France and Italy many of the gardening 'bibles' are written with a cooler climate in mind than the Mediterranean regions of these countries.

The greatest problem of all in the Mediterranean is water, or rather the lack of it. At the outset one can dismiss France since there is seldom a water shortage and the only problem is the expense. Even in the most arid regions of the Languedoc one can turn on a tap at any time of the day and get pure drinking water. However, all water consumption is metered in France and in the drier regions can cost a great deal.

The other place which tends to have no water problems is the Dalmatian coast with one of the highest rainfalls in Europe. This is due to the mountains immediately behind the coastal region. Beware plants with the word *dalmaticum* in their names if they cannot be watered often and well.

When the Moors came to Spain one of the first things they brought to an arid land was the science of irrigation and to this day series of linked wells can be seen in many parts of what had been Moorish territory. Today, there are few communities that do not have piped water (frequently rationed in high summer) and only lonely farmsteads or *cortijos* have to resort to their own well. There is an immense shortage of water in Spain, in Europe second only to Greece, and you only have to travel through Murcia, the garden of Spain, to see what lack of rain can do. Often watering your garden from the municipal supply will be forbidden in which case you must fall back on a well if you are lucky enough to have one (and with water in it) or on to a holding tank which has taken water from the bath and washbasins. The water lorry is a common sight in Spain and southern Italy in high summer and is for drinking only.

Greece has probably the greatest water problem in Europe. In *A Book of Mediterranean Food*, Elizabeth David mentions that 'Greek gourmets know exactly where the best cheese, olives, oil, oranges, figs, melons, wine and even water (in a country where water is often scarce, this is not really so surprising) are to be found and go to immense trouble to procure them.' That was first written in 1950 but remains true today. Geography is against Greece and the Greeks have spent thousands of years trying to overcome the fact. Short of a permanent and unrationed water supply (which must be rare in all but the largest towns), or a well of your own, the only thing to do is save every drop you can and never throw down a drain that which can be usefully and safely stored or poured on the land. Even without water many bulbs can be grown as well as all the labiates which thrive in poor, dry ground with little water. Many of the wild flowers endemic to Greece are of bulbous origin.

Every traveller to Greece remarks on the variously coloured house-leeks covering the roofs of whitewashed houses. These plants go months and months without a drop of water. They are not only very decorative but to a degree act as an insulator both in winter and summer. The Greeks plant them on roofs to deflect lightning. Apparently you can even eat them – the taste is said to be akin to spinach. What more obliging plant could one ask for?

As for Greece so for the eastern Mediterranean though Israel is unique in that it actually utilizes almost 90% of its water sources. Indeed, the country has arrived at a stage where any further water requirements must come from desalinated sources. Eilat, a resort on the Red Sea, depends entirely on sea-water. This full use of the country's water resources has resulted in both the coastal plain and the interior of the country being turned into a vast market garden the produce of which is largely exported. The Israelis are the first people in the Mediterranean to plant forests with a view to decreasing the ambient temperature.

The African coast bordering the Mediterranean is the driest place in the whole area. Much of the land is at sea-level or only just above, much of it is desert. The coast of Egypt enjoys not only the majority of the rainfall in North Africa but also a fairly high humidity – around 70–75% the year round in Alexandria. People complain about not being able to eat dinner outside in the evening because they are soaking wet before the end of the meal. Elsewhere along the coast the rainfall

13

is usually under 25cm/10in a year until Algeria where it can be as much as 100cm/40in a year. Algiers itself gets about 75cm/30in. Although enjoying much the same climate as the western Mediterranean in winter, during which time all the annual rain falls, Algeria suffers in the summers from the scirocco coming up from the Sahara which dries up the whole country. She is therefore forced to rely on storage and subsequent irrigation.

The most fortunate country along this coast is Morocco since not only is the climate influenced by the Mediterranean sea and the Atlantic ocean but also the High Atlas remain covered in snow until midsummer which reduces the temperature. It must be admitted, though, that the Atlantic coast of Morocco is rather cooler than the Mediterranean.

Finally, there are many places in the region which have microclimates, usually of an advantageous nature. Sanremo in northern Italy is one which is well known. Within the Bay of Sanremo and inland until the foothills climb to around 300m/1000ft, the temperature does not vary by more than 10°C/18°F annually. It is, therefore, never too hot and in winter it is rarely necessary to wear an overcoat. The distances between one micro-climate and another can be surprisingly short. For instance Nice is considerably more humid than Cannes at any time of the year. All the Mediterranean islands have their own special climates, some very different from the nearby mainland.

Micro-climates, usually with protection in mind, can be created in gardens by using hedges or walls. Sometimes, the land configuration can cause a disadvantageous micro-climate in a garden. By its very nature, a micro-climate is something to take advantage of or to control. It is the overall climate of the region you live in which you must accept and respect.

The following list gives the average midday temperatures for December, March, June and September; whether the area in question is subject to frost; the annual rainfall which is taken to fall mainly between October – April unless otherwise stated; together with the direction of the main wind.

Place	Dec		March		June		Sept		Frost	Wind
Gibraltar	17°C	63°F	18°C	65°F	27°C	81°F	27°C	81°F	No.	From sea
Malaga	17°C	63°F	18°C	65°F	27°C	81°F	28°C	82°F	No.	From sea
Almeria	17°C	63°F	19°C	66°F	26°C	79°F	27°C	81°F	No.	From sea
Alicante	17°C	63°F	18°C	65°F	28°C	82°F	29°C	84°F	No.	From sea
Valencia	16°C	61°F	18°C	65°F	26°C	79°F	27°C	81°F	Yes	Sea and Mts
Perpignan	13°C	55°F	16°C	61°F	26°C	79°F	25°C	77°F	Yes	Mountain
Marseilles	11°C	52°F	15°C	59°F	26°C	79°F	25°C	77°F	Slight	Mistral
Nice	13°C	55°F	15°C	58°F	24°C	75°F	30°C	86°F	No	Mountain
Sanremo	15°C	59°F	16°C	61°F	25°C	77°F	24°C	75°F	No	Very little
Genoa	12°C	54°F	14°C	57°F	24°C	75°F	24°C	75°F	Yes	From sea
Florence	11°C	52°F	14°C	57°F	27°C	81°F	26°C	79°F	Yes	General
Ajaccio	15°C	59°F	15°C	59°F	25°C	77°F	26°C	79°F	No	From sea
Cagliari	16°C	61°F	17°C	63°F	27°C	81°F	27°C	81°F	No	Maestrale
Naples	14°C	57°F	15°C	59°F	26°C	79°F	27°C	81°F	No	Sea and Mts.
Palermo	18°C	65°F	17°C	63°F	27°C	81°F	28°C	82°F	No	Very little
Bari	14°C	57°F	14°C	57°F	28°C	82°F	26°C	79°F	No	Sea and Mts.
Ancona	10°C	50°F	13°C	55°F	24°C	75°F	23°C	73°F	Slight	Bora
Ravenna	8°C	46°F	13°C	55°F	26°C	79°F	24°C	75°F	Yes	Bora
Venice	8°C	46°F	12°C	54°F	25°C	77°F	19°C	66°F	Yes	Bora
Trieste	9°C	48°F	12°C	54°F	25°C	77°F	24°C	75°F	Yes	Bora
Split	12°C	54°F	14°C	57°F	27°C	81°F	20°C	54°F	Slight	Bora
Corfu	16°C	61°F	16°C	61°F	26°C	82°F	28°C	82°F	No	Levante
Athens	15°C	59°F	16°C	61°F	30°C	86°F	29°C	84°F	No	Tramontana
Thessalonika	11°C	52°F	14°C	57°F	29°C	84°F	28°C	82°F	Slight	From sea
Izmir	11°C	52°F	13°C	56°F	28°C	83°F	27°C	81°F	Yes	Sea and Mts.
Famagusta	19°C	67°F	19°C	67°F	32°C	90°F	33°C	92°F	No	From sea
Aleppo	12°C	54°F	18°C	65°F	34°C	94°F	33°C	92°F	No	From Mts.
Beirut	18°C	65°F	19°C	67°F	28°C	83°F	27°C	81°F	No	From sea
Haifa	20°C	68°F	22°C	72°F	29°C	85°F	31°C	88°F	No	From sea
Alexandria	20°C	68°F	23°C	73°F	29°C	85°F	30°C	86°F	No	From sea
Malta	16°C	61°F	16°C	61°F	26°C	79°F	27°C	81°F	No	From sea
Tunis	16°C	61°F	18°C	65°F	29°C	84°F	31°C	87°F	No	From sea
Algiers	16°C	61°F	17°C	63°F	26°C	78°F	27°C	81°F	No	From sea
Oran	17°C	63°F	18°C	65°F	25°C	77°F	27°C	81°F	No	From sea

2

Making a New Garden

There can be few prospects more daunting to a gardener than a new house surrounded by vast quantities of clay-laden sub-soil with not a vestige of anything growing in it except some rosebay willow herb and thistle. Builders are rarely to be relied upon to put the top-soil aside and replace it once the work is finished. Indeed, a new owner is lucky if the contractor has been kind enough to remove all the detritus left on site. My own builder demolished a small shepherd's hut on the land leaving stones and rubble where they fell to be added to the rest of his mess. In the end we were forced to level the land and make a rockery. The best thing one can say about this arrangement is that the drainage is superb.

IMPROVING THE SOIL

Purchasing soil is fraught with difficulties not least because most soil for sale in the Mediterranean is chiefly clay and stones. Often local horticulturists will help by putting you in touch with wholesale suppliers to the trade (*they* do not buy earth in 50 litre bags) or with a local earth-moving concern. This latter will simply bring, in a series of lorry trips, the result of his latest site-excavation. This is probably one of the cheapest methods and can prove excellent as a base for top dressing with at least 30cm/12in of good quality bagged potting compost. In northern Italy and parts of France it is possible to purchase by the lorry load compost which has been worked over by earthworms. Called *terra di lombrico* or *terre de lombric* it is dark and rich, and mixed in equal proportions with your own soil will prove good enough for most shrubs and flowers. It works excellently also as a top dressing on poor soils. It has two main detractions; its price, which is high; and very occasionally it is the result of industrial rather than vegetable waste and there may be traces of undesirable minerals present – mercury, for instance. Lucky gardeners in the United States are able to start their own earthworm farms by buying a nucleus rather as one does with bees and gradually working over their soil and increasing the number of earthworms. The outlay may seem expensive but at the end of a year such a nucleus (and its progeny) can produce several *tons* of excellent topsoil.

When it is impossible to purchase earth or compost you can make you own by mixing washed river sand and peat in the proportions of .50 cubic metres/.65 cubic yards of peat to 2 cubic metres/2.6 cubic yards of sand. Most peat (much of it German from Luneburg Heath) is sold in large bags of .17 cubic metres/.22 cubic yards and you would need three bags to get .50 cubic metres/.65 cubic yards. Peat in French is *la tourbe*, in Spanish *la turba* and in Italian *la torba*. Keep all ingredients dry when mixing. It is a very hard task indeed and a cement mixer saves much back breaking work. This amount of 'compost' will be adequate for approximately 100 sq.m/1000 sq.ft. If you want rather more water-retaining quality then increase the quantity of peat but do not over-peat your 'compost' or it can become water-logged in the torrential autumn and spring rains. In any event you should not have a higher proportion of peat than one third to two thirds sand. This mixture is far from ideal and to it you must add nourishment in the form of manure which is sold in granulated form virtually everywhere. Some slow-acting blood and bone would be useful also at about 60gr/2oz to the sq.m/sq.yard. In the months to come add all the humus you can, much of which will have been made from composting the weeds and 'green manure' on your own (and others'?) land.

An alternative recipe for making your own 'soil' is to make 50% sand with 25% crushed fine tree bark and 25% peat. Horticultural perlite or vermiculite can be used instead of crushed bark and it has the advantage of being very light. However, its very lightness makes it difficult to mix with other things without a mechanical or an electric mixer. It can be done by hand but it must be done with small quantities at a time.

SALT IN THE SOIL

There are frequent saline pockets all along the Mediterranean coast and although there are plants which happily live in a salt laden atmosphere there are very few which actually relish having their roots in salt-laden soil. A list of those which will tolerate such treatment is given below and further details will be found in the plant directory.

Presented with salt laden soil you have three choices when planning a garden. You can change the soil completely which is unbelievably expensive unless you limit yourself to pots, tubs and raised beds. Also you should bear in mind that if the garden soil is salt laden so, in all probability, is the air. Wind storms can bring in a great deal of extra salt as anyone who has covered their precious plantings with covers can vouch. Next morning there are bucketfuls of sand and salt. Sea air is also full of salt in certain areas and the Mediterranean is fairly salt being virtually an inland sea.

Alternatively you can treat the soil by adding prodigious amounts of gypsum which is hydrous calcium sulphate and is best known to the public in the form of plaster of Paris. You will need, by volume, about one third gypsum to two-thirds soil and a cement mixer makes everything easier. All the better if you are able to add *river* sand, chopped bark or peat, no matter how small the quantities. You will end up with a growing medium which has a very high pH content but there are many, many more plants tolerant of this than there are of saline soil. You will have to choose your first plants very carefully and you should grow annuals from seed to begin with. Gypsophila, pinks and many of the labiates like a high pH.

There are two main schools of thought about how to remove salt from your soil without using gypsum. One says you should leach it out by frequent heavy waterings which is not always easy where saline soils occur. The other school says this is the worst thing you can do because each time you water heavily you push down the less saline topsoil into the very saline sub-soil and you are, therefore, sitting on a time bomb since as your top soil goes down yearly the roots of your plants will find themselves in salt laden soil. Probably the best thing you can do is add gypsum, top dress your soil at least once a year with a peat/bark/fertilizer mixture to a depth of about 30cm/12in and grow shallow rooting or salt tolerant plants. Among these latter are, *Acacia arabica, A. cyanaphylla, A. decurrens, A. farnesiana*; most of the aloe family; *Atriplex canescens, A. lentiformis*; some of the callistemons; *Calotropis procera*; *Casuarina stricta*; *Cortaderia selloana* – the pampas grass; *Dodonea viscosa*; *Ficus nitida* (Indian laurel); most of the ice plants; *Leucophyllym frutescens*; *Nerium oleander*; *Olea europea*, the European olive; *Parkinsonia aculeata* (Jerusalem thorn); *Pinus eldarica*, the Russian pine, which I have never seen look anything but scrubby and sad but apparently it *can* be well grown; the pomegranate, *Punica granatum*; some, though not all, *Robinia* species; *Schinus molle*; *Sesbania aegyptica*, but not the red flowered type; and finally *Zizyphus jujuba*.

ALKALINE SOIL

If you think your soil is going to be very alkaline indeed or if you are near a desert or at the sea side and near sand dunes then add Sequestrene 138Fe in granules and water in well. I have found it a disaster to try and mix sequestrene into the sand and peat mixture. The distribution is rather uneven and it is best to scatter it on top afterwards at the rate of approximately 30–35gr/1 oz per sq.metre/ sq.yard. Alternatively you can mix the sequestrene with the blood and bone meal if you wish and scatter this on top of the soil. Sequestrene 138Fe is made by Ciba Geigy and will probably be the most expensive additive you will use on your Mediterranean garden. If you feel it will be essential to your garden never buy it in less than 1 kilo packets – the tiny 100 gr packets are prohibitively expensive. It keeps well.

PREPARING THE GROUND

Before you plant so much as a daisy, do get the construction side over and make sure the land is properly drained and can cope with the heavy autumn rains which are common throughout the northern part of the Mediterranean Basin. Electric cables for garden lighting, water conduits for irrigation, gas pipes, drain pipes and pipes to and from water reservoirs, should all go in before the lawn is made or paving laid and the shrub border planted. Remember also to make sure that all but the plastic irrigation pipes are deep enough under the soil since they can easily break with heavy garden machinery going over them from time to time.

The area you wish to cultivate should be thoroughly cleared, either by hand or with the help of a brush-cutter and if there are any perennial weeds these should be killed either by the use of paraquat (Gramoxone by I.C.I. for instance) or of glyphosate (such as Roundup by Monsanto). Often in the growing season it is necessary to make as many as four applications of weedkiller as new weeds appear. Thistles come more or less last and are among the most difficult to kill. Thereafter, dig over or better still, rotavate, top dress and then plant. Incidentally, never mix glyphosate weedkillers with anything else or it will nullify the effect. Also always respect the manufacturer's directions on the packet. Mixing weedkiller too strong can actually stop it working at all which is not what you are seeking at such expense! Thereafter, plant ground cover or use mulches to suppress weeds. Although chopped bark is the most pleasant to look at, black plastic often does an even better job particularly where new hedges are concerned.

If you have some spare ground which is not going to be used for some time, this could be used to plant lupin or other plants specifically offered for green manuring. The French often use annual rye grass for this purpose but I think that this is a mistake as it is far too difficult to remove all the roots and unless one is very quick about digging it in, it will have seeded itself. It is not easy to incorporate this 'green manure' without a rotavator. Also, I have found that it is better to plant in spring and rotavate it in summer than to plant in autumn and rotavate in spring.

Those who would like to have a climber on one or more walls of the house should bear in mind that the walls of buildings often leach lime into the soil for more than twenty years which can cause washed-out looking wisteria or roses. Often a large container is better for climbers of medium vigour. In any event do not plant right up against the wall and always dig out a large hole and replace the soil with relatively rich compost. Wall plants need feeding much more frequently than the rest of the garden with the possible exception of wisteria and stephanotis which seem to flower better with a less rich diet. Incidentally both respond well from a flowering point of view to root-pruning and I can think of nothing more difficult than root-pruning a climber planted hard against a house wall!

STARTING PLANTING

If you are lucky enough to have a new house on an already partially or fully planted site count your blessings. Although you may not approve of your predecessor's taste you can take your time with re-planting whereas the owner of a bare patch must plant with a view to getting a desirable effect in record time. Never under-estimate the value of pots in such circumstances. They can quickly furnish a barren patch, a blank facade or an empty terrace. Even annuals in pots are a useful addition and are cheap and easy to obtain.

Every garden is different and there are no set rules about what to plant first except that probably the lawn, if there is to be one, should be done first, though not always. Of course, it is not ideal to plant trees behind a shrub border once the shrubs are growing but it can be done provided great care is taken. Often, in an effort to get a garden going, only the summer and autumn are thought of and winter and spring can prove very bare. Bulbs, except for the newest varieties of tulips, are still very good value for money and provide a wonderful display at time when there is little else in the garden. Most, including tulips, can be left in from year to year to increase naturally and continue to do their good work. Of course, you cannot expect such wonderful flowering during the second year but over a period of five years or so you will find most of the bulbs have increased and their slight reduction in flowering size will be amply compensated by their sheer number.

PLANTS TO AVOID

Everyone with a new, bare garden wants a list of rampers, spreaders and giants. Before giving a list of those which can be useful in such circumstances perhaps a word of warning would not come amiss. Among the ground cover plants are some rampagers which should not be admitted to any civilized garden. That I have them in my own and enjoy them most of the time is no excuse for their behaviour. Periwinkle, *Vinca major*, rightly called *misère* in French, covers vast spaces with its rather boring green leaves at a terrifying rate. It is very difficult to eradicate. The variegated form is much less rampaging and is an asset to a shady part of any garden. *V. minor* on the other hand, although difficult to eradicate also, at least does not rampage and because the leaves are smaller one is more aware of the pretty blue flowers which one hardly notices with *Vinca major*. *Ajuga reptans* in all its forms other than the cultivars *A. r.* 'Burgundy Glow' and *A. r.* 'Burgundy Red' should be avoided as it is far too invasive. This latter has rather pretty 'sops-in-wine' colouring and looks good under shrubs as a ground cover. But it too spreads everywhere though luckily is easy to pull up and hand on to your unsuspecting friends. I suppose every gardener gets given a cutting or pot of Bouncing Bet, *Saponaria officinalis*. Whatever you do, do not put it in your rockery! One plant can cover a square yard in a season. Putting up with its aggressive habits for the sake of its rather ordinary pink flowers in mid summer is hardly worthwhile. Always cut off the dead flowers and do not let seeds form for every one will germinate far and wide. I love the veronica family but must admit that *Veronica filiformis* is not one of its better members and is generally counted as a weed in this part of the world. She pops up all over my garden sometimes huge distances from her starting point and the pale blue flowers quickly succumb to Mediterranean sunshine leaving nothing but a tangle of washed out pale green leaves. *Cerastium tomentosum* and *Campanula carpatica* are difficult to remove and every little bit of white root will take. *Cerastium* should be clipped back hard after flowering and again tidied up just before winter or it will be a sodden mess in spring. Also I have found that it, like closely planted lavender, harbours not only lizards but snakes which are never pleasant to come across. *Solidago, Physalis,* all the Michaelmas daisies, great and small and *Hypericum calycinum* or St John's Wort are great stayers and not easily shown the door.

PLANTS FOR QUICK EFFECT

Among the goodies, *Phuopsis stylosa* with its bright pink flowers quickly fills a space as does the taller (1.5m/5ft) *Silphium perfoliatum.* Among my favourites for filling large blanks are *Brachyglottis* 'Sunshine', which should be allowed 1 sq.m/1 sq. yd; *Phormium tenax*, or New Zealand flax, which needs about the same amount of space but grows to 2.50m/ 8ft. It is wind resistant and excellent for seaside gardens. However, it does need occasional watering. One plant which seems to need no watering at all but of course, like so many, does even better with a moderate amount, is perovskia from Afghanistan which flowers late and long – a good six to seven weeks between August and October. Its only demands are well drained, gritty soil and staking against wind. It hates rain once fully grown and takes a couple of days to recover from a thunderstorm. *P. atriplicifolia* is the commonest species of which there is a good cultivar 'Blue Spire' which has violet-blue flowers above soft grey foliage.

Macleaya cordata probably holds the record for growth in a season at 2.5m/8ft. It will take over if left to its own devices. It has tall spikes of ivory flowers. A purchased plant of *Fatsia japonica* of middling size planted in a border will quickly use up quite a lot of space and create a certain amount of shade. It looks absolutely splendid under-planted with variegated plants such as hostas, Canary ivy, euonymus or periwinkle.

An annual planting of *Ricinus communis* at the back of a border can be useful for filling up large gaps – though one should remember its seeds are deadly poisonous and the flowering heads should be cut off as they arrive. I would never normally have this plant in my garden since I find its foliage rather coarse and flashy but it can be very useful in a brand new one. That giant of giants, *Gunnera* is not really suited to a Mediterranean garden without a large pond or lake and its leaves quickly dry up in the sun so it must be planted in partial shade.

The F1 hybrids of *Impatiens*, or Busy Lizzie, cover very quickly provided they are well watered and given a little fertilizer each week. Do not plant too close together – they grow vigorously – 40cm/15in in each direction is quite enough. Begonias, again of the sort you buy for bedding out, *B. semperflorens*, really live up to their name and continue flowering until the first frost. They expand greatly with a little nourishment and plenty of water and cover large amounts of bare ground quite quickly. If you are able to dead-head them so much the better.

Fuchsias quickly use up a lot of space given sufficient water and nourishment. Partial shade is best and the pink fuchsias appear to do better than the white hybrids.

Of the grasses and bamboos, *Miscanthus*, both green *M. floridus* and *M. sinensis*, and bronze *M. saccharensis* immediately spring to mind. They should be cut back hard each spring to produce new shoots which will grow to 2m/6ft. However, do remember that they are a form of sugar cane and are even more difficult to remove than the bamboo family so choose your site carefully. Most bamboos are invasive (occasionally this is desirable but not generally) but the shorter bamboos such as *Arundaria viridistriata* can easily be kept in their place. *Phyllostachys* is a cane which will grow as much as 5m/15ft in a season, rather like a small tree and indeed I have seen 'woodland' created with them. Rather tender, their roots are removable for the first season or so but thereafter, become permanent fixtures.

HEDGING AND FENCING

The question of hedging or fencing your land has to be considered from many aspects, not least price. Chain-link fencing *can* be clothed and made attractive but a living hedge is best. In built-up areas, on housing estates for example, the law is often very strict. In France, for example, you cannot plant a tree less than 2m/6ft from the road; a hedge must be at least 50cm/20in inside your own boundary and not more than 2m/6ft high. The local town hall will supply the necessary information.

France, because of fire-blight, is trying to discourage the planting of pyracantha as hedging. The deeper you are in the country the less problem you will have about what you can plant and where. In Italy, at the moment, there are no restrictions on what hedge you may plant except if you live on what is known as a *strada panoramica* in which case you should not block the view for more than 20m/66ft at a time.

Apart from the ubiquitous Japanese laurel, Portugal laurel and privet, all of which are much loved in the Mediterranean for some reason and it cannot only be that they grow well, there are many hedging plants which give better value. *Punica granatum* makes a beautiful hedge with bright red flowers in the season and if you have a cold enough winter you will get pomegranates. *Plumbago capensis* flowers from May to the end of October and its bright sky blue flowers have a wonderfully cooling effect in hot sun. Apart from lavender and rosemary hedges which are naturally low you can plant higher shrubs such as berberis, Natal plum (*Carissa grandiflora*), Mexican orange blossom (*Choisya ternata*), Judas tree (*Cercis siliquastrum*) grown espalier-fashion, all the cotoneasters, *Elaeagnus × ebbingei*, escallonia, griselinia, myrtle, oleander (*Nerium oleander*), pittosporum both plain and variegated, raphiolepis, suitable roses, spiraea (in partial shade or the flowers quickly brown), Cape honeysuckle (*Tecomaria capensis*), *Teucrium fruticans* and laurustinus (*Viburnum tinus*).

PARASOLS AND FURNITURE

You will need somewhere to sit in your garden and possibly somewhere to eat as well. Unless you are very lucky and have a large shade-giving tree you will have to make your own shade. This can be done by means of small or medium beach umbrellas or the wonderful large shade umbrellas such as are seen on Italian piazzas, or by blinds. Both the latter are expensive but will last several seasons if properly cared for and always well attached or tied down. One gust of wind can ruin a large umbrella or awning. It is always best to have this type of equipment in dralon or acrylic rather than in cotton which quickly rots. As to garden furniture the Mediterranean garden is one which can take a lot of white, even in plastic or ABS, though of course wood, and especially well oiled teak, still looks best of all. However a dining table and chairs of teak are not only expensive but far more difficult to store in winter than stacking or folding chairs and a table which comes to pieces for storage. It is unwise, unless you are very well protected to leave furniture out in the garden when you are not there (or sometimes even when you are) since it will eventually be stolen. Heavy terracotta pots, tubs, even plants, all develop a tendency to 'walk' after a time. Stone seating obviously does not but stone is not very comfortable to sit on for long.

SWIMMING POOLS

If you are going to instal a swimming pool, do bear in mind when siting it that for some unknown reason people, particularly children, *scream* in water. Therefore, do not put it where your afternoon nap will be disturbed. Pools are not particularly attractive *per se* and they are rarely properly landscaped. The pool does *not* have to be bright pale blue or turquoise but can be dark coloured also. I have seen emerald green, midnight blue, black and dark brown pools which were really rather beautiful. Dark colours also help heat the water but dark browny greens should be avoided as they tend to make the water look rather unhealthy. In much of the Mediterranean, pool-owners do not have to worry about frost and can, therefore, have free-form cement pools which are much prettier and infinitely easier to integrate into the landscape. The often rectangular lines of less-expensive pools can be softened by judiciously placed pots of flowering plants. However, most plants are very chlorine sensitive. Among the less sensitive are juniper, eschscholtzia, pelargonium, begonia, *Brachyglottis* 'Sunshine', *Erythrina crista-galli*, non-variegated ivy and myrtle. Unfortunately, succulents and cacti appear to succumb quickly. There are now many swimming pool products on the market which contain either very little

25

chlorine indeed or none or at all. Indeed I.C.I. boast that with certain of their products you can actually drink the water. Using such products can greatly increase the variety of plants you can use round a swimming pool. Blue Crystal by Aquatech Ltd. of Newbury is among the best chlorine-free swimming pool care products

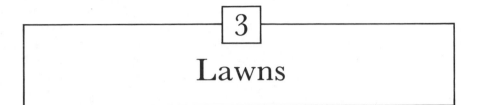

3

Lawns

Before embarking on planting grass consider carefully the ten main requirements of *any* lawn, no matter where it is.

1. The right site.
2. The right soil.
3. A *permanent* and plentiful water supply.
4. The right lawn seed mixture.
5. The correct ratio of sun and shade.
6. Correct feeding.
7. Mowing every week in the growing season.
8. Constant weeding.
9. Bi-annual scarification and de-thatching.
10. Proper tools such as lawn mower, roller, strimmer, scarifier and de-thatcher.

Is a lawn worth all this work, worry and expense? For a lot of northern Europeans and Americans in the Mediterranean region the answer is undoubtedly yes. To many of those not from the Mediterranean the sight of green grass is a precious thing and such people will go to immense lengths to obtain and keep a good lawn. Although I know I should not, I devote a disproportionate amount of time and expense to keeping my grass in good condition. It is a sad truth that in England I would be ashamed of what passes as a lawn in my Italian garden.

If the area concerned is less than 100 sq.m/1100 sq.ft then forget about grass and have paving instead. If you cannot guarantee a watering at least every other day during the period May to September either because you are absent or have no one to do this chore for you then it would be unwise to have a lawn.

1. THE RIGHT SITE

This is the most important requirement. It is no use siting a lawn without considering drainage, sun, shade, water supply or its difficulty of upkeep. A great number of Mediterranean gardens are on slopes and/or terraces which does not make things any easier. Builders often put water tanks, septic tanks or conduits more or less anywhere and usually without consulting the owner of the property. Sometimes these are not even covered by 30cm/12in of soil and you cannot grow a lawn successfully with that depth of soil. Lucky the owner who knows where his drainage and soil pipes are. Architects rarely consider the garden as an integral part of the house which I find surprising since a well-thought out garden can enhance any architecture, good or bad.

If you are fortunate enough to build your house keep the top soil, excavated for the foundations, apart in large heaps for use later when laying a lawn. Try, in any event, to keep any top soil you can lay your hands on one side for future use. It will save you a fortune in purchased soil.

Trees already *in situ* can pose a problem. Even if they are ugly most countries now insist you keep them if they are still alive and you will usually need *written* permission to remove them. The average fine in France and Italy begins at around £100 sterling for removing a tree without permission so it pays to get into contact with the local Ministry of Agriculture's forestry people before removing anything. You can get their address from your local town hall or from the local police. However, as will be seen later, you will need almost all the trees you can muster. You may find that such trees play havoc with the level of a lawn. Covering the roots with soil is *not* the answer – 30cm/12in of extra soil over the roots can quickly kill a tree. Building a retaining wall round them which is at least 60cm/24in bigger than the diameter of the trunk is one of the easiest ways of preserving trees and these structures can look rather attractive in dry stone walling or with a stucco or rough rendered finish either in white or the colour of the house. I have also seen this type of walling done in stained wood. Of course if the lawn is vast there is nothing to stop your having a depression where a clump of trees occur. This can look particularly attractive if you plant the tree surround thickly with the various wild cyclamens or with colchicums for autumn colour and with bulbs for late winter and spring.

The perfect site is one which slopes very slightly, drains well, has good loamy soil, some shade, not too much sun, not too much foot traffic and an easy access to a plentiful water supply – rather a daunting list. However, you can cheat to a certain extent by changing the soil, using fertilizer, installing drainage if necessary and affording shade by planting trees and shrubs. Even so far as water is concerned you can help matters by using types of grass which are less greedy in their requirements.

2. THE RIGHT SOIL

The average soil in the Mediterranean region – largely clay and stones – is not suited to grass all year round. Clay tends to dry up hard and let the rainwater run-off. Stones hold the sun's heat and dry out the surrounding clayey soil. You must, therefore, clean the soil of stone for at least 45cm/18in down though of course you can leave in small pebbles for drainage. If you do not do this you will quickly get patches of dying, dried up grass.

The best grass areas in Europe are in the Lake District of England, Ireland, Central France, Switzerland, Austria and the steppes of Russia. The Alpine meadows are fed all winter, often from November to April, with the contents of the cow byres and this addition is gently watered in by melting snow. No private Mediterranean gardener could do likewise since the cost would be prohibitive, the smell dreadful and the snow which 'transports' the nutrient into the ground, unavailable. The soil of these grassy places is a rich friable loam. The combined rainfall/snowfall is triple that of any place in the Mediterranean. We know only too well that rainfall, or lack of it, is to a certain degree responsible for soil types. Much of the best grass – though by no means all – is grown on acid or neutral soil. Most Mediterranean soil, though again, not all, is alkaline. Therefore, you must not expect too much. Changing your soil is part of the plan. Removing stones, adding peat, humus, top soil, fertilizers, even water-beads, all help but nothing can imitate nature on such a large scale.

Pretty as it can look grass should never come right up to the walls of a house. There should be a concrete, stone or tiled surround to the house of at least 1–1.3m/3–4ft. If you have the slightest doubt about the land draining towards the house have drainage pipes put in by a professional; it will save a lot of headaches and money later on.

3. A GOOD WATER SUPPLY

Merely sprinkling a lawn simply brings the roots closer to the surface for the sun to parch. You need deep soaking to a depth of about 30cm/12in though you can get away with 15cm/6in at a pinch if the lawn is not in full sun all the time. A thorough soak every two days is better than a sprinkling everyday. Automatic or semi-automatic watering is best. Trying to water a lawn with a hose is dreadful for the gardener and inefficient for the lawn. Automatic watering is the sort which has pipes laid under the lawn and the 'pop-up' systems such as those made by Gardena and Toro Rainbird are not expensive and save both time and water. They can have special clocks attached, so the lawn can be watered when the owner is away. Semi-automatic watering is done with hose-attachments – but they use much more water as they are not particularly efficient.

A great deal of water is thrown away which could be used on the land. Tanks and containers should be filled with bath water. Do not use kitchen water, as detergent is bad for the entire vegetable kingdom. Small amounts of soap on the other hand are quite a good insecticide. Alternatively there are now on the market tiny pumps for use with an electric drill which, coupled with a hose and its attachments, can pump out bathwater directly on to the lawn or into a tank.

However, the most important thing to emphasize is that if you have not got a permanent water supply or a back-up supply when the former is rationed you should not consider having a lawn. Remember also that although trees on a lawn help with shade and ultimately with the amount of water used, they themselves also use up a considerable amount.

4. THE RIGHT LAWN SEED MIXTURE

Closely clipped fine grasses simply will not grow or look good without constant water. Many lawns in the region are composed of plants which are normally considered coarse grasses such as perennial rye grass (*Lolium perenne*) and meadow grasses. Clover is frequently used for its lush green pile. However, it is expensive and using one part clover to four parts of conventional seed considerably increases the cost of making a lawn. For the ecology minded a mixture of equal amounts of Dutch clover (*Trifolium repens*), achillea and camomile (*Anthemis nobilis*) with a small amount of your local thyme (*Thymus vulgaris* or *Thymus serpyllum*) makes a very lush carpet (though it needs frequent cutting to make the plants spread and reduce the size of the clover leaf) in even the hottest summer because it has its own large reserves of sodium and nitrogen. However, you must not expect a smooth sward but rather a sheet of green.

Virtually all lawn seed mixtures for the north of the region use a basic 30–50% annual or perennial rye grass. The annual seeds itself, if allowed, and both these grasses can stand a certain amount of drought once they are established, and tolerate sun as well as a coldish winter. However, neither type spreads quickly or easily but stays in bunches and therefore rye grass should always be mixed with one of the fescues and at least one of the bent grasses, agrostis species, which are of a finer texture and spread easily. Agrostis are the most beautiful of lawn grasses being fine textured but they do not stand up to wear or excessive heat on their own but need the company of more resistant grasses. Top quality lawn seed mixtures always have a proportion of agrostis in them. Never use bents or fescues in the southern part of the Mediterranean Basin – they will dry up as they germinate.

All over the Mediterranean lawns are made of doob, or Bermuda grass (*Cynodon dactylon*), and the Imperial War Graves Commission use this plant for their cemetery lawns in southern Europe. Although it stands up superlatively well to heat, it has a very obvious dormant season during which it often becomes unattractively brown if the weather gets cold enough. It will not take much frost either. However, you can, in very hot areas, overseed the area in early winter with Italian rye grass (*Lolium perenne*) which will more or less disappear when the Bermuda grass comes up again. Its other drawback is that it is fairly demanding in maintenance and pesticide which the other grasses are not and of all the grasses needs the most fertilizer. It is one of the few 'lawns' available as plants but except where a lot of water is available I would advise seed since there is no transplanting shock to cope with. Bermuda grass is certainly the most commonly planted item in the plant kingdom, even surpassing rice.

Dichondra micrantha is another ground cover that will do duty as a lawn where grass simply will not grow but it will not stand cold. It cannot be sat on since it stains clothing. It has a slight clover-like appearance with tiny round leaves and well fertilized it is a pleasant, lush green.

When seeding a lawn remember to incorporate an anti-ant powder, preferably carbaryl which is bio-degradable. Otherwise you will find in a matter of hours that millions of ants have removed every vestige of seed and made neat little piles of it around the edges of your future lawn. Much of the seed is transported to 'stores' under rocks. If carbaryl does not work, then use other chemicals such as lindane but as they are extremely poisonous you must keep the family pets away from the place for at least four to six weeks and constantly water in the product. With kittens and puppies keep them away for at least three to four *months* since they eat everything.

Most of the lawn seed mentioned above is available in Western Europe although you may have to go to a specialist outlet or an agricultural seedsman. So far as Bermuda or doob grass is concerned you can buy this throughout the Mediterranean region but only as *Cynodon dactylon* and for cultivars (which are not only better looking but stronger and need less feeding) you must go to the United States. There they offer as many as ten or twelve different varieties and probably the best for the Mediterranean region are 'Santa Ana', 'Ormond' and 'Sunturf' – all available from California nurseries. They are all salt resistant and therefore ideal for the seaside.

5. THE CORRECT RATIO OF SUN AND SHADE

Try to plant your lawn so that it does not get full mid-day sun. No grass likes eight hours of sunshine a day – even with copious water. Err on the side of shade but of course not dense shade which can encourage moss. Trees help a lot though they are not the entire answer. I am always amazed at just how much intense sunshine grass will tolerate. If all the other requirements can be met sun will do less harm than if they cannot. Never mow a lawn in the middle of the day nor in full sun.

6. CORRECT FEEDING

Probably more than any other plant in the garden, grass needs rich feeding. This is not only because it is constantly being cut but it is also constantly being mistreated not only by people walking, playing or lying on it and by extremes of temperature. Many of the commercial fertilizers are too high in nitrogen and an ideal mixture for the Mediterranean region is 4%N (nitrogen), 8%P (phosphorus) and 10%K (potassium). This should be used at the time of seeding in the spring or autumn at the rate of 35–50 gr. per sq.m/1–1½ oz. per sq.yd. In the case of Bermuda grass you will need to give a fertilizer every two months but for ordinary grasses this is too much.

The French tend to sow grass rather more densely at around 80 gr. per sq.m/2½ oz. per sq.yd and certainly you get quick, if expensive, results that way. Autumn fertilizer should be of the slow release type if possible. Very often magnesium is added at about 1% – so much the better since it improves colour and health. The same amount can be used once or twice a year. Do not over fertilize your soil. It only causes more work and mowing, and encourages weeds and disease. The French make a fertilizer called 'Coup de Fouet' (it comes in various makes). Being too rich in nitrogen and more suitable for cooler areas, this should not be used on lawns in the Mediterranean.

7. MOWING

Mowing should be done with a good quality mower which does not tear at the grass but cuts it cleanly. This may seem unnecessary to say except that the majority of gardeners appear to use a blunt instrument to tear off the top layer of grass. Mowers, like knives or scissors, need sharpening from time to time. Before buying a mower without a grassbox bear in mind that raking up dried grass (a fire hazard in the region and ugly to look at) is, literally, a death-dealing pastime. Mowing heights are quite different from northern Europe – think in terms of at least 5–7.5cm/2–3in. The soil does not bake so hard with longer grass and the grass keeps greener.

8. WEEDING

The moment you see a weed remove it or it will grow bigger and stronger by the minute. Provided you sow the grass closely the weeding should be minimal and fertilizer/selective weedkillers should not be needed. Certain weeds such as plantago and creeping buttercup are hard to eradicate as is a particular type of couch grass peculiar to the

Mediterranean. Glyphosate in the form of liquid on a small sponge stroked on to the offending plant works best. Selective weedkillers can be used on all the lawns except those containing clover which itself tends to keep out interlopers by its dense spreading mat. Clover will need a specific clovercide which means going to a specialist outlet rather than just to a garden centre or supermarket.

One of the most irritating lawn weeds in parts of the Mediterranean is prunella and where a selective weedkiller has left this untouched, two applications of Iotox, made by Fisons, at about a month's interval will usually deal with this problem. Selective weedkillers must be used on a totally calm day which is not easy to find in the region. It is so easy for a small gust of wind to blow broadleaf weedkiller on to nearby flower beds.

9. BI-ANNUAL SCARIFICATION AND DE-THATCHING

Many modern lawn mowers have a small attachment which will turn the machine into a scarifier. Otherwise you will need to buy a small machine, preferably electrically or mechanically driven. Do not be tempted by so called scarifiers you can strap on to your feet. With Mediterranean soil they do not work and are very hard on the wearer. De-thatching can be done with a rake or stiff nylon brush and if you occasionally sweep with the latter de-thatching should not become a problem. Thatch can quickly kill off parts of a lawn to say nothing of causing moss in the right climatic conditions. You will need to scarify at least twice a year in late autumn and early summer. If you have bulbs in the grass you cannot do anything until they have died down but if you have nothing else growing there then late spring is an excellent time to scarify and de-thatch.

You pass the machine over once and then rake up the debris. The lawn looks like a battlefield but quickly recovers. Then pass the machine over once again at right angles to the previous direction. The Americans have what is known as a power rake to do this sort of work. In Europe a certain amount of hand cleaning and raking is still the norm. Once cleaned you can re-seed bare patches if necessary. Always water well after scarifying or de-thatching.

10. THE RIGHT TOOLS

Electric mowers have become very much safer throughout Europe and can safely be used in most countries. If you have doubts buy a small earth-trip to interpose between you and the machine. They are certainly the easiest mowers to use. I am surprised to see how well they deal with relatively long grass compared with a few years ago when they would not cut more than 7.5cm/3in of grass without becoming blocked. The next easiest but infinitely more expensive are the petrol driven mowers (either reel or cylinder) which start like a car by turning an ignition key. Next down are the less sophisticated sort with the pull start which I (and most other women) find almost impossible to get going. If you have a lot of grass to cut, then use a mower which does not need to be pushed. Finally, there are the old-fashioned cylinder mowers which you push and which are very hard work in heat.

Whether you have a reel, cylinder or rotary mower is up to you and merely a matter of taste. If you want a striped lawn then only a cylinder will produce this finish. Personally, if I had a lot of grass, I would plump for a reel mower with key ignition. As I have very little I have an electric rotary mower.

Whatever your mower you *must* have a proper grassbox attached. The best modern mowers suck up the clippings but even an ordinary mower where the force of cutting throws the clippings into the box is better than having to rake up the lawn every time. This is why some Flymo rotary machines are not ideal for this part of the world although they are wonderful for cutting slopes.

A strimmer for cutting the edges is vital unless you already have a brush cutter which will do the job just as well. 'By his edges shall ye know him' is supposed to be the motto of the good gardener and certainly overgrown edges to a lawn look very untidy. A roller, except when laying a lawn, is less vital in the Mediterranean region than elsewhere and I have found the land scarcely ever develops bumps and depressions. Scarifiers and rakes (powered or otherwise) become essential once the lawn is well established.

By and large because the soil is so clay ridden and hard, lawns do not suffer greatly from insect infestations and for the same reason moles are virtually unknown in Mediterranean lawns. However, certain types of web-worm and white worms eat the roots and in such cases the dead patches must be dug out, new earth put in and the space re-seeded after having been treated against the problem. Carbaryl is excellent and if this fails there are several specific pesticides available usually containing lindane (see chapter on pests and diseases).

A word of warning: You may be persuaded by someone or a nurseryman (who certainly does not have a lawn) to use zoysia grass since it is a deep dark green and drought resistant. Do not listen. You cannot walk on zoysia grass without damaging it and it does not lend itself to frequent cutting. For a patch of green here and there in a dry landscape it is excellent – as a lawn it is useless. It is slightly different if the zoysia grass comes from the United States when almost certainly it will be a hybrid of Z. *matrella* which can be mown. All the same it is doubtful if zoysia grass offers many advantages over Bermuda grass and the latter is infinitely easier to procure.

Perhaps it would be a good idea to read this chapter through a second time and then calculate carefully (and truthfully!) the cost of creating and keeping up a lawn and the cost of random stone paving or tiling the same area. You may well change your mind.

Rock Gardens and Water Gardens

ROCK GARDENS

Before embarking on a rockery do bear in mind that such a garden is always labour intensive. Therefore, it is not for the absentee gardener or the person who hates weeding. Even a small rockery takes at least two hours' maintenance a week over a year and most of this work is concentrated into late spring and summer.

A proper rock garden at sea level is not really possible since the sun is too hot, the soil too full of clay or chalk and furthermore, on flat land the average attempt at creating a rock garden will resemble Reginald Farrer's 'dog's grave'. However, if you have land sloping down to the sea or even down to a meadow, then you can help nature by arranging rocks in such a way that they provide the right environment for the plants you choose. Such an arrangement should follow the general lie of the rocks which are already nearby.

A rock garden is the most difficult type of garden to create success-fully. It requires not only great skill but also great taste. Most people tend to make mistakes the first time but subsequently are more successful. Alas, rocks are difficult to move and one is forced to live with one's mistakes. Getting professional gardeners to help is not always the answer since although they may be better at the nuts and bolts of arranging a rockery they are almost certain to be worse than you in the matter of taste. A proper garden or landscape designer whose work you have seen and admired can help rather more. However, if he suggests not having such a feature in your garden then abide by his advice.

Unless you live above 750m/2500ft forget about alpines which need not only poor, well draining soil, which you can easily imitate, but also dry, freezing conditions in winter which you cannot offer. Damp, poorly drained soil such as is found in the northern Mediterranean, is death to almost all alpines in winter. However, with many of the Mediterranean natives a very successful type of rockery can be made which will be more like a sloping lawn with rocky outcrops. A certain amount of skill is still needed and you should choose your rocks very carefully to go with the others already in the garden. The Ligurian coast, the limestone Karst coast around Trieste and the eastern Adriatic, the southern coast of France and the Spanish Costa Brava are all ideal for creating this type of rockery sloping towards the sea. You do not, of course, have to live anywhere near the sea to make a similar sloping garden. Even if you confine yourself to Mediterranean natives such as cistus, the labiate family, dwarf lavenders, prostrate rosemary, cyclamen and bulbs you will still achieve a most attractive effect and you will know that the plants can survive all the worst aspects of a Mediterranean climate.

In spite of the rather natural or casual look a well made rockery should have, it will take a great deal of careful planning to achieve this effect. So far as placing the rocks is concerned you must think big. You need only four or five really large boulders (perhaps you have one in place already in which case so much the better) of about 1–1.3m/3–4ft long by as much wide. These should be buried in the soil by about two thirds of their height making sure there are no empty pockets where a plant's questing roots will find no soil. It will cost quite a lot to purchase these and even more to haul them to your garden. Since you will be spending quite large sums of money you might as well have a professional to arrange them for you. Too many amateurs suffer from bad backs and even hernias as a result of heaving around large stones.

Normally the south east is considered the best aspect for a rockery – the south being too hot and drying for the plants. In the Mediterranean these two sites would quickly dry up and need constant watering. In fact any site except these two would be acceptable – even south west provided you are prepared to limit the type of plants you use. Do not site a rockery near a building, under trees or near a wall. You should use bulbs as much as possible since they can give a great deal of early spring colour when there is little else in the garden. In high summer take advantage of the Mediterranean natives such as the labiate family and various members of the daisy family. There are many small evergreen trees such junipers, pines and cypress which can be used. By all means plant in large clumps so the rockery does not look like a rich fruit cake but do be careful about using large areas of ground cover without some punctuation since your rocks will soon disappear and the whole sight will be difficult to digest. The same goes for invasive plants which should not be allowed into a rockery.

No matter how you may long to grow acid-loving plants do not try and change the nature of your rockery soil in order to accommodate them. You will be doomed to disappointment since the neutral rain-water will wash over the (almost certainly limestone) rocks and render all the soil alkaline too. It is better to grow such treasures in pots or in stone troughs elsewhere where they are very sheltered. However, for those who cannot forgo heathers there are two species which will grow well in the Mediterranean. They are *Erica* × *darleyensis* and *E. herbacea* (syn. *E. carnea*). They tend to look a bit scrubby in high summer and should be protected by some deciduous planting which will have disappeared by the time their own flowering season has arrived.

The problem of falling leaves on a rockery should be left until late spring if possible, when they can either be blown off if you have the right machinery or the whole rockery can be top dressed with fine chopped bark. By the time the bark has disappeared the leaves will have rotted into the soil. Bark improves drainage and prevents weeds germinating, in particular clover which seems to come from nowhere.

Strictly speaking you should never use fertilizer on a rockery. However, since a rockery in the Mediterranean has no, or very few, alpines and since the autumn and spring rain quickly wash out such nutrient as there is in the soil you could use a very mild fertilizer such as N.P.K.5–10-10 or even simple bone meal at half the normal dosage.

Suitable plants for a Mediterranean rockery are:- acaena, dwarf aquilegia, anemone, arabis, armeria, aubrieta (northern Mediterranean only), chionodoxa, cistus, crocus, cyclamen, dwarf cytisus, erica, dwarf dianthus, draba, erigeron, erinus, dwarf gypsophila, helianthemum, helichrysum, hepatica (in shade), hypericum, iberis, dwarf lavender, dwarf narcissus, nierembergia, dwarf phlox, potentilla, primula, ramonda, prostrate rosemary, saxifrages, scilla, sedums, the various creeping or dwarf thymes, dwarf tulips and veronica.

39

WATER GARDENS

Water is scarce in the Mediterranean region and therefore a pond or lake is not a common sight. Because of the climate water must move or be oxygenated, either by fish or by plants, otherwise mosquitoes will take up residence and make outside dining a misery to say nothing of having sheets of green algae where there should be a limpid pool.

Large fountains are expensive to instal and although the water circulates with a submersible pump this can be rather irritating to have on all the time. The old Moorish pools with one or two jets in the middle are an ideal answer to having water in the garden for both beauty and practicality since in a crisis, provided there are no fish, you can use the water for plants. Personally, I do not find tinkling water particularly restful but this is a matter of taste. The Spanish make clever small round fountains in stone which are ideal as a focal point in a small garden or on a terrace. Of course, they need to be fitted before the garden and/or terrace is completed otherwise there is a lot of messy work to hide. At all costs avoid the free-form fibreglass pools which look most unnatural. The most Mediterranean thing of all is to have a raised round or octagonal pool, with or without a fountain, and preferably with some fish or aquatic plants. This can be made of waterproofed concrete which can be either rendered and painted, faced in stone or tiles or even clothed with dark stained wood.

Waterside plants are relatively uncommon in the Mediterranean garden since the weather is against them in all except the proper natural marshes such as you find in the Camargue, Venice and parts of the south of Spain. However, proper water plants are fairly common and provided you are prepared to spend a certain amount of money and a great deal of care creating a water garden is not particularly difficult. It is not as labour intensive as a rockery but you must be prepared to drain and clean out the container every three or four years, and prune or discard the aquatic plants, otherwise something beautiful can become quickly overgrown and rather squalid.

When planting your artificial lake or pond (so much the better if you have a natural garden stream which can feed it) do remember that certain aquatic plants hate having their leaves constantly splashed by water from a fountain, so you should think carefully about having one if, for instance, you want water lilies. Fish, on the other hand, keep a pool free of algae and never touch water lilies. The most ordinary goldfish will do but at least buy them from a reputable dealer specializing in water gardens. Pet shops tend to assume you are going to keep everything indoors which is not the case. Also make sure the fish you choose do not rush and bite any hand unsuspectingly put into the water (Koi carp can be quite vicious as I have found to my cost). People always seem rather surprised when told that fish will require feeding, not necessarily every day but certainly at least twice a week until the insect population is enough to keep them happy in between times. And what makes them happy can make you miserable in turn! Depending on your winter climate they either need feeding every two days or even a little more often since the insect population will be reduced or, if the pond ices over, will need a hole or holes made in the ice to allow the air to pass in. Do not smash a hole, as the shock waves can kill the fish. Use either a hairdryer on the lowest heat or a heated, wet pad of cloth. You can buy open mesh plastic balls to prevent ice closing on the whole pond. Unless you have chosen the tropical sort, most fish will survive very cold weather. In the country you may need to net the pool against herons and other wading birds but this is not particularly common and easily dealt with. Aquatic plants can grow up through the netting if it is put on at a suitable time. Black thread, stretched across the top of the pond will also prevent birds from landing.

Pools, ponds and artificial lakes should be professionally installed since do-it-yourself installations tend to leak sooner or later with disastrous results. Avoid butyl sheeting pools – they quickly disintegrate in the Mediterranean heat and you can never successfully camouflage their edges. Properly made cement pools are best – either rectangular if the garden is to be a formal one or free form if it is on the wild side. You will need proper drainage facilities even though they are only to be used on rare occasions. In Italy anything over 10,000 litres (not very big) will need a separate septic tank as you are not allowed to drain into the municipal sewer or, in the country, into your normal household septic tank.

What to plant is a matter of taste and it is more important to say what *not* to plant. The most notorious of all is the water hyacinth (*Eichornia crasspipes*, which blocks the Amazon and Orinoco Rivers for miles and makes shipping impossible), commonly available in every Mediterranean aquatic nursery. Charming as it may be, it grows like a weed and quickly kills infinitely more desirable aquatics in its desire for space. Another ramper is *Elodea crispa* which behaves in precisely the same way and specializes in killing expensive water lilies and nelumbiums. The third shocker and water lily eater is what is commonly known as floating heart (*Nymphoides peltata*) which is not worth having in spite of its beautiful yellow flowers in midsummer.

Water lilies (nymphaea species) can be over vigorous and you should think in terms of re-planting at least every two years. The flowers come in a number of colours and bloom from spring to the end of summer. Occasionally, after flowering, they tend to stand up above the water rather than float but this can be avoided by choosing varieties of *N. marliacea* which are more or less guaranteed to continue floating. They are planted in containers with at least 30cm/12in above their crowns. Unless you see something you really long for you will find anyone with water lilies will be overjoyed to give you a few. Not so pink-flowered nelumbiums (*Lotus nelumbo* species) which again grow in containers but instead of floating rise 60–90cm/2–3ft above the water. Occasionally they come at double that height which can be rather overpowering. Although they increase they do so rather less rapidly than water lilies and need dividing about every six or seven years. Some fish have a tendency to nibble at lotus roots but not to the extent of damaging or killing them.

No pool, pond or lake should be covered by more than a third with floating plants or its oxygenation will go awry and fish will suffer. Also, more than most places, do not be tempted to plant trees too near your pool since their roots can quickly break up its foundation. Be very wary of the weeping willow – it is far too greedy for the average Mediterranean environment. The only exception to this is where you have a large, natural lake but even then, in a hot summer, you will see the water level go down quite remarkably.

As with rockeries, though to a lesser extent, a water garden is not for the absentee gardener unless one can guarantee help three or four times a year when it is needed.

5

The Mediterranean
Kitchen Garden

If you are limited for space and have to choose one or the other then choose a fruit garden. If you are not in permanent residence but more of an absentee gardener, again, choose to have a fruit garden. There are a few perennial vegetables such as asparagus, spinach beet, Jerusalem artichokes and globe artichokes, but the majority of vegetables and salads need fairly constant care. That is not to say a fruit garden needs no care but on a domestic scale such work is distinctly seasonal and not onerous.

Moreover, planting fruit trees, bushes and vines can serve more than one purpose. A grape vine will provide a shady arbour; almond, apricot or peach trees can line a drive or avenue and provide shade; currant bushes, properly pruned each year, can make an attractive and useful hedge; and nut trees, if you are prepared to wait, can be extremely decorative. Indeed, apart from preparing the ground properly, a *sine qua non* for virtually everything in the garden, pruning at the right season and giving the standard winter wash (see chapter on pests and diseases) fruit trees will stand a surprising amount of neglect.

Except at altitude (i.e. above 500m/1650ft) the Mediterranean offers a wealth of sub-tropical and temperate fruits from citrus to peaches, pistachios to Japanese medlars. However, a fruit which does not grow well is the apple (the winters are not cool enough in most places) and to a lesser degree the pear. If you can grow this latter at above 400m/ 1300ft so much the better since it appears to like a slightly harder winter than the average Mediterranean garden offers. Bear in mind that the best pears come from Central Europe, Belgium and Luxembourg and you will understand why their taste is not always wonderful when grown further south.

No matter what tree, bush or vine you are going to plant, it is a good idea to prepare the ground as well as you can. In the case of many fruits such as the vine, apricots and figs, stones do not matter; on the contrary they can help to conserve heat in the soil, but in all cases the ground can do with improved drainage and added humus.

One of the most important pieces of advice is to buy your fruit trees in the country in which you live. That may sound obvious but many people in northern Italy particularly in the Piedmont, buy from France since they have certain plum and peach varieties which are virtually disease free and better flavoured. Many of these are not suitable for use farther south and the first real Mediterranean summer will kill them. Therefore, be very circumspect about ordering from abroad and only do so if it is really necessary as with mirabelles or certain pear varieties; in any event, in the northern Mediterranean, both need to be grown at altitude.

FRUIT AND NUTS

ALMOND *Amygdalus communis*

Whatever the variety, this tree needs warm, alkaline and stoney soil. Spring frosts are to be feared since it flowers early and once the blossom is frosted you will get almonds with black slime inside instead of nuts. It is one of the most beautiful trees in the area, which you can either train or let grow as it wishes and it stands drought very well. Always get a local variety – Spanish almonds do not do well in the South of France.

APRICOT *Prunus armeniaca*

This fruit will grow all over the Mediterranean area up to an altitude of about 600m/2000ft. It rather likes a chilly winter though not too much frost. The best apricots come from Turkey but the Italians, Spaniards and French, in that order, also have good varieties. Usually the tree is grown as a large open bush or pyramid but occasionally, in slightly colder areas, it may be espaliered. Apricot trees planted facing south-east are said to give bigger and better fruit. A good idea, if space is limited, is to have an early, medium and late variety so you do not have to collect all the fruit at once but can space it out between June and August.

Apricot trees need very little pruning except to prevent them getting too tall to collect the fruit – any such work should be done in February–March before the blossom comes out. They do not usually suffer from pests and diseases but a winter tar oil wash or a branded product which does the same thing is an excellent idea. They do best with plenty of organic manure but if you cannot get that, use a fertilizer low in nitrogen and high in potassium and phosphates. Always pick the fruit just before complete ripeness – usually the day before you need it.

CHERRY *Prunus avium* and *P. cerasus*

Northern Mediterranean only. You will need occasional water in late spring and early summer for your cherries to do well.

P. avium are the sweet cherries and are usually grown as half standard or standard trees. They take three or four years from planting to fruit properly. Do not feed until they are at least four years old and never give any form of nitrogen. The bigarreau varieties such as 'Napoleon', 'Burlat' and 'Moreau' appear to do best in this climate. Check carefully whether your cherries have the right pollinators – cropping can be poor if this is not taken account of. Where cherry trees are not commonly on sale, for instance in the south of Spain, it usually means they do not do well. Prune sweet cherries in winter, only during the first few years and thereafter to keep a tidy, manageable tree. Both bacterial canker and chlorosis can be a problem (see chapter on pests and diseases). You can net against birds or put the (shortened) trees in a fruit cage or have a bird scarer. Wasps can be an occasional problem too.

P. cerasus, or sour cherry, includes the morello, the amarena and the marasca, or amarasca, from which Maraschino is made.

All are self-fertile and although they need pruning each year, removing at least one third of the new growth, they are virtually pest and disease free. They are usually grown as fans in the region in clean, open ground. Unless you can find farmyard manure then use a fertilizer low in nitrogen and high in potash. These cherries should be cut off the tree (never pick or you will tear the tender bark) and can be used for black cherry jam, tarts and liqueurs.

CHESTNUT *Castanea sativa*

The Spanish sweet chestnut is a large tree and one which you will plant for your grandchildren rather than for yourself – so choose the position carefully and not too near the house. In thirty years it will provide enviable shade. Usually one chestnut tree in a garden is enough. Virtually pest and disease free except for rodents after the nuts. It needs no pruning.

CITRUS

This family includes the lemon, lime, orange, tangerine, mandarin, grapefruit, etc. They are all evergreen but in cold conditions may well drop their leaves in which case forget about fruit in the coming year, since they will be using up all their energy refoliating. If this becomes a common occurrence it means they are not getting enough winter protection. In the south of France you can grow citrus successfully only in the various suitable micro-climates found between Hyères and Menton. You will soon discover whether your property has been blessed with a suitable micro-climate.

The most tender citrus of all is the lime (*C. aurantifolia*) which can be grown only in the southern Mediterranean Basin. It prefers desert or tropical, rather than sub-tropical, conditions. Once adult it produces fruit all year round.

The next most sensitive is the grapefruit (*C.* × *paradisi*) and like the lime it prefers desert conditions. You cannot make it fruit unless it can be kept out all year round. It forms a very decorative large bush. It is generally for the southern Mediterranean Basin only, though I have seen it successfully grown on the Costa del Sol in Spain.

Lemons (*C. limon*) are very sensitive to cold and to excessive sunshine. By and large where you see lemons growing successfully you can count on growing all the following forms of citrus. Unlike oranges, lemons can take up to a year to ripen on the tree. There is a cultivar called 'Quatre Saisons' which flowers and fruits throughout the year.

The Seville orange (*C. aurantium*), like the lemon, is of tropical origin and will not stand much frost though will tolerate cold winds. This tends to be the orange tree used for lining streets and decorating gardens.

The mandarin or tangerine (*C. reticulata* syn. *C. nobilis*) will tolerate quite a bit of cold and a few degrees of frost after the fruit has been gathered. It is fairly wind tolerant also but wind can make for dry, pithy fruits.

The sweet orange (*C. sinensis*) which is found in several varieties – 'Washington Navel', 'Valencia', 'Navel', 'Navelino', 'Maltese' and 'California' are commonly seen. It grows best where the weather is slightly doubtful. For flavour it needs a coldish winter but does not like frost, snow or wet feet. Consequently professional growers spend a great deal of their time cossetting their sweet orange trees.

If you are at all doubtful grow your citrus trees in pots until you can be sure of your weather. Generally, with the exception of the Seville orange, the sweeter the orange the spinier the tree – the spines can be quite vicious. They need to be planted in an open but not too windy position in good friable earth which means you will have to improve your basic Mediterranean soil with humus and manure. The whole citrus family resents disturbance and in pots prefers to be rather potbound. They need no pruning except to remove dead wood. However, citrus plants are very subject to red spider and scale attack as well as chlorosis and this can make them a doubtful proposition for the absentee gardener. On the other hand, I rented a house in Spain for a year where nothing had been touched for five years and the citrus trees were in perfect condition – so you never can tell.

CURRANTS *Ribes*

Black currants (*R. nigrum*) grow neither tidily nor well in the Mediterranean region and in the northern part they are susceptible to mildew. You should stick to red and white currants (which are *R. sativum*, the white being a natural seedling lacking the red pigment); both can be grown on cordons or you can make a hedge from properly pruned bushes. In winter when the plants are bare and dormant they should be pruned by approximately one third but do not do this to black currants which fruit on the previous season's wood. All the currants are subject to attack by aphids and red spider. In a damp summer, or with automatic watering sprays, mildew can be a problem.

FIG *Ficus carica*

Considered by some to be *the* Mediterranean fruit. It needs no special conditions and is hardy throughout the Mediterranean region. It dislikes wet feet and heavy feeding which makes for leaves rather than fruit. Greek and Turkish figs are said to be the best but virtually every Mediterranean country produces excellent figs and it is best to choose named varieties in the country in which you live. Depending on where you live you may or may not get two crops a year. Figs form in autumn and remain on the tree ripening in the following spring. Summer and autumn fruiting varieties are better for being given a little water if possible once the fruit has formed until it is ripe. Keep such watering regular or cracked fruit can result. The fruit travel and keep badly so should be picked just before use. No pruning is needed except to keep the tree within bounds and it is virtually disease and pest free. Wasps can be a problem if you leave fruit on the ground.

GRAPE *Vitis vinifera*

Although they are among the most tolerant of fruit, grapes will not grow in desert conditions unless a great deal of time and money is spent improving their habitat. They are hardy in the whole Mediterranean region. They need pruning every year to produce good fruit (or wine) and even those trained on a pergola are improved by a bit of tidying up. Do not overfeed or you will get light, sappy growth which will succumb to the first frost. For the northern Mediterranean you are limited only by what your local district allows you to plant. If it is for wine there are very strict rules in France, Italy and Spain. However, there is no such problem with table grapes. In the southern Mediterranean the choice is much more limited and probably the best white grape for eating is 'Dattier de Beyrouth' which is extremely prolific even in dry conditions. If you are making hedges or pergolas from grape vines, make sure the supporting structure is really strong – it will have to last for years and it may be worth while to think of using metal rather than wood.

A whole book could be written on the pests and diseases of the vine. The many fungus diseases can be kept under control by using two different fungicides at fortnightly intervals. Except by way of prevention do not spray for fungus diseases until you see mildew or grey mould. Often professional wine growers keep a rosebush at the end of each row. This gets fungus problems approximately a week before the vines are attacked and you can then spray preventatively. However, do spray against the many pests (caterpillars, weevils and various flies) which can be devastating.

HAZELNUT *Corylus avellana* and *C. colurna*

This bush or tree grows wild in many parts of the Mediterranean and in some places, such as Turkey and Italy, the Turkish hazel (*C. colurna*) is cultivated on a large scale. Both it and the ordinary hazel (*C. avellana*) are easy to grow, tolerant of drought, hardy, and seem to be free of pests and diseases except for nut weevils which bore holes in the fruit. This can be prevented by spraying in winter. Once the nuts have been infected brown rot can set in in which case everything must be cleared up and burnt. Spray with a suitable fungicide immediately and with a product such as ICI's Clean Up once the tree is dormant. Pruning consists of keeping the middle of the bush open and shortening old shoots in March after flowering. Nuts form on the previous year's wood.

LOQUAT or JAPANESE MEDLAR *Eriobotrya japonica*

This is much grown as an ornamental tree and occasionally you see the small, yellow, oval fruit in shops. This makes good jam, tarts and ice creams. However, it bruises easily and does not travel well. It can be grown in virtually all the northern Mediterranean and in the Levant, Morocco and Algeria. It is a most attractive evergreen shade tree with rich glossy green toothed leaves. However, to get good fruit it needs plenty of water so this must be taken into account when planting.

MELON *Cucumis melo*

Melons may be grown throughout the Mediterranean. They are an annual vine of which there are many varieties. You can try using seed from a melon you have enjoyed but it may not be viable. Purchased seed often comes in the form of F1 hybrids and this is probably the best way for a beginner. Depending on your climate you sow in peat pots indoors and plant out at the three leaf stage or you can sow seed where it is to grow. Plant at least 45cm/18in apart in rich, well manured soil. Usually you do not need to pollinate artificially plants which are growing outside. Once the fruit is the size of your fist start giving plenty of water with a little liquid manure and when they are full size just give water until they ripen. Try and stagger plants or you can end up with too many melons at a time. Never allow more than four or five melons to a plant to come to maturity, even if they are the tiny sort such as 'Cavaillon' or 'Ogen'. Certain melon seeds coming from America are not allowed to be planted in E.E.C. countries. This is not because of disease but for commercial reasons. You will have to do a lot of planning to get American or Israeli melon seed into an

E.E.C. country – whatever you do, do not have it sent direct. Better to have someone bring it or send it from a less suspect country in letter form – Switzerland or Austria for example.

NECTARINE see PEACH

PEACH *Prunus persica*

This is one of the most important Mediterranean fruits. There are many varieties with white or yellow flesh as well as smooth skinned types known as *nectarines* or *brugnons* in French. Some taste ambrosial and others like cheap scented cotton wool. It is always best to buy the peach trees normally used in your part of the country though it can be said that neither the Spanish nor Italians are very adventurous in the matter of varieties. The commonest available varieties are 'Hale', 'Amsden' and 'Redhaven' and there are better varieties on sale as trees than as fruit. Peaches do not travel well nor does the tree last long – ten years is a good age. Peach trees prefer alkaline soil with quite a few stones to which you add humus and organic or chemical fertilizer. They are hardy in the Mediterranean, do not mind wind and need little pruning. You must decide what shape is best for your garden or orchard – they come as half-standards, pyramids, espaliers, goblets or fans for walls (usually totally unnecessary in the Mediterranean). Peaches fruit on the previous year's wood and you should bear this in mind when pruning. This should be done by removing a number of fruiting branches the moment the fruit has been picked. If non-fruiting branches need to be removed this can be done at the same time (August or September) or when the tree is dormant. Both peaches and apricots produce far too much fruit and at least half should be removed, either by you or by the wind – otherwise the fruit will all be small and rather tasteless. Do not do this too soon since you may well end up with an empty tree having removed half yourself and the wind removing the rest. It is best to wait until mid or end May to do this.

Peaches are subject to many diseases and pests. The worst diseases are bacterial canker and peach leaf curl which you should spray against when the tree is dormant in January or February, depending on where you live. Bacterial canker can be a very real problem and so can occasional mildew. The main pests are blackfly, greenfly, earwigs, wasps, red spider and two sorts of larvae one of which enters the fruit and causes it to drop even in its green state and the other enters the fruit and virtually demolishes the whole stone, leaving the fruit whole and seemingly perfect. You get an unpleasant surprise when cutting the peach in half. All the pests can be sprayed against – see chapter on pests and diseases.

PEAR *Pyrus communis*

Pears can be grown only in the northern Mediterranean and then only successfully at an altitude above 400m/1300ft. Even then they are not always wonderful and it is best to stick to late maturing varieties such as 'Conference', 'Doyenné du Comice' and 'Royale'. 'Williams Bon Chrétien' which ripens in September can be good but can quickly rot. In any event do not have more than one tree of each variety. Pears will not give good fruit unless you plant their proper pollinator. They need well manured soil, protection from wind but they need little pruning when young. Later you will have to reduce the size of the tree, since it can grow very high indeed, bearing in mind that pears are borne on wood which is three or four years old. They need rather more frequent watering than most fruit trees otherwise their fruit can crack. The main pests are birds, aphids and red spider. The main diseases are fireblight (notifiable to the local Ministry of Agriculture), bacterial canker, brown rot and mildew. All can be prevented by proper spraying at the right time (see chapter on pests and diseases). This is not a fruit tree for the absentee gardener who has no-one to spray for him or occasionally water the trees.

PISTACHIO *Pistacia vera*

Southern Mediterranean, southern Italy, Greece. A medium size nut tree of about 10m/30ft the green fruit of which is known mostly from pistachio ice cream or salted nuts. Easy to grow but it needs male and female to produce nuts. It will tolerate great drought once established – indeed the flavour is said to be better – but absolutely no frost. There are many different varieties in the countries where this nut is commercialized ranging from the small pistachio from Sfax in Tunisia to the extra large sort in the Near East and Turkey. Although it sometimes fruits at three years the main fruiting comes at around ten or twelve years, at approximately 9–11kg/20–25lb per tree.

PLUM and DAMSON *Prunus domestica* and *P. damascena*

These will not grow well unless you can guarantee a certain amount of cold weather in winter and therefore they are suitable for the northern Mediterranean only. They will succeed in Spain in northern Catalonia and in Italy north of the Piombino Peninsula. At altitude you will have more success and can even grow mirabelles if you are in France. Both plums and damsons need rich soil with plenty of humus – not always easy to provide in the Mediterranean. They also like high nitrogen fertilizers plus some extra potash. They tend to crop well one year and badly the next. They are subject to attack by aphids, birds and red spider. Bacterial canker and brown rot are their main diseases (see chapter on pests and diseases).

POMEGRANATE *Punica granatum*

This 5m/15ft fruit tree will grow in virtually any soil, tolerate drought and produce fruit in November. To have good tasting fruit you must have a coldish winter so desert or mountainous conditions are ideal. The flowers are scarlet and very decorative. It needs no pruning and is free of pests and diseases. The fruits are best made into syrups (grenadine) or jellies for eating with game.

QUINCE *Cydonia oblonga*

Hardy throughout the Mediterranean. A very attractive shade tree ideal for courtyards and patios though it takes rather long to grow to full size. It has dark green foliage, which turns a brilliant yellow in autumn and there are white, pear-like blossoms in spring. You either love or hate the taste of quince – no Victorian apple pie was considered good without it – but even if you hate the fruit it is an excellent deciduous tree in its own right. It is disease free apart from a tendency to brown rot which can easily be prevented by spraying in winter when it is dormant. However, many pests like its fruit including aphids, caterpillars, codling moth, sawfly and red spider (see chapter on pests and diseases). The fruit is strong smelling and can affect the taste of other fruit stored nearby.

RASPBERRY *Rubus idaeus*

Northern Mediterranean only. Not an ideal Mediterranean crop since the plant becomes dormant in heat and often before the fruit has had time to ripen. Cutting the canes hard back to produce autumn fruit ('Lloyd George' for example) or using an autumn variety (say September) does not appear to be the answer. However, at altitude you may have a slightly better chance since the heat comes that bit later. Raspberries need rich, moisture retaining soil which is difficult to find or reproduce in the Mediterranean. They should have a potash rich fertilizer in late winter and a light dressing of sulphate of ammonia in mid-spring. Although the flavour is good the amount is always poor compared with more temperate climes. Virus diseases seem to be no problem here but aphids and red spider are. Pruning consists of cutting out the canes which have fruited in the previous year.

STRAWBERRY *Fragaria* × *ananassa*

Although for the northern Mediterranean only, these are a better bet than raspberries. If possible, it is better to plant strawberries which do not produce runners otherwise you will end up working very hard in boiling sunshine. The ever bearing varieties, which are the only type which are virus prone in the Mediterranean, quickly exhaust themselves even with generous amounts of feeding. In any event think in terms of only three crops from a plant and then renew them. They are always best in their second year. Those living in France are considerably luckier than those living in Spain or Italy though the former produces good varieties on the fruit market. In any event, in Spain strawberries are so cheap it is almost not worthwhile growing them. Italy seems to produce only about two or three varieties, all designed to be eaten with orange- or lemon-juice and sugar, or in sweet red wine, without which they are poorly flavoured. Birds, slugs and snails and strawberry beetle all munch strawberries with relish. Eelworms and aphids are the biggest pest problem.

WALNUT *Juglans regia*

Whole of the Mediterranean except North Africa, Israel and Lebanon. The common walnut makes a handsome tree – eventually. It really is something you plant for the long term since, unless you are very young indeed, you are unlikely to live to see it at its best. Be careful where you site it since little will grow under it due to the juglone which is imparted by mature trees to the surrounding soil. It can start cropping as little as ten years after planting but this is rare. The main enemies are rodents and birds which attack and/or eat the nuts. Apart from honey fungus (see chapter on pests and diseases) the tree is disease free.

Vegetables

This list will not include salads such as lettuce, *escarole*, endive, *radicchio* and oak-leaf lettuce all of which can be obtained in the shops easily or can be bought as small plants for setting out in the vegetable plot or in containers. They are all very easy to grow from seed. One or two salads should be added to this list such as the Mediterranean natives rocket (*Eruca sativa*) and purslane (*Portulaca oleracea*) which is one of the main ingredients of the Lebanese *tabbouleh* salad. Rocket is easy to grow and gives a sharp peppery taste to a salad. It is best served with other salad greens. Purslane is an acquired taste for some, particularly cooked, when it is too like slimy spinach to be enjoyed. However, raw, it is an interesting and unusual salad herb.

As mentioned before there are a few perennial vegetables but their tendency is take over the plot in your absence, particularly in the case of Florence fennel and Jerusalem artichokes. Except to clean the ground it really is not worth growing potatoes unless you are a devotee of potato salad and need a firm, waxy potato which hardly exists in the region. The same goes for most of the root vegetables. Below is a selection of vegetables commonly grown outside in the Mediterranean region.

ARTICHOKE *Cynara scolymus*

The globe artichoke is a Mediterranean native, easily grown provided you choose the right variety. In southern Spain, southern Italy, parts of Greece and the whole of the southern Mediterranean Basin you should get two crops a year; one at the end of summer and another at the end of April or beginning of May. In the early twentieth century the French discovered that the Provençal artichoke grew more easily in Brittany and this region now produces over eighty per cent of all French artichokes. The climate is distinctly humid in Brittany and the soil acid. It is, therefore, important that you do not try to grow Brittany varieties such as 'Vert de Laon' or 'Camus de Bretagne' unless you can assure copious daily watering. Throughout Mediterranean Italy only one variety is grown which is the pointed, prickly, violet type. If you want other sorts you must sow from seed and bide your time. The exception is 'Palla Romana' which is round headed but considerably smaller than the Brittany types and with less flavour than the violet sort. Italians eat very young artichokes raw with vinaigrette or with *bagna cauda*. Violet artichokes are grown in Provence, Algeria, Morocco and Egypt; to a lesser degree, in Greece and Turkey. Spain grows both sorts, round and pointed, green and violet, and does so on a commercial scale.

In many countries year-old plants can be purchased for planting out and this can be one of the best and easiest ways of starting an artichoke patch. Since artichokes do not give of their best until after three years you should organise your plantation so that there are always one or two year-old plants to take over from those you have thrown out.

It is a comforting thought that the further south you are the less your artichokes will be attacked. In wetter climes mildew and various fungus diseases can be a problem (try to avoid wetting the leaves when watering). Use a general fungicide if this is the problem but withhold it three weeks before harvesting. Again, the hotter the weather the less pests attack but alas the universally present artichoke moth *Vanessa carduii* and its caterpillars may defoliate the plant leaving just the veins. Any anti-caterpillar spray will deal with this.

ASPARAGUS *Asparagus officinalis*

Northern Mediterranean only. Not a difficult crop to grow and now there are several varieties from France which are male only (the female sort produces only berries). These are available in France, Spain and to a certain extent in Italy where you have to buy them in rather larger quantities than the average home gardener would wish. Perhaps such a purchase could be shared between three or four people. Asparagus can be started from seed but it is easier to start with one or two year old 'crowns'. It depends on taste and where you live as to which asparagus to plant. France and Spain both have white (with violet tips) and green asparagus; Italy and the rest of the Mediterranean tends to have more green than white. In the Mediterranean the crop should always be grown in a raised bed in well manured bought-in potting soil, thus ensuring a healthy beginning. Once the foliage has turned yellow in early autumn clip it off. Do not cut the asparagus spears until the crowns are three years old. Top dress with rich organic manure (salt is not necessary in the Mediterranean) every year just before new vegetation shows or in winter if the weather is not cold. Always hand weed an asparagus bed since the plants are shallow rooting. The asparagus beetle and the asparagus fly are the main pests and are easily dealt with (see chapter on pests and diseases). Asparagus rust is rare in the Mediterranean but if it does occur pull up everything and do not start an asparagus plantation for at least five years. Clean the soil with a fungicide applied every six months for two or three years.

AUBERGINE *Solanum melongena*

A very delicate plant, cousin to a tomato but far more tender; it will not tolerate temperatures under 18°C/65°F so be very circumspect about putting the plants out too early. They will need support and grow to about 1m/3ft or so. Pinch out the tips to encourage bushiness as you would a tomato. Always wear gloves when handling aubergine plants since they are very prickly and some people are allergic to the fine hairs covering the leaves. Aubergines come sausage shaped or round, violet, black, dark brown or white though they all taste virtually the same. They need a fair amount of watering and plenty of feeding. It is a good idea to mulch the plants if you can. Pests rarely attack aubergines but mildew can be a problem at times. Do not spray with fungicide within three weeks of harvesting.

AVOCADO PEAR *Persea gratissima* or *P. americana*

This bush or tree is a native of the wetter regions of Mexico and of Guatemala. Therefore, it should not be grown in the Mediterranean region unless you have a permanent source of water from which you can allow daily about 40 litres (about 9 gallons) for an average tree or about half that amount for two avocado bushes. This is its only demand and the warmer parts of the Mediterranean i.e. where lemons are easily grown, are perfect for its culture. Moreover, the low humidity lessens the danger of insect and disease attack. Avocado trees or bushes are not normally self-fertile and you should plant at least two. In fact bushes are best for ease of culture and harvesting otherwise you will find yourself shinning up a tall tree to get a couple of avocados since they tend to fruit high rather than low.

There are three basic types of avocado the Mexican which is the easiest to grow and the most resistant to cold; the Guatemalan which has a somewhat horny skin but is unsuitable for the Mediterranean climate; the West Indian which produces slightly larger fruit and is the most commonly cultivated in the Mediterranean. There are many cultivars of this type, mostly American, which are on sale at specialist outlets. The best are 'Anaheim', 'Haas', 'Fuerte' and 'Topa-topa' and the French have hybridized a great deal from this type. All plants are grafted onto Mexican rootstock. Never expect fruit from an ungrafted plant.

Dig out a fairly large hole for each bush and replace the soil with rich, well draining compost. Plant approximately 3.5m/12ft apart for bushes and 7m/20ft for trees. Feed as you would for citrus. Avocados occasionally suffer from scab in the Mediterranean but usually it is very mild and damages only the skin and rather as with a potato can be ignored. There are also occasional infestations of thrips.

CUCUMBER *Cucumis sativus*

A much used vegetable except in Italy. In Greece, Egypt and parts of North Africa there is a per capita consumption of at least one a day. All can be grown outside once the temperature is above 18–21°C/65–70°F, allowing each plant at least 1m sq./1 yd sq. Give wire or string horizontal supports up to a height of about 1m/3ft around which the cucumber tendrils will twine. Daily watering is necessary. In the Mediterranean cucumbers are subject to few diseases but red spider, nematodes and cucumber fly are all common (see chapter on pests and diseases). Cucumber mosaic is hardly known in the Mediterranean but if it does occur clean the patch, burn the plants and do not plant cucumbers or related species for at least five years.

FLORENCE FENNEL *Foeniculum dulce*

Much cultivated in Italy and France for its white bulbs which are useful in salads or cooked *au gratin*, it is very easy to grow. Seeds should be sown 50cm/18in apart in rows about 30cm/1ft apart. Once the bulbs form, you cover them with about 30cm/1ft of earth to blanch them. When harvesting you cut down or dig up the whole plant. There is no point in letting the plant produce a second crop since the bulbs will be extremely small and difficult to use. Overwatered plants produce a rather tasteless bulb and therefore you should limit watering to the minimum necessary for survival. The leaves can be used as a flavouring, especially good with fish, as can the dried stalks for oven baked or barbecued fish. Neither let your fennel seed (every seed germinates) nor leave it in the ground since it will quickly take over and is difficult to eradicate after two or three years.

OLIVE *Olea europaea*

Although originating in the Near East this tree has become a symbol of the Mediterranean. It is most accommodating, standing up to virtually any sort of weather, including snow at times, but not damp. The Huguenot French tried to grow olives in the Cape Province of South Africa but the atmosphere was too damp in winter and the trees died. On average you should not have winters where the temperature is constantly lower than 2°C/35°F but the occasional really cold snap will not disturb well established trees.

The first decision you must make is whether you want olives for oil or olives for eating and in the latter case green or black. By and large in Greece, Cyprus and the Levant you will find only black olives for eating. This does not mean you cannot grow green olives for the same purpose, just that it will be difficult to find them. The four most popular green table olives are 'Picholine' (*Uova di Piccione* in Italian), 'Sevillana' (Spanish), 'Ascolana' and 'San Agostino' (both Italian).

Before purchasing olive trees for oil at least make sure you like the taste since the olive oils of Spain, the Levant, Greece and southern Italy are heavy and fruity and not to everyone's taste. Some may prefer the oil of the South of France, Liguria, Tuscany and Umbria in Italy which is light, pale coloured and not so powerful. There are many varieties for oil production and it is best to ask for the local sort rather than branch out with something unfamiliar. The only exception to this is for table olives of which 'Sevillana' is the finest of its kind.

Although the olive is not subject to many pests or diseases the few which do attack can be devastating. Thrips, olive flies and suckers – bringing disease with them – can devastate a crop though, luckily, not the tree. Arsenate of lead is the antidote commonly used in the area but there are plenty less dangerous substances which work just as well (see chapter on pests and diseases). Usually only one fungus attacks olive trees and that is cycloconium. It is difficult to miss as all the leaves become black over a very short period. This can lead to total defoliation. Normally you should spray against this in January or February by way of prevention and then once again in mid-autumn.

The most effective cycloconium fungicide is Ciba-Geigy's Oxiram but if this is not available then use a local remedy. It can be used in mid-season if need be. Follow the maker's instruction and never exceed the stated dose. Whatever you do, do not listen to locals who tell you to prune the tree hard to cure the problem and improve fruiting – it will not. In any event how can removing branches that are sometimes as much as 100 years old renew the tree next season and what has that to do with killing fungus?

Olives are harvested from November to the beginning of February. If you have many trees then it is wise to use an abcission agent (Ciba-Geigy's Alsol is the best known), which causes the fruit to drop. You spray the trees one evening and, having put down nets beforehand, collect the olives next morning. Otherwise you collect over a period of approximately two months since ripe olives remain tenaciously on the tree.

Olives must be treated before eating to eliminate the bitter gluco-sides. This is particularly so with green olives though black olives can often be dropped into a cold solution of salt and water (about 4 tablespoons of sea salt to 550ml/1pt of water). One of the simplest ways is to pierce the olive all over (a flower arranger's pin holder is quite useful but a fork will do the trick as well if more slowly) and put in cold water. Change the water every day for ten days and then put in whatever pickle you prefer with or without herbs, spices, garlic, etc. Some people sterilize olives but this tends to change the taste some-what. When collecting eating olives use a wide container and never put too many in together as they bruise easily which looks unattractive once pickled.

Olives for oil are best taken to the local co-operative or olive mill. The remaining pulp which can be made into briquettes is very useful for burning in household fires. The smell is delicious and they burn a long time.

PEA *Pisum sativum*

The ordinary garden pea as known in western Europe does not grow well in the Mediterranean as it becomes dormant at 16–21°C/65–70°F. It can be grown in spring above 400m/1300ft if you start the peas in slight heat and then put outside early but it is difficult to get a good crop.

PEPPER *Capsicum annuum*

This vegetable grows throughout the Mediterranean with the greatest of ease provided you improve the soil to make it rich and well drained. It can also be grown conveniently in raised beds. Peppers should be sown in February and planted out in the open in March at about 60cm/2ft apart. Provide support and tie in new growth as and when necessary. They are virtually pest and disease free but in a damp, warm summer mildew can be a problem. Spray with copper sulphate when young, before the fruit has formed, and with a fungicide should this problem appear later.

SWEET CORN *Zea mays*

Although one sees fields of maize throughout the Mediterranean this is mainly for cattle and chickens and known as *grano Turco* in Italy where it is cultivated on a vast scale. Anyone trying to cook it and eat it will be disappointed. Sweetcorn is becoming rather more common in the northern Mediterranean region and is very easy to grow. Stagger sowings and start as early as you dare – you need a minimum night temperature of 18°C/65°F. The plants need to be spaced 50cm/18in apart and 75cm/30in between rows. They need much watering otherwise the corn will be starchy – ideal for cattle but not for humans. Generally pest and disease free.

TOMATO *Lycopersicon esculentum*

Another member of the cold-shy solanum family which grows remarkably well throughout the whole region. Except for the plum tomato usually sold as 'Roma' it is best not to try and grow any variety which has small, regular fruits since these are more suited to greenhouse culture. Most Mediterranean tomatoes are large, rather ugly looking fruit but with a far better flavour than anything grown north of Paris. One of the most commonly grown is 'Marmande' or 'Super Marmande' and eighty per cent of France's tomato production is of this cultivar grown in the Vaucluse. Sow seed from January to March, either under cover or in the open, but make sure you have a night temperature of a minimum of 18°C/65°F before planting out. For plum tomatoes slightly higher temperatures are needed. Give good support – there is no such thing as a bush tomato in the Mediterranean – 2m/6ft is not too high. Pinch out tips to make the plant branch out. Plant in rich soil – they do not mind clay – and water well. Tomatoes should be watered each time they flag. Give liquid manure at least once a week, or use a specially balanced tomato fertilizer.

Tomatoes are subject to many pests and diseases the most dangerous of which is tobacco mosaic. Keeping the soil clean and free of insects helps to prevent this disease but there is no cure. If your plants succumb, burn them and do not plant any member of the solanum family, including potatoes, in the same place for some years. Tomato canker, anthracnose and *Alternaria solani* are all fungus diseases which can be prevented by simply spraying with copper sulphate early in the season. All sorts of flies attack tomatoes and a general insecticide sprayed every fortnight should prevent their depredations. Cease spraying at least three weeks before harvesting fruit.

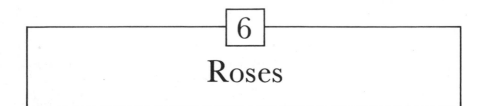

6

Roses

Many roses are native to the Mediterranean and most non-natives thrive in its frequently clay-laden soil. Gardeners new to the area should revise all their old ideas about how and where to grow roses and should choose only hybrids known to stand up to the intense summer heat and sun. All the species roses, except Scotch and Austrian briars, stand up well to heat – indeed the baking they get in the summer serves them well in winter and prevents die-back.

First of all, buy hybrid roses which have been raised either in the region in which you live or in one with a very similar climate. In France many of the large rose growers have nurseries in the north and many of their roses are poor doers in the south. People living in Spain do not have this problem since virtually all Spain enjoys a hot, dry summer. Although Italy is similar to Spain it is as well to remember that the most important rose breeding areas of the Veneto and Piemonte are cooler in summer than the rest of the country and roses grown in these districts may not do so well in hotter climates.

Some of the very best roses for a Mediterranean garden are the modern English shrub roses bred by David Austin which, provided you dead head at the appropriate time, will flower three or four times a year given good weather until mid-November. Indeed, their first and last flowering are the best of the three or four. Many of the Hybrid Musk roses such as 'Moonlight', 'Penelope', 'Felicia' and 'Cornelia' flower virtually non-stop. Of course, flowering as they do, such roses will need rather more feeding than shrub roses normally do.

Choose a position for your roses which is cool in summer compared with the rest of the garden. This is often difficult because it frequently means choosing a spot which is positively cold in winter. Above all do *not* plant in direct sun. Planted in bright sun, your roses will bloom quickly and the flowers will often not last the day but 'blow' by lunchtime. Strangely enough, drought is less of a problem than sun and most established roses will tolerate quite dry conditions. Dappled shade is best.

It is as well to change the type of systemic or ordinary fungicide you use frequently since it has been found that the roses (or the pests) often become used to a product. This can be rather expensive and swapping products with a friend or neighbour can lessen the cost provided you grow similar things and have similar problems. Living in an area where roses are grown for the north European florists' market I find it difficult to find really good sprays that work since the professional growers use such strong products (often unnecessarily) that mine must seem like plain water to the various fungi and insects.

Fungus diseases in the Mediterranean region are probably worse where you have professional horticulturalists nearby. There are three main offenders which in order of seriousness are black spot, powdery mildew and rose rust.

Certain roses are mildew-prone, such as 'Albertine', 'American Pillar', many of the Gallica group, 'Dorothy Perkins', 'Duke of Windsor', 'Elmshorn', 'Europeana', 'Frau Karl Druschki', 'Iceberg', 'Kathleen Harrop', 'La Reine Victoria', 'Little Dorrit', 'Masquerade', 'Madame Pierre Oger', 'Nevada', 'Nuits de Young', 'Reine des Violettes', 'Sander's White', 'Serenade', 'Superstar', 'Tour de Malakoff', 'Variegata di Bologna', 'William Lobb' and 'Zéphirine Drouhin'. Although not listed as one of the classic susceptibles I have a white banksian rose which quickly succumbs to mildew if I forget to dose it with fungicide. Susceptible shrubs should not be planted where watering is by oscillating spray or where mildew is known to exist on nearby roses. Lack of air circulation can also cause mildew.

It is a very great temptation in warm climates to let roses continue to bloom until Christmas. This is not a good thing to do for two important reasons. The first is that it encourages insects and diseases to 'winter over', breed and increase in comfort. If you must have roses on your Christmas table restrict yourself to allowing one or two bushes only to flower and thereafter remove flowers and buds. The second reason is that the rose needs a rest period to recuperate from flowering its head off all summer. In the Mediterranean region gentle winter pruning is better and a tidy up or more serious pruning can be given mid-to late March.

In spring established bushes should have an application of fertilizer in the proportions of N (Nitrogen), P (Phosphorus), K (Potassium), 5:10:5, to get them going. Organic or inorganic really does not matter but the advantage of the former is that it adds humus and benefits all soils both light and sandy, heavy and clay. This is the mixture to be used throughout the season whilst remembering that shrub roses need very much less feeding.

There are many climbers and a few shrub roses which usually cannot be grown outside in an unreliable climate such as that of Great Britain, much of France and parts of northern Spain, but which will quickly establish themselves in the Mediterranean region. Most will flower for four or five weeks at a time and then either intermittently throughout the season or once again in September or early October when the weather cools down. *Rosa banksiae*, which has small double flowers in clusters, will do this, particularly in its sweetly scented white form, as opposed to the more common yellow, provided it is not exposed to too much sun. It is particularly beautiful in its white form when allowed to mix with wisteria, though in France and northern Italy one cannot always guarantee simultaneous flowering. There is a single version of *R. banksiae* called *R. b. normalis* which is less subject to mildew, though equally tender, and a single yellow form *R. b. n.* 'Lutea'.

One of the most famous fragile roses, *R. brunonii* 'La Mortola', whose antecedents are still argued about, will take slight frost once established but not in the first two years or so. It makes a vast quantity of growth to a height of about 3.6m/12ft. The leaves are grey-green and the sweetly-scented flowers single white with very prominent yellow stamens. It is less subject to mildew than many tender roses. If you cannot grow this because of cold winters, then try *R. sinowilsonii* which has similar flowers though very different, almost evergreen, foliage and which tolerates several degrees of frost.

Three Noisette roses which are usually found only in greenhouses north of the Loire, are 'Desprez à Fleur Jaune' (also known as 'Jaune Desprez'), 'Lamarque' and 'Maréchal Niel'. Although they are all yellow, they are very different. 'Desprez à Fleur Jaune' is a warm yellow with peach shading, highly scented and considerably less tender than 'Lamarque' whose lemon-coloured petals fade almost to white. 'Maréchal Niel' has Tea rose shaped yellow buds which hang down and seem to be made for viewing from below. None of these three will tolerate *any* frost. Lastly, 'Climbing Sombreuil', an old Tea rose from South Carolina with creamy white double flowers which does fabulously well by the sea on the Côte d'Azur, the Italian Riviera and the Costa Brava. Elsewhere, the humidity is not high enough until one reaches Alexandria where the sun is too harsh and shade too difficult to find.

7

Drought Resistant Plants

Alas, there are parts of the Mediterranean region which can be just as dry as the Libyan desert in summer but without its superb drainage. A combination of rock hard clay soil, no water and low humidity augurs well for little other than certain cacti and desert succulents. If you are able to cheat a little and/or can use clean, waste water then you can have the odd pot of colour from pelargoniums, petunias, certain euphorbias, salvias or erythrina, but the choice is not great.

Apart from palms, and some of these need a little water from time to time even though they put down roots which are two-thirds of their height above ground, there are very few trees which can survive a desert-like climate. The acacia family, mostly coming from Australia, has a Middle Eastern cousin known as the Arabian acacia, *Acacia arabica*. No-one would want it if there were alternatives but it is commonly on sale from one end of North Africa to the other. It has the usual mimosa-like flowers one expects with the acacias but for a very short period. Provided you can give it some physical protection from passing domestic animals such as goats and camels it will give quite good evergreen shade. Another tree, frequently used as a street lining tree, is the mop-headed *Melia azadirachta* (syn. *Azadirachta indica*) a relation of the azedarach (*Melia azedarach*). It grows to about 10m/30ft, is evergreen and has white flowers in panicles.

Prosopis species do well in desert areas and are commonly known in the south-west and south-east United States and South America as mesquites. The Americans have many hybrids but in the Mediterranean region you are likely to find only *Prosopis juliflora*, the commonest of the species, and *P. spicigera*, native to Saudi Arabia. They are grown for their shade-giving properties rather than anything else. Deprived

66

of water or in an excessively windy situation they develop a twisted stem which can be very dramatic against a white wall (not a house wall though since its roots can go 30m/100ft down) or a blue sky. The small yellow flowers are insignificant. It is laughingly easy to grow from seed and should be planted out when the plant is around three years old.

A south-west Asian pine which almost enjoys a desert atmosphere is *Pinus eldarica*, sometimes called the Quetta or Afghan pine. Its temperature range is from -10°C/15°F to 40°C/105°F and in such conditions it will still grow up to 75cm/30in a year. When old enough, it can be pruned to an umbrella shape.

The very common Jerusalem thorn (*Parkinsonia aculeata*) will give a brilliant display of yellow flowers in April but thereafter, to keep itself alive, will drop its flowers, leaves and even small branches. It perks up in the autumn rains.

Atriplex which comes in both tree and shrub form and is very drought and salt tolerant. The most undemanding of all is the shrubby *A. semi-baccata*. All atriplex respond to occasional very deep watering but once established will go six months without a drop. They look dreadful after such suffering but soon come back to life once water is available.

Several members of the fig (*Ficus*) family tolerate drought, in particular *F. pseudosycamoris*. Others will lose their leaves and only water and time will bring them back.

Leucophyllum frutescens is sometimes imported from the United States, adapts remarkably well to drought, and in the southern Mediterranean region appears to be quite free of the many diseases to which it is prone in its native land. Known as Texas Ranger, it is green when well watered but becomes more and more silver as drought takes hold. It seems impossible to kill. *Teucrium fruticans* behaves in more or less the same manner but it can look very miserable without water over a long period.

Datura species are all happier with water but can jog along for months at a time without any – but you must not expect summer-long flowers. Since they make ideal pot plants it is possible to cheat and use waste water for such plants. They are quite happy growing on a terrace or covered veranda.

Provided you choose carefully, bulbs can be an immense source of garden colour in the most drought ridden area. Anyone who has seen the Moroccan *bled* (desert) in springtime will vouch for that. The Anatolian Plateau is another case in point where for an incredibly short season between a bitterly cold winter and unrelentingly hot summer the whole area is covered in flowering bulbs. For most really dry gardens the narcissus, crocus and tulip hybrids are useless. They may bloom for a day then shrivel up. But there is a vast number of tulip species, many of which are natives of the Near East which will do well. These include *T. fosteriana, T. greigii, T. kauffmannia, T. batalinii, T. clusiana, T. pulchella, T. tubergeniana* and one of the loveliest, *T. whittalli*, to name but a few. Then there are the cyclamen family, puschkinia, chionodoxa, grape hyacinths, *Anemone blanda, Iris chamaeiris, I. pumila, I. p. attica, I. danfordiae, I. reticulata* and that most useful of all, the Algerian iris (*I. unguicularis*, syn. *I. stylosa*). This last flowers for three or four months in the winter/spring period. It has beautiful pale mauve flowers and there is a much sought after white form. Its leaves can be cut back hard in summer for tidiness sake and they will grow again by Christmas. It is one of the most reliable irises imaginable.

Another frequently untapped source of spring colour are the many tender South African bulbs such as acidanthera, agapanthus, crocosmia, freesia, gladiolus, the climber gloriosa, hippeastrum (pots only), ixia, nerine, sparaxis, scilla (not all) and the arum lily. Admittedly agapanthus need some water since they are not really bulbs and hippeastrums (better known as amaryllis) blooms better with water and fertilizer. Day lilies (hemerocallis) come up increasing year after year. Many of these bulbs, corms or tubers will have to be obtained from specialist nurseries but given the sterling service they will perform it is well worthwhile going to this trouble and expense. Only the Algerian iris is commonly available in the southern Mediterranean – someone will usually give you a clump for nothing. After that you keep dividing it up every three or four years.

Virtually all the succulent forms of euphorbia as well as most forms of kalanchoe, aeonium, echeveria, jovibarba, crassula and cacti will grow well without water once established and some never need it. However, certain cacti are native to the high Andes and similar terrain and rely on night dews for water. This type of climate is not available to them in the Mediterranean region (except occasionally at altitude) and they will quickly succumb. Most forms of opuntia do well, as will aloes, agaves, dasylirions and yuccas. Ice-plants such as mesembryanthemum, drosanthus and lampranthus together with sedum and sempervivum manage months without water.

Of the grey-leaved plants many of the labiates are long suffering, lavender in particular, as is perovskia from Afghanistan, which has the advantage of being hardy, santolina and some of the artemisias. As with so many drought tolerant plants, with the exception of the succulents and cacti, they all appreciate an occasional deep drink.

No matter where you live you can organize things so that your house and terrace are surrounded by a tiny oasis of succulent plants as ground cover, clumps of pampas grass and perhaps the odd pot with a shrub which requires water only very rarely. The more protected from the sun this pot is (or these pots are) the better the results you will have for your trouble.

8

Pests and Diseases

There are gardeners, particularly in Italy and Spain, who would put hunters at the top of their pest list. Accompanied by their dogs, they tramp over other people's land with never a care for any plant life. I have friends in Tuscany who swear they never have a cat or dog which survives more than two hunting seasons. Others, also in Italy, keep replacement glass for their greenhouses always to hand against the depredations of trigger-happy hunters who shoot at anything including songbirds. Until Italy changes the law which currently allows hunters to do more or less what they like where they like, this type of damage will continue.

Farmers can also be careless and allow their livestock to stray. Pigs can do tremendous damage to a lawn, to say nothing of flower and vegetable beds. Alas, one is not allowed to take more than preventative action. Electric fences are fairly effective at keeping animals out (and in, for that matter) but are also quite expensive. Every country has different laws regarding electric fences and it is as well to make enquiries as to what is required where you live.

Against rodents the situation is only a little better. I cannot be sure which munch my bulbs but I have seen both dead rats and fieldmice on my land. Hares and rabbits, especially in winter when there is not much to eat except in private gardens, come in and kill trees, particularly fruit trees, by eating the bark. Tree protectors or tree tape are the only answer. Aluminium foil wrapped and tied round the base of the trunk for the dormant period as a temporary measure can be quite effective.

If you know rats to be a real problem, the local municipal or regional

Sanitary Department will send someone to kill them with cyanide or special raticide. In parts of France this service is free but usually you have to pay. Raticides containing warfarin, a powerful anti-coagulant, are commonly on sale in Italy and pet owners should be very careful when allowing their cats to stray and when taking their dogs for walks near private houses or large farms. This type of raticide together with snail and slug pellets based on metaldehyde cause a great number of animal deaths. In Italy the most common cause of death in domestic pets is poisoning and there must be hundreds of deaths which are not reported.

Moles are supposed to be kept away by planting the caper spurge (*Euphorbia lathyrus*). It did not work for me but it is a handsome, drought resistant plant and worth trying in its own right. Moles do not like clay soil and therefore most Mediterranean gardens are spared this pest. A professional mole catcher is able to identify the main runs and trap them where you may well be bamboozled into treating a secondary or tributary run and get nowhere. Alternatively, cyanide gas can be used by a suitably qualified person, not a member of the public. All in all, getting rid of rodents can be dangerous and is for a professional to carry out. Small anti-mole 'bombs' compounded of sulphur, potassium and nitrate are harmless to most pets and are on sale to the public from Aurouze s.a.r.l., 8 rue des Halles, Paris 75001. You drop a lighted 'bomb' into the run which disperses gas for about fifteen minutes and kills the inhabitants. Alternatively a sonar device is currently being advertised in French, Italian and Spanish gardening magazines which emits an ultrasonic hum which keeps most rodents away.

Hedgehogs do an immense amount of good in the garden munching all sorts of harmful insects and so should be encouraged unless you keep chickens since they also like eggs. Woodlice appear to be their 'caviar'.

Crows and pigeons can be a great nuisance, especially in winter. Nets are the answer to keeping fruit undamaged; otherwise use conventional birdscarers. The French manufacture a bird scarer based on an electric wire which emits a very high pitched note which birds appear to hate. It is totally harmless and is advertised from time to time in the principal gardening magazines. The municipality will often help if the situation demands. Otherwise shooting is a possibility and so are seeds coated with a product which sends the birds to sleep. They are then collected and I suppose disposed of humanely. Many corvicides are based on strychnine and cause a terrible and painful death to any bird (not always the crows you are after). Therefore, if you can use any other method do so.

Mole-crickets (*Grillotalpa grillotalpa*) are crickets, not moles, but suggest the latter by their fur and digging ability. They are extraordinarily ugly, 10cm/4in long, and rather frightening to come across. They do an immense amount of damage to plants by eating just above the roots and although they eat other insects as well, the harm and destruction they cause outstrips any benefit they may bring to the garden. The main method of destruction is to use bait made from bran which has been poisoned with either lindane or dieldrine. In some countries, France and Italy certainly, retailers of agricultural products sell a specific poison against them.

There are probably some plants which suffer from no pest, disease or fungus, but they must be rare. The most common insect pests and plant diseases with their antidotes are given in the list below. Insect colouring may change slightly from country to country. Scorpions for instance, are black in most of Europe but become lighter, or redder, and more dangerous, in North Africa and the eastern Mediterranean. The reddest red spider I have ever seen was in Cosenza in southern Italy and his brother in France is anaemic looking in comparison. Red spiders live in the open in most of the Mediterranean region if the temperature is right. It is probably one of the most difficult insects to destroy and specific acaricides must be used. Some are mentioned below but there are many others on the market both for the professional and amateur gardener.

It is assumed that many Mediterranean gardeners will try to buy insecticides in the U.K. whenever possible since they are cheaper and more plentiful in that country and there is considerably more choice. However certain insects do not occur there and insecticides against these must be purchased in the country of the pest.

We are all brain washed by advertising and the gardening press to believe that for every pest and disease there is a chemical antidote. Often there is not and when there is it is far too strong or does not work as well as simple mechanical or biological control. For some reason we are now more likely to spray insects on plants than to pick them off by hand. Nor do we give enough credit to the many natural predators such as toads, frogs, hedgehogs, the praying mantis, lacewings and certain beetles which live on insects. Even wasps, dirty and unpleasant as they are, have many members of the family which are parasites on caterpillars. Then there are the pathogens which in the form of fungi, viruses or bacteria attack garden insects and cause them to die. The most commonly known is *Bacillus thuringiensis*. Sprayed on fruit trees, for example, it causes the feeding caterpillars to die and thus end the evolution cycle. This ecologically sound anti-tortrix and codling moth spray is on sale only in France in the Mediterranean region and then it has to be sought out. The big chemical giants with whole divisions devoted to agro-chemicals are not great admirers of such an inexpensive and efficient spray.

Finally, never forget that one of the finest insecticides is soap and water. It is very useful when you have nothing else more powerful to hand and very few insects thrive on daily spraying of this.

PEST AND DISEASE LIST

ALGAE see MOSS

ANTS

(Fr: *fourmis*, (f); It: *formiche* (f); Sp: *hormigas* (f)). A very real problem in the whole of the Mediterranean area. Ants come in every size and variety from virtually invisible to almost 2.5cm/1in long. Most common are the Argentine ants which are also the most difficult to eradicate. Their most irritating habit apart from spreading aphids and disease is removing newly sown seed – particularly grass seed and the ground must be treated *before* sowing. Panant (PBI), Poudre Anti-fourmis (Sovilo, KB) and Ant-Killer Dust (ICI) all help as do carbaryl based powders. Where these are not obtainable use Lindane powder at 3–4%. All anti-ant powders are dangerous to pets and need to be well watered in. Do not allow pets to eat treated grass for some months. Treatment lasts approximately four to six months.

APHIDS

(Fr: *pucerons*, (m); It: *afidi*, (m); Sp: *pulgones*, (m)). As plentiful in the Mediterranean as in the rest of Europe. Roses, fruit trees, particularly cherry and pear, and dozens of other plants become affected once they arrive in a garden. Once thoroughly infested, a plant will be covered with a blackish-grey sooty mould and then the ants move in and spread the aphids all over the garden. Systemic insecticides at regular intervals help. Specific insecticides are: Bio Long-last and Crop Saver (PBI), Sybol 2, Abol Derris Dust, Rapid (all ICI), Nexion, Bactospeine Jardin, Omnitox, Roxion 100 (all Sovilo), Dimecron (CG).

APPLE and PEAR PESTS

(Fr: *les maladies des pommiers et des poiriers*; It: *le malattie di fruttiferi*; Sp: *las enfermededes de los manzanos y perales*). There are so many things which apple and pear trees can suffer from that it is best to spray for prevention rather than cure. If you give your apples and/or pears a winter tar wash which is based on phenols and is easily obtainable in most countries, followed by a regular programme of spraying against the various pests and diseases which can strike, you should be safe. Many of the specifics for apples and pears can be used elsewhere in the garden and therefore, in the long run, are not expensive. Winter washes include Clean-up (ICI), Liquide Total (Sovilo), Oleodiazinon and Oleo Supracide (CG). Specifics are: Bio Long-last, Fenitrothion (both PBI), Sybol 2, Sybol 2 Dust (both ICI), Delan Liquide, Kothrin, Roxion 100 (all Sovilo).

BEES (MINING)

(Fr: *abeilles découpeuses*, (f); It: *api pungente*, (f); Sp: *abejas minadores*, (f)). These are solitary bees, not belonging to a hive, which slice off pieces of leaf in order to build their nests. If you spray against them you spray against all the honey bees as well. Pick off the offending leaves if necessary but do not try to get rid of the bees themselves.

BLACKFLY

(Fr: *mouche noire*, (f); It: *mosca nera*, (f); Sp: *pulgon negro*, (f)). This fly is an absolute scourge in northern Italy particularly where broad beans are grown for the immensely enthusiastic local market. The professionals use very strong insecticides and therefore you, in turn, must use something equally strong. Although neither aphids nor the common black fly which occurs on roses, this broad bean black fly requires much the same treatment, except in market garden areas, where you should use the same insecticides as neighbouring market gardeners.

BLACK LEG

(Fr: *jambe-noire*, (f); It: *gamba nera*, (f); Sp: *pierna negra*,(f)). As its names suggest it is the stem of the plant which is affected by a parasitic fungus which causes it to become black and diseased. The plant dies of it and there is no cure but to pull it up and throw it out or burn it. Chinese asters, pelargoniums (particularly cuttings) and potatoes are usually the main victims. On no account put the dead plant on the compost heap. Do not plant the same type of plant in the same area for some seasons. Cheshunt Compound (PBI), Bordeaux mixture (*Bouillie Bordelaise*) which is found throughout France, or Dory Mildiou (Sovilo) all help.

BLACKSPOT

(Fr: *marsonia* or *la maladie des tâches noires*, (f); It: *malattia* or *mala nera*, (f); Sp. *mancha negra*, (f)). This is a fungus spread by spores which tends to attack mainly roses and then only where there is very pure air i.e. seldom in cities and places where there is a great deal of road traffic. People living at an altitude between 300–750m/1000–2500ft are almost certain to have it in their garden unless they are extra careful – and lucky. Signs are yellowing leaves with *fringed* blackspots. Never let the leaves fall onto the ground without picking them up. The same goes for prunings. In the winter use a tar-oil emulsion on the bare bush or tree and the soil. In season use systemic fungicides and/or Bordeaux mixture. Some authorities believe the disease is due to an excess of nitrogen and therefore in areas subject to blackspot it is best to use a fertilizer higher in potash and phosphates with a little magnesium rather than a standard rose fertilizer. Sequestrene can also help in alkaline areas since chlorosis weakens a plant. Multirose (PBI), Nimrod-T, Roseclear (both ICI), Funginex (Sovilo), Rodimil 45WP (CG).

BOTRYTIS

(Fr: *botrytis*, (m); It: *botrite*, (f); Sp: *botrytis*, (m)). This fungus disease is present in many forms in most gardens, even those which are squeaky clean. It particularly attacks bulbous forms of plant life. Grey mould is a form of botrytis as is tulip fire. Use proprietary fungicides, thiram based powders and copper sulphate. In dire cases it will be necessary to throw away the affected plants or bulbs. Do not grow susceptible plants where you have had this disease. Apron 35 SD, Motecide C 50 (both CG). Also same treatment as for blackspot.

BROWN ROT

(Fr: *monilose*, (f) or *monilia*, (f); It: *marciume di frutta*, (m); Sp: *podredumbre*, (f)). Can affect most types of fruit in the Mediterranean. Common in pears and peaches particularly. A fungus, *Sclerotinia fructigena*, is the culprit and it enters the semi-ripe to ripe fruit and causes a brown central rot. In turn the fruit shrivels but remains on the tree. If you suspect this disease and it is very easy to check, remove all the fruit, make sure it has not entered the branch of the fruit tree and spray with copper sulphate or a proprietary fungicide. Do this again in winter when attending to your fruit tree since the fungus can easily winter over in the tree. Do not put the shrivelled fruit or the prunings on the compost heap. Benlate (PBI), Sybol 2 (ICI), Peltar (Sovilo), Tilt, Topas (both CG).

CABBAGE ROOT FLY

(Fr: *cecidomyie*, (f); It: *mosca del cavolo*, (f); Sp: *mosca de la col*, (f)). The brassica family seems far too susceptible to insects and diseases to bother to grow it. However, if you do, the cabbage root fly lays its eggs just below soil level and the maggots which hatch out eat the roots of cabbage, turnips, radishes, wallflowers, etc. A soil drench is the only answer, usually the specific one for this purpose is based on diazinon and this can be combined with the use of lindane if you must. Basudin 5G (CG), Bromophos (PBI), Sybol 2 (ICI), Nexagan MG5 (Sovilo).

CAPSID BUGS

(Fr: *pucerons verts*, (m), *punaises des fruits*, (f); It: *cimici di fruttifere*, (f); Sp: *aranuelos del manzano*, (m)). Although there are many different sorts of capsid bugs the two most commonly found in Mediterranean gardens are the fruit capsid bug and the common green. Both are sucking insects. Tattered leaves are the sign. The first can be stopped dead in its tracks by being scrupulous about tar washing your fruit (and other) trees in winter and spring. The green capsid bug can be controlled to a certain extent by keeping your garden as weed free as possible and using a general garden insecticide at frequent intervals. More than one generation can be born in a season and overwintering in the Mediterranean is no problem for them. Bio Longlast (PBI), Picket or Picket G (ICI), Liquide Total, Total Verger (both Sovilo), Dimecron (CG).

Pests and Diseases

CANKER, FUNGAL and BACTERIAL

(Fr: *chancre*, (m); It: *cancro*, (m); Sp: *cancro* (m)). Fungal canker is usual found on apple and pear trees and manifests itself by shrinkage of the bark and sometimes red growths in winter. The bacterial canker on the other hand is often accompanied by gumming on branches of stone fruit trees. Remember also that cherries and to a lesser degree apricots should be pruned in late summer *while still growing* to prevent silver leaf disease and other fungus problems. Having both diseases on one tree will almost certainly kill it. In all cases you must either cut the canker out and back to a healthy part of the tree or remove the entire branch. You then paint the wounds with one of the following fungicides:- Arbrex (PBI), Nimrod-T, Clean-up (both ICI), Funginex (Sovilo,) Topas (CG). As prevention, use Ventine 90 (CG).

CATERPILLARS

(Fr: *chenilles*, (f); It: *bruchi*, (m) or *cingoli*, (m); Sp: *orugas* (f)). The problem with having butterflies in your garden is that they all lay eggs which in turn become caterpillars and eat your plants. It should not be forgotten that all moths also give rise to larvae or caterpillars some of which can do immense damage in the garden to say nothing of clothes. Use one of the proprietary insecticides which give quite good control. Bio Longlast, Fenitrothion (both PBI), Picket (ICI), Liquide Total, Liquide Verger (both Sovilo), Basudin (CG).

CATS and DOGS

Cats are in some ways a bigger menace than dogs since they are nocturnal, invisible by night and love soft earth. Use stretched cotton over the precious crop (you cannot hope to protect your entire garden), pepper sprinkled on the bed, sprigs of holly underneath the flowers or shrubs which later on will do *you* damage. Some recommend the inner tube of a bicycle tyre on the nearby lawn which cats will think is a snake and give a wide berth. Dogs, I am frequently told, can be disciplined. You can become rather bad tempered imposing such discipline and it depends mightily on the breed as to whether your wishes will be fulfilled or not. Dogs also hate pepper and mustard dust. The French market an anti-cat and dog powder (which is, ominously, mustard yellow) which is efficacious for about ten days. If a dog does anoint a precious plant wash it immediately and very

77

thoroughly. Some people recommend a strong smelling disinfectant but I cannot believe the plant will like that. Otherwise your dog, being a creature of habit, will keep going back to that spot.

CHAFER BEETLE

(Fr: *hanneton commun*, (m); It: *coleottero*, (m)). This could be the cause of tattered and holed leaves on your plants. Chafer beetles attack fruit, roses, shrubs and many flowers. Their small, rather plump worms live in the soil until it is time for them to emerge as fully grown chafer beetles. It is no use treating your plants if you do not treat your lawn and grass land. The following are the main proprietary insecticides but if the infestation is great then you will need one containing lindane. Hexyl (PBI), Sybol 2 (ICI), Nexion 20 (Sovilo). Drenching the soil in winter and spring can help as well; use Sybol 2 (ICI).

CHAFER GRUB

(Fr: *ver blanc*, (m); It: *vermo biancho*, (m); Sp: *gusano blanco*, (m)). The offspring of the above, sometimes called Joe Bassett. They can be recognised by their fat creamy white bodies 4cm/1½in long. They should be killed on the spot if found when digging and the ground should be treated as above.

CHLOROSIS

(Fr: *chlorose*, (f); It: *clorosi*, (m); Sp: *clorosis ferrica*,(f)). This occurs very commonly in the Mediterranean since much of the water from both rivers and taps is saturated with calcium and other alkaline elements. It is recognisable by the yellowing leaves which still have bright green veining. Eventually the plant can sicken and die of what is basically a lack of the micro-element iron or rather its inability to absorb it due to the presence of too much alkali. There are many anti-chlorosis products marketed from blue-ing powders for hydrangeas based mostly on alum, to a form of acid for dissolving the alkaline in water. The latter, *Décalcairisant pour eau d'arrosage* manufactured by Truffaut in France is *very* expensive. The product that I have found the most satisfactory is Ciba-Geigy's Sequestrene 138Fe. It is ruinously expensive but if you must grow azaleas, certain Chinese and South African bulbs, lapageria, etc., it is invaluable. You should grow such calcifuge plants in pots to avoid really huge bills. Using pure peat is not necessarily the whole answer to growing such plants successfully if alkaline water is all that is available. It is essential to have a combination of acid soil, non-calcareous stones and soft water. This is where Sequestrene can help. Follow the directions on the pack and do not overdose. It is said you can use Sequestrene as a foliar treatment but in the dry summer atmosphere of the Mediterranean (a time when the plants suffer most) I have found this treatment can damage most acid loving plants except camellias. In winter and early spring when there is plenty of rain, Sequestrene granules can be sprinkled around the plants and raked in at about 30 gr. per sq. metre. The rain or sprinkler will do the work for you.

CLUB ROOT

(Fr: *hernie des crucifères*, (f); It: *ernia del cavolo*; Sp: *hernia de la col*(f)). Attacks wallflowers as well as cabbages but is not very common in the Mediterranean as the soil is mostly too dry and alkaline. Easily recognisable by the thickened roots and the general poor and shrivelled condition of the plant. Calomel Dust (PBI), Club Root Control (ICI), Folcap, Peltar (both Sovilo).

CUCKOO SPIT see FROG HOPPERS

CUTWORMS

(Fr: *vers des choux*, (m); It: *vermi di cavolo*, (m); Sp: *gusanos de la col*, (m). Not a worm at all, and not, mercifully, very common in the Mediterranean, this is a type of caterpillar which works at, or just below, soil level and at night so it is not easy to see. However, next morning will soon tell the sorry tale if this pest has arrived in your garden. Lots of dead seedlings and plants nipped off at ground level. Bromophos (PBI), Sybol 2 Dust (ICI), Nexion 20 (Sovilo), Fenom P (CG).

DAMPING OFF

(Fr: *fonte des semis*, (f); It: *marciume di pianta o di semi*, (m); Sp: *damping-off*, (m)). The Mediterranean climate is perfect for damping off as is a greenhouse. It is caused by one of the most dramatically coloured and beautiful of the fungi and only the demise of your precious seedlings stops your taking an interest in it. The only answer is prevention. When planting seeds use sterilized compost, drench it in fungicide, plant seeds, water well and spray again with fungicide. If you are not using new containers make sure your old ones are clean and sterilized in a solution of a quarter of household bleach and to three quarters water. Do not sow too thickly since this type of sowing is the first to be attacked by damping off. Put the container into a *new* plastic bag, tie and do not remove bag until the first seedlings show. Keep in an airy, though not windy, location. It almost always works. Whether you keep up the fungicide treatment thereafter is for you to judge but normally it is not necessary. Alternatively you can stir into the soil some specially made fungicidal powder or coat the seeds with it. Certain of these powders are good for preventing fungus diseases in bulbs such as tulips, aroids and lilies. Finally, there are seeds, mostly F1 hybrids, which are already treated with a special coating against fungal diseases. They cost extra but for certain susceptible types it is a good idea. Fonginex Poudre (Sovilo), Fongarid (CG).

DIEBACK

(Fr: *dessiccation du bois*, (f); It: *avvizzimento*, (m); Sp: *desecacion* (f)). Almost always caused by bad pruning or no pruning at all when the wind has damaged stems. Gradually the damaged stem dies back to the main stem of the plant. Sometimes, though rarely, it can kill it. Trim the plant back to healthy wood and in the case of roses and most shrubs to where there is a healthy bud waiting to shoot. Paint the cuts with Arbrex (PBI) or a 50/50 water and household bleach solution or *mastic des vignerons* which is available all over France, or at least with melted (but not too hot) candlewax.

EARWIGS

(Fr: *perce-oreilles*, (f) or *forfécules*, (f); It: *forfecchie*, (f); Sp: *tijeretas*, (f)). These pests do not confine themselves to dahlias in the Mediterranean but eat everything they land on destroying petals, leaves and fruit. Bio Long-last, Hexyl (both PBI), Picket, Picket-G, Sybol 2 (all ICI), Nexion 2 (Sovilo), Dimecron (CG).

EELWORMS

(Fr: *nematodes*, (f) or *anguillules*, (f); It: *nematodi*, (f); Sp: *nematodas*, (f) or *angullulas*, (f)). Eelworms are only one sort of nematode. It is very difficult to be sure whether you have nematodes in your soil since the damage they cause can be very similar to that of leatherjackets, chafer bugs and other soil grubs. If nematodes are diagnosed then uproot all the plants, burn them or throw them away but not on the compost heap. Do not use the soil for the same plants for some years – at least five or six. Use soil drenches on the land concerned such as Sybol 2 (ICI).

FIRE BLIGHT

(Fr: *feu bactérien*. In Italian and Spanish this disease is usually known by its rather charming Latin name of *Erwinia amylovora* but alas there the charm ends). Fire blight affects the cotoneaster family as well as pyracantha and hawthorns. The disease pounces at flowering time by entering the plant through the nectaries ultimately causing the leaves to turn brown. The following spring cankers appear at the base of the plant which in turn spread the disease further. In France, Spain and Italy this is a notifiable disease though taken really seriously only by the French. You report it to your local Ministry of Health office. France is trying to ban the use of pyracantha in public hedging schemes to combat this disease and you cannot import into France, *even with a phyto-sanitary certificate*, pyracantha, cotoneaster, malus, certain prunus and crataegus. The standard treatment is drastic pruning back to at least 60cm/2ft into good wood but in France you must burn the affected plant.

FLEA BEETLES

(Fr: *altises*, (f); It: *altiche delle crucifere*, (f); Sp: *altisas*, (f)). A small black and yellow beetle which, for its size, does a great deal of damage to all the brassica family, certain salad crops, particularly in their seedling stage, and stock seedlings. Use Bio Long-last, Hexyl, Liquid Derris (all PBI), Sybol 2 Dust (ICI), Nexion 20 (Sovilo), Dimecron (CG).

FROG HOPPERS

You never see the offending animal which lays its eggs on the stems of your lavender and other plants then covers them with a frothy watery mess. Lavender seems to stand up quite well to these depredations but other plants do not. In the first instance spray off the froth with a jet from the hose or if you are short of water pick it off with a damp cloth.

If such methods do not work then use Hexyl, Malathion Greenfly Killer (both PBI), Sybol 2 (ICI), Nexion 20 (Sovilo).

GREENFLY see APHIDS

GREY MOULD

(Fr: *pourriture grise*, (f); It: *patina grigio-biancastra*, (f) or *muffa grigia*, (f); Sp: *moho gris* or *mildiu gris*, (m)). Unlike ordinary mildew, grey mould comes in spots and patches on the leaves, stems and even flowers of plants. Can spread very rapidly. Prevention by using systemic fungicides is easier than cure though Dithane 945, Multirose, Systhane (all PBI), Nimrod-T, Roseclear (both ICI), Peltar (Sovilo), Fongarid (CG) applied at regular intervals all help.

HONEY FUNGUS

(Latin: *armillariella*; Fr: *armillaria*, (f); It: *armillaria*, (f); Sp: *armilaria*, (f)). This is probably the most dangerous of all the fungus infestations apart from silver leaf (which appears to be extremely rare in the Mediterranean) and at present there is no real cure. Some of its main victims are rhododendrons, privet, elaeagnus, conifers and roses though any plant can be attacked. Luckily it seems to be relatively rare in the Mediterranean area perhaps because of the great summer heat and lack of moisture for propagation purposes. It is not the spores of this fungus which spread the disease but the long, black, thread-like rhizomorphs which are able to enter the roots of the host plant. On trees and shrubs honey fungus shows as white fans under the bark. Death inevitably follows soon after. Above all keep the garden clean and free of dead wood. Armilatox (PBI) can help but will not cure. Dig out all the offending soil and roots or sterilize with creosote or formalin at 2–3% solution. Fongarid (CG) applied to the soil can help also. Using such a sterilizing agent as the first two will mean you cannot plant anything for a couple of years but it is better than having honey fungus present in your garden. You can use Fongarid at the time of planting but do not think of in terms of a cure but rather as a preventative.

LEAF HOPPERS

(Fr: *cicadelles aphophores*, (f); It: *cicadelli*, (f); Sp: *cicadellas*, (f)). Very small pale green insects which leave pale mottled flecks on leaves, particularly roses. Malathion, Fenitrothion (both PBI), Sybol 2, Picket G (both ICI), Nexion 20, Liquid Total (both Sovilo).

LEAF MINERS

(Fr: *mineuses des feuilles*, (f); It: *miniatori fogliari*, (m); Sp: *minadores de hojas*, (f)). They make blotches and blisters on chrysanthemum and rose leaves in particular and sometimes attack philadelphus. In the vegetable garden they appear to like salads and the beet family. Spray with Hexyl, Malathion (both PBI), Picket G, Sybol 2 (ICI), Liquid Total (Sovilo), Trigard (CG).

LEATHERJACKETS

These are the legless grubs of crane flics which live on the roots of plants, principally grass but they can be killed with any anti-slug/snail powder or pellets. See also Slugs and Snails.

LICHEN

(Fr: *lichen*, (m); It: *lichene*, (m); Sp: *liquen*, (m)). See Moss.

MAGGOTS IN FRUIT

(Fr: *vers des fruits*, (m); It: *larve di frutta*, (f); Sp: *gusanos de fruta*, (m)). These need no description! Usually it is a question of your sins finding you out since if you tar wash in winter and spray at the required intervals this pest should not occur. Bio Long-last, Fenitriothon (both PBI), Sybol 2, Picket, Picket G (all ICI), Kothrin (Sovilo) are all useful. See also Apple and Pear Pests.

MEALY BUG

(Fr: *cochenilles farineuses des serres*, (f); It: *cocciniglie cotonose*, (f); Sp: *cochinillas*, (f)). These bugs occur mostly in the warm conditions of the greenhouse or on houseplants. In the latter case use Baby Bio House Plant insecticide (PBI) and in the greenhouse use Fumite Smoke. Outside use Sybol 2 (ICI), Roxion 100, Sovion (in winter), Anti-cochenilles (in spring and summer) (all Sovilo), Supracid(e) or Basudin (both CG).

83

MILDEW

(Fr: *mildiou*, (m); It: *muffa*, (f); Sp: *mildiu* (m) or *moho*(m)). Very common on roses and in the greenhouse. It is best to use a couple of systemic fungicides every two alternate weeks. Once it has arrived in a garden it can spread like wildfire to all other plants. Other anti-mildew specifics are Multirose, Systhane (both PBI), Nimrod-T, Roseclear (both ICI), Funginex, Folcap (both Sovilo), Ridomil (CG).

MILLIPEDES

(Fr: *millepattes*, (f); It: *millepiedi*, (m); Sp: *cienpies*, (m)). Slug Guard lightly raked into soil (PBI) or Agrolimace (Sovilo).Gamma-HCH dust in the soil gives some protection. See also Slugs and Snails.

MOLE-CRICKETS

(Fr: *courtillière*, (f); It: *grillotalpa*, (f); Sp: *grillotopo*, (m)). Unpleasant insects which build their nests in the soil about 10–12cm/4–5in deep and in doing so damage the roots of plants, causing their death. If found these nests should be destroyed at once. A planting of tomatoes is one of their favourite haunts and a strawberry patch can also harbour them. Occasionally you are able to catch one in which case kill it at once since they have an extraordinary digging ability and can make as much mess as a mole and there are usually more of them. No soil is too hard or baked. There are specific insecticides against them such as Sovicortil by Sovilo in France and Basudin 10 Granules (CG) elsewhere but in many parts of the Mediterranean one has to rely on lindane based powders or liquids to eradicate them.

MOSS, LICHEN and ALGAE

(Fr: *mousses*,, (f), *lichen*, (m) et *algues*, (f); It: *muschio*, (m), *lichene* (m) *e alghe*, (f); Sp: *musgo*, (m), *liquen*, (m) *y algas* (f)). Use Bio Moss Killer (PBI). Iron Sulphate crystals help but remember they will turn stone, cement, tiling, etc., permanently brown, so try to paint it only on the offending moss or lichen. Unless it has become slippery or dangerous lichen can be most attractive, particularly on old stone pots and tubs. The various forms of algae arrive in ponds and lakes due to lack of oxygen. Providing aquatic plants such as waterlilies is one answer – so are fish and so are water fowl. If you do not have fish you will certainly get mosquitoes! If you can avoid using anti-algae agents do so since they tend to inhibit growth of any plant life.

PEACH LEAF CURL

(Fr: *cloque du pecher*, (f); It: *tafrina di pesche*, (f); Sp: *torque del durazuero*, (m)). Affects the entire prunus family with the possible exception of apricots. In the Mediterranean, almonds and the small damson-like plums seem more likely to suffer than peaches themselves. It is recognisable from the reddish blistered leaves which eventually drop. Not only is prevention, by spraying in January or February, better than cure it is doubtful that a cure within the season is possible in this part of the world. Once the leaves have fallen in autumn, the same spray can be used against *coryneum* which causes holes in the leaves and later can affect the branches causing the death of the tree. Most of the stone-fruit trees can be infected with these diseases if you do not bother to spray. As a cure Dithane 945 (PBI) is good, for prevention use a winter wash of Clean-Up (ICI), Anti-cloque (Sovilo), Anti-cloque du pecher (KB Jardin), Motecide or Topas (both CG) or Bordeaux mixture.

PEAR LEAF MITES

(Fr: *psylle commune du poirier*, (f); It: *psylle*, (f); Sp: *psilas*, (f)). When the tiny fruit has set on the pear tree and does not get any bigger it is probably due to pear leaf mite. Eventually the fruit drops and if it is opened up it will be found to be full of small grubs. It is often worth sprinkling a dust such as Sybol 2 in early spring to prevent the pear leaf mite's return. Poor growing conditions and/or poor hygiene are the usual cause. Fenitrothion, Hexyl (both PBI), Sybol 2 (ICI), Neoron (CG). Winter wash with Clean-up (ICI), Kothrin (Sovilo), Oleo-Basudin (CG).

RATS, MICE AND FIELDMICE

(Fr: *rats*, (m), *souris*, (f) *et mulots*, (m); It: *ratti, topi e ghiri*, (all m); Sp: *ratas*, (f), *ratones*, (m), *y campanoles*, (m)). The trouble starts from October onwards until, in colder parts, the mice and fieldmice hibernate. They all love bulbs, the more expensive the better, so never leave expensive lilies in the open ground. Always protect your pots by storing them in a cold greenhouse or in a rat and mice proof shed.

Many spring bulbs are not planted deeply enough and almost offer themselves to the mice. Tulips, narcissi and daffodils can be at least 23cm/9in deep – even at 30cm/12in tulips come up happily. Snowdrops, winter aconites and grape hyacinths are all favourites of these rodents so plant as deeply as possible, preferably in small wire cages for extra protection. Otherwise use one of the following, remembering they are all dangerous to household pets – Racumin Mouse or Rat bait (PBI), Ratak bait (ICI), Super Sovitox for rats and mice, Rimitox for fieldmice (both Sovilo).

RED SPIDER, FRUIT TREE RED SPIDER

(Fr: *araignée rouge (des fruitiers)*, (f); It: *ragnetto rosso (di fruttifere)*, (m); Sp: *araña roja*, (f)). All the red spider tribe, which are mites not spiders, live in the open in the Mediterranean area – some are out all the year round, others only in high summer. They are extremely difficult to eradicate. They do a great deal of damage to the leaves of plants growth. Bio Longlast, Liquid Derris (both PBI), Sybol 2, Fumite Smoke in greenhouse (both ICI), Sovifol (Sovilo), Akar (for citrus only) (CG) and Neoron (CG).

ROSE CHAFER

(Fr: *cétoine dorée*, (f); It: *cetonia dorata*, (f) or *maggiolino* (m); Sp: *escarabajo de rosas*, (m)). These beetles are handsome as beetles go and are related to the ancient Egyptian scarab. They have a metallic green and bronze carapace and make a great deal of noise when flying. They particularly like single roses with prominent stamens but also bore into white and pink roses, ceanothus and lilac. They are virtually impossible to get rid of since they lay their eggs in the soil which hatch out in the same way as the ordinary chafer beetle. The grub has a dark head and three pairs of dark legs on a cream coloured body. They should be killed immediately. The treatment is identical to an ordinary chafer beetle and should be carried out on all dug beds, lawns, etc. – everywhere in fact. Hexyl (PBI), Picket, Sybol 2 (ICI), Sovinexit granules in soil, Liquide Total (both Sovilo) and Insectes du Sol (KB).

RUST

(Fr: *rouille*, (f); It: *rugine*, (f); Sp: *royas*, (m)). Although relatively common on roses and pelargoniums in the Mediterranean this quickly responds to fungicide. However, the carnation rust is not so easy to eradicate and along the coast in France and N. Italy it seems to be part and parcel of carnation culture whether under glass or in the open. Perhaps if you use non-French fungicides you will get better results. Dithane 945 (PBI) is not sold in France or Italy but Nimrod-T (ICI) is as is Topas (CG). Fonginex from Sovilo is excellent against rose rust but probably most of the carnations in the area are resistant to it.

SAN JOSE SCALE

(Fr: *pou de San Jose*, (f); It: *cocciniglie*, (f) *o pulci di San Jose*, (m); Sp: *piojo de San Jose*, (m)). This is the disease, together with fire blight (see above), which all customs authorities take most seriously. You cannot import anything from a country known to have San Jose Scale. A phyto-sanitary certificate stating a plant is healthy is worthless if it comes from such a country. The main problem is that there can be as many as five generations in a year (the females give birth to live young and do not lay eggs) and all the females are soon capable of increasing the population. The first signs are tiny red rings on both fruit (either developing or fully ripe) and leaves, and these are an indication that the infestation in thoroughly established. It is a notifiable disease in France and Italy and Spain. An acaricide will keep it under control but usually the local Health Authority will advise you what to do.

In the Mediterranean area Algeria, Morocco, the Lebanon and Syria are known to have San Jose Scale. At the moment Turkey and Greece are free but it is wise to check with their Embassies before importing anything. Neoron 25, Suprac and Supracid(e) 40 WP (all CG) will all help. However, if you tar wash or spray your fruit in late winter this should kill the hibernating females.

SAWFLY

(Fr: *hoplocampe*, (f); It: *oplocampa*, (f); Sp: *hoplocampa*, (f)). These 'flies' lay their eggs in the fruit blossom which hatch as caterpillar/grubs in the fruit itself. The fruit drops to the ground in June and the caterpillars leave to hatch out as sawflies. Spray at petal fall to prevent the grubs entering the fruit and keep the soil underneath the tree clean to prevent caterpillars. Spraying at the required intervals (see under the various fruit entries) will prevent this pest. Fenitrothion (PBI), Sybol 2,

Picket-G (both ICI), Kothrin, Liquide Total (both Sovilo), Supra-cid(e) (CG).

SCALE INSECTS

(Fr: *poux*, (m) or *chenilles bourrues*, (f); It: *cocciniglie* (f) or *pulci*, (m); Sp: *piojos*, (m)). Not immediately apparent at first – they have to be looked for on the branches of trees, shrubs and plants. They appear as tiny excrescences, often the same colour as the plant itself or the wood of the branch. On fruit trees a winter wash and other spraying should prevent them. Remember always to spray *under* the leaves as well as on top. Particularly prevalent in the greenhouse and it needs concerted action to eradicate them. Sometimes they have a puffed up appearance, hence the *bourrue* in French. Bio Longlast (PBI), Sybol 2. Dormant plants: Clean-up (ICI), Delan Liquide (Sovilo), Supracide/Ultracide (CG).

SLUGS and SNAILS

(Fr: *limaces*, (f) *et escargots* (m); It: *limmacie e lumache* (both f); Sp: *limacos*, (m) *y caracoles*, (f)). There is nothing slugs and snails do not like but salads, hostas and tuberous plants seem to be among their favourites. Never leave windfalls on the ground since it will only encourage them. When not based on methiocarb most of the slug baits are based on metaldehyde which can cause a quick and painful death to dogs and cats – there is no antidote at present, so beer in a saucer or a slug trap is harmless to all except the slugs and works well though clearing it up each day is rather nauseating. Slug Gard (PBI), Mini Blue Slug Pellets (ICI), Agrolimace, Agrolimace bleu, Limagel (all Sovilo), Metaclor (CG). Fertosan, available only in the U.K., is excellent and not dangerous to domestic animals.

SOOTY MOULD see APHIDS

THRIPS

(Thrips in French, Italian and Spanish, pronounced without sounding the 'h'). These are extremely small black (or sometimes dirty yellow) flies which are virtually invisible. They arrive in thundery weather and roses seem their favourite flower. They can do quite a bit of damage but they are not too difficult to eradicate. Spray with Fenitrothion (PBI), Sybol 2, Picket, Picket-G (all ICI), Liquide Total (Sovilo), Dimecron (CG).

TORTRIX MOTH/CATERPILLAR

(Fr: *tordeuse rouleuse*, (f); It: *tortricidi*, (m); Sp: *pollilas*, (f)). Easy to recognise because the leaves of ornamental shrubs, roses and fruit trees seem to be spun together with silken thread. Sometimes fruit is covered in the same way. Their progeny, brown or green caterpillars, can do a lot of damage on their own account to say nothing of becoming tortrix moths themselves one day. Spray with Fenitrothion, Hexyl (both PBI) Sybol 2, Picket, Picket-G (all ICI), Nexion 20 (Sovilo) Supracid(e) or Basudin (both CG).

TULIP FIRE

(Fr: *feu de tulipe*, (m); It: *marciume di tulipano*, (m); Sp: *botrytis de tulipan*, (m)). This is a form of botrytis and you should always dust your bulbs with a good fungicide before planting them (which also discourages rodents who dislike the smell). It is easy to recognise by a grey mould on the bulbs or new leaves or the burnt edges of the tulip leaves. Sometimes there are even earlier signs such as sad, soft first growth. Destroy all bulbs with botrytis and wait a couple of years before planting susceptible subjects in the same place. As it is soil borne stir some fungicidal powder into the soil before planting. As with so many things in the garden prevention is not only better than cure but cure is often impossible. Dithane 945 (PBI), Peltar, Folcap (both Sovilo), Apron 35SD (CG).

VINE WEEVIL

(Fr: *altise de vigne*, (f); It: *altiche di vite*, (m); Sp: *gorgojo de la vid*, (m)). Very simple to recognise since the vines look very unhealthy with all the leaves holed and the fruit damaged. Vine weevils winter over in the soil doing a great deal of damage to the roots of the vines as well The eggs are laid on the soil rather than in it and the larvae can be recognised easily as they are legless. As with so many fruit crops vines need a great deal of spraying at required intervals. Never try to resuscitate an old vineyard since disease and pests will be lurking everywhere. Better by far to pull everything up, thoroughly clean the soil and replant with vigorous new vines which within three years will give you far better crops than the old. This does not count for an old vine on a house or outbuilding but again you should spray for various pests at the required time. See also under Vines. Fenitrothion, Hexyl (both PBI), Sybol 2 solution as soil drench (ICI) Nexion 20, Kothrin (both Sovilo), Basudin (CG).

WASPS

(Fr: *guêpes* (f); It: *vespe*, (f); Sp: *avispas*(f)). Apart from being the greatest enemies of honey bees they are both dirty and unpleasant. First of all try and find the nest. Letter boxes, bird boxes, holes in trees and even inside garden lamps are all favourite places. In letter boxes and lamp globes you can lay a folded paper tissue soaked in insecticide but you cannot do the same in a bird box. It is best to take this sort of thing away in summer to avoid squatters such as wasps. You should do this sort of work when the wasps are away from their nests and not at dusk as so many people advise, when you will almost certainly be stung by at least one of the thousands that are in residence. Wasp traps that end up drowning the wasps slowly are not only horrid but can trap bees as well so should not be used. Waspend (ICI).

WHITE FLIES

(Fr: *pucerons blancs*, (m); It: *mosche bianche*, (f); Sp: *pulgones blancos*, (m)). The tiny nymphs of the white flies can often be found on the underside of leaves of many plants both indoors and out. They suck the leaves dry and then excrete a type of honeydew which in turn leads to sooty moulds and, in the Mediterranean, thousands of ants which is often the first sign of the infection. Once the flies and honeydew are gone the ants will leave also. Pyrethrum dust can be excellent but otherwise you can use one of the following:- Bio Longlast (PBI), Picket-G, Sybol 2 (both ICI), Trigard (CG).

WIREWORMS

(Fr: *taupins*, (m); It: *enteride*, (f); Sp: *gusanos alambres*, (m)). These are the larvae of the click beetle and they live in the soil. They are a dirty yellowy brown with a tough carapace. If you have these in your garden you can plant potatoes with a view to cleaning the soil (they will be inedible because they will be so infested) or you can use soil cleansing dusts and liquids. Once found in a Mediterranean garden, count on at least two to three years-finally to banish them. Italians tend to call wireworms *millepiedi* which they are not. Bromophos before planting (PBI), Sybol 2 Dust (ICI), Sovinexit granules (Sovilo), Insectes du sol (KB and Truffaut).

WOODLICE

(Fr: *cloportes*, (f); It: *onischi*, (m); Sp: *cochenillas*, (f)). For some reason woodlice are never taken seriously though they can do great damage. All anti slug products work well, so does keeping places free of debris. Scrubbing out their favourite haunts with Jeyes fluid, carbolic or bleach also helps.

9

Weeds and Weedkillers

Weeds are part and parcel of every cultivator's life. If there are not too many, remove them manually or by machine. In between rows of vegetables use a black plastic mulch and/or hoe once a week. It is a quick way to deal with them and if you had your head chopped off once a week you would soon give up the struggle.

There are some weeds which require special treatment. Certain perennials require a poison that goes right into the plant and its roots. Bindweed is one and Truffaut in France make a specific bindweed killer called *Désherbant pour fraisiers*. Many years ago I was found by our jobbing gardener trying to get to the bottom of bindweed to root it out. He told me that he had been a well-digger for many years and had seen the white roots of bindweed 4m/14ft down. I now use glyphosate in the form of Roundup made by Monsanto and available worldwide.

Another plant difficult to eradicate is the common valerian (*Centranthus ruber*) which can be a pest in many Mediterranean gardens. It seems to tolerate the most ghastly conditions. I have never dug as far as 4m/14ft but I have seen the large starchy roots of this valerian over 2m/6ft down in a bank. These two, together with the dog rose, thistle (very painful to deal with by hand even with gloves on) and plantain are my own main weed problems. I do not worry too much about annual weeds and confine myself to not letting them seed.

Apart from the fact that it is not pleasant to look at a jumble of weeds or to try and find vegetables growing in a patch of thistles it is important to remember that weeds rob the soil of both nutrient and water which could be usefully used by the cultivated plant. Having cleared your soil, mulching is the best answer to keep weeds down. In the vegetable garden this can be black plastic made specially for the purpose. The new sort has minute holes punched in it which let rain and garden water pass through. Wooden boards are also good but do not use straw which is a fire hazard, as are pine needles. Grass clippings are probably the most easily available mulch (provided they have not been dosed with a selective weedkiller). Gravel is not a good mulch in the Mediterranean since it becomes and remains too hot. Peat is excellent but needs to be thoroughly and constantly wetted otherwise it will blow all over the place. Coarse sawdust which has been weathered, mixed with peat, is also quite good. However, do not use sawdust which is too resinous since most plants will not like this and it can present a fire hazard. The best of all is chopped bark which is not available everywhere. It gives a rich, dark finish to flower beds and for rose growers who will not underplant their Hybrid Teas it is the perfect answer. A mulch not only smothers weeds (it will smother your treasured seedlings as well unfortunately), but will keep the soil moist longer.

I compost all my weeds. There are some whose hard seeds survive the heat and chemical processes of decomposition but they are few. I sometimes use sulphate of ammonia as an accelerator and the seeds cannot possibly enjoy this.

When all else fails weedkillers are the answer, selective or otherwise. On a lawn it is the best method of treatment since digging up weeds can leave an unsightly mess. The similarly unsightly mess left by the broad-leaved weedkiller is less enduring and usually scrapes off leaving little trace. This is, of course, no good if you use clover in your lawn but the matted roots of clover and creeping fescues will not usually allow any interlopers. Underneath woody shrubs and rose bushes a selective weedkiller, together with a pre-emergence inhibitor if possible, such as simazine, can save several days' work.

Reclaiming land for cultivation which has become overgrown with bramble, kermes oak, wild clematis, cistus, oxalis, etc., can be a heartbreaking task. For a start, it is difficult if not impossible to get to the root of the plant and manual removal nearly always leaves something behind to grow even more strongly in less crowded conditions. Moreover, the roots of some plants such as cistus and certain grasses perform a useful task in keeping walls and banks from falling down and removal of their roots may well mean the collapse of the wall or bank. Weedkillers, those containing glyphosate in particular, and several applications of them, are the only answer no matter how ecology minded you may be.

93

To clean land for cultivation be sure to use a product which allows you to sow within three weeks of the treatment. Paraquat for example enables sowing *five hours* later and glyphosate allows sowing the moment the weeds have been killed. Some French products work with ammonium sulphate which cause the weeds to outgrow their own strength due to the immense dose of nitrogen. This is excellent where the infestation is not great and composed mostly of annual weeds.

The only problem with using weedkillers is that one application is not enough because there are weeds for every season so, except for planting largish shrubs and trees, do not count on having totally clean land for at least a whole season. Thereafter, you will have to cope with the odd strong annual which has established itself well and truly due to lack of local competition. Dandelions and plantago are among the greatest offenders of this sort.

There are several brush-killing products after whose use the ground must be tilled by machine. In order not to waste the product and to see what you are doing, it is best to hack down at least half the growth before spraying with the brush-killer. Often products used in agriculture do a better job on neglected land than a general garden herbicide. These are not generally available and it is necessary to get them from specialist outlets. Very often products for agricultural use are stronger than what is on sale to the general public – they are certainly cheaper. However, in both Spain and Italy and to a certain extent in France, herbicides and insecticides are coded according to their toxicity and occasionally you may find it impossible to buy the product you need.

Apart from following the instructions to the letter, and not putting in a bit extra to be sure (this can often lead to the product working less well than usual), do spray only on a totally windless day. Even on what seemed to be a perfect day without a breeze I managed to kill some geraniums about 3m/10ft from where I was spraying paraquat. When spraying with all but the gentlest weedkillers, protective clothing, gloves and rubber, non-absorbent shoes are necessary.

Never use sodium chlorate for several reasons. It is a fire hazard. It stays in the soil for far too long, going further and further down over the years. It can leach into other parts of the garden due to abundant autumn rainfall and it can pollute ponds, lakes and even rivers.

Many herbicides are deadly poisons, sometimes with no antidote and no matter how safe they may be in the garden they are not particularly safe for humans and pets. Many modern lawn grass seeds have been previously treated either with an agent to repel birds or with a broadleaf weed inhibitor. Both of these are poisonous to any dog or cat eating this grass and pet owners should check that they are not buying treated seed. Apart from the obvious move of taking the animal to the vet if you think it has been poisoned, charcoal in its food (either as biscuits or as tablets) for a week or ten days is a marvellous purifier and dogs seem quite happy to eat it.

Lastly, there is no point in using a poison on weeds when ten minutes with a hoe is all that is needed and there is no point in weeding only to leave the ground unplanted.

Every country has its own manufacturers of herbicides and weedkillers. The giants – Ciba-Geigy, Monsanto, ICI, Fisons and Bayer – are everywhere. They are usually more expensive than local brands but some of them manufacture unique products such as Ciba-Geigy's Sequestrene and only Monsanto's glyphosate weedkiller is available in the Mediterranean, though in the U.K. it is available from Murphy in various forms. For the commoner weedkillers and insecticides smaller firms such as KB Jardin, Sovilo, Sem, Truffaut (France), P.B.I. (U.K.), etc., often offer better value for money, as do some of the bigger supermarket chains. In Italy often, but not always, the local *Consorzio Agrario* (an agricultural co-operative) stock weedkillers and insecticides at reasonable prices.

GLYPHOSATE

Generally found as Roundup by Monsanto – this name is used world wide. In the U.K., Murphy market it as Tumbleweed. The treated ground can be replanted as soon as the weeds have died down. Poisonous but the least dangerous of all. Never mix with anything else or it will not work.

SIMAZINE

Gives approximately nine months' protection from weeds on paths, rose and shrub plantations, orchards, raspberries, etc. The chemical prevents weed seeds from germinating. Often used in conjunction with paraquat. Do not use where there is peaty soil or peat based compost or mulch. Gesastop from Ciba-Geigy is available throughout the Mediterranean but most countries have at least one or two makers of their own.

PARAQUAT

The most commonly used weedkiller in the Mediterranean. The cheapest way to purchase it is from agricultural outlets (usually for the winegrowers). Both Ciba-Geigy and ICI products such as Gramoxone are available virtually everywhere.

AMETRYN 24D

Selective broad leaf weedkiller. Gesapax from Ciba-Geigy is available almost everywhere. Verdone from ICI in the U.K. and Liseron-Pur Gazon from Ets. Clause in France are two others.

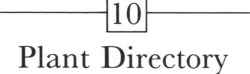

Plant Directory

Note: In the plant descriptions a code is used to indicate the zones in which plants may be grown and the watering conditions they prefer. The code is explained below. The temperature zones have been devised especially for this book and do *not* correspond to the International Hardiness Zones.

TEMPERATURE ZONES

ZONE A

Coastal regions in the N. and S. Mediterranean Basin including Apulia, E. Sicily, Cyprus, Costa del Sol in Spain, coasts of Turkey and E. Greece, Israel, Lebanon, Syrian coasts, N. Africa. No frost at all. Tender plants need no winter protection but choose carefully since water demands can be great in summer in an area notoriously short of water. Perfect for most succulents and cacti. No protection needed for citrus except limes. Sun and lack of water are greatest enemies. Pelargoniums continue to grow throughout the winter.

ZONE B

Lower night temperatures (down to 5°C/40°F) and occasional slight frost. Includes the Mediterranean coast of France, N., W. and E. coasts of Italy (down to Gargano Peninsula) and inland up to 2–300m/660–1000ft, western coasts of Greece and all the islands, Spanish eastern coasts to Valencia. Citrus can stay outside (except lime and grapefruit) but may need occasional protection from frost (netting of trees, soil warming). Very delicate plants such as natives of Brazil, Uruguay, South Africa, Australia, etc. may need

97

winter protection and are best grown in pots so they can be taken in at the coldest period. Pelargoniums can become dormant in winter but for the most part need no winter protection.

ZONE C

An area almost always at an altitude of more than 800m/2,600ft, subject to occasional frosts and even light snow which does not settle (or very rarely). Plants which are hardy in the average Mediterranean climate to 300–400m/ 1000–1300ft above sea-level but are not necessarily hardy further north in Europe or at greater altitude. If in doubt put your more precious plants in tubs and take in to a cold greenhouse for winter protection. This includes all pelargoniums.

PLANT TYPES AND THEIR WATER REQUIREMENTS

TYPE 1

Either tolerates or definitely requires dry conditions. Such plants normally need absolutely perfect drainage so, in most areas, dig out the Mediterranean clay and make a mixture of one part garden soil, one part peat, two parts fine gravel or sand.

TYPE 2

Grows in the most commonly found Mediterreanean garden conditions. Water only once a week but with long, deep soaks of at least fifteen minutes, or when leaves and flowers flag. In very dry areas it is as well to put in plastic or clay watering pipes close to the plant at the time of planting which will direct the water to the roots. This not only conserves water but any 'cheating' on watering you may be obliged to resort to will be less noticeable.

TYPE 3

Thirsty plants which you should only grow where you have an enviable water supply throughout the year or where you can grow them in pots. Hydrangeas, all the S. American climbers, cyperus, impatiens, certain poplars and the willows spring to mind although there are many others.

TYPE 4

There are a number of plants which require what could be called jungle conditions but which are so beautiful that they are well worth growing in pots in the Mediterranean region. The first thing to remember is that they must never be exposed to temperatures lower than 10°C/50°F and only as low as that very rarely. Secondly, they need hot, damp shade which can be obtained by placing the pots under a veranda, pergola or a not too densely clothed tree. To keep up the damp conditions they need permanently moist soil (do not try to achieve this in parts of S. Spain, N. Africa or S. Italy where water is permanently short) and some will need spraying or syringing several times a day in order to simulate the very high humidity lacking in the Mediterranean region. For instance humidity runs from 30% in the day to 75% in the evening in Alexandria, Egypt which is exceptionally high for the region. Elsewhere it can be as low as 25%. However, most of the northern states of S. America have an humidity of around 85–90%. Only by experimenting will you be able to tell the requirements of a plant in your particular region. Provided you are prepared to take this sort of trouble you can grow anthurium, aralia, tropical begonias, beloperone, bilbergia, brunfelsia, dracaena (the small sort, not the Dragon tree), lapageria, tropical fuchsia, tropical hibiscus, orchids, philodendron, strobilanthes, spathiphyllum, tillandsia, tibouchina, *Tradescantia fuscata* and many, many others. These sort of conditions are rather better for camellias and the rhododendron family than exposing them to the full Mediterranean sun and aridity but do watch out for fungus diseases.

DIRECTORY

Note: The area of origin shown applies only to the species described

ABELIA (*Caprifoliaceae*)

Very decorative deciduous (except where shown) shrubs all with tubular flowers. They are frost tender but will tolerate a certain amount of drought when well established, though their scent is better when watered. *Origin*: China except where otherwise shown. *Zone*: A. *Water*: 2. *Pruning*: Cut off dead and damaged growth only. If hard pruning is necessary, due to frost, the shrub will throw up new shoots in late spring. *Propagation*: Cuttings, with heel if possible, in early autumn or layering in spring. Wait at least a year before removing layered plant from its parent.

Abelia chinensis

A. chinensis. White/blush flowers late May–June. H 2m/6ft. Scarce.

A. 'Edward Goucher'. Rose pink flowers June–July. H 1.6–2m/5–6ft.

A. floribunda. Origin: Mexico. Semi-evergreen. Crimson flowers late July–October. One of the nicest but very tender. H 3m/10ft.

A. × *grandiflora*. Semi-evergreen. Mid pink flowers June–September. Fairly hardy. H 2m/6ft.

A. g. prostata. As above but prostrate with a spread of 1.6m/5ft. Hardier than most.

A. schumanii. Mauve pink flowers August–September. H 2m/6ft. Very tender.

A. triflora. White/blush pink flowers June. H 5m/16ft. Hardiest of all.

ABUTILON (*Malvaceae*)

Attractive, deciduous, flowering shrubs and climbers. *Origin*: Middle East to Iran. All the varieties described flower from April–September. *Temperature*: Zones A and B. *Water*: Type 2. *Soil*: Not important though if very chalky or poor add peat and humus. Sun is essential. *Pruning*: None except to cut out dead wood. *Propagation*: By cuttings taken in early summer and rooted in a sandy compost with the help of hormone rooting powder or liquid. The night temperature should not drop below 16°C/55°F for propagation purposes. Seed can also be used. *A. vitifolium* often seeds itself. All flower from April to September.

A. 'Ashford Red'. Open, saucer shaped single flowers with salmon red petals. H 2–2.5m/6–8ft.

A. 'Cloth of Gold'. Yellow saucer shaped flowers. H as above.

A. *megapotamicum*. The most dramatic of all with red and yellow bell shaped flowers. H 1.6m/ 5ft. There is a variegated version which rather detracts from the flowers.

A. *ochsenii* 'Patrick Synge'. Lavender saucer shaped flowers with purple centres. H 3m/10ft.

A. *striatum*. Striped red and yellow flowers which are not so pretty as *A. megapotamicum*. H 2–3m/ 6–10ft

Abutilon vitifolium

A. *vitifolium*. Lavender hollyhock shaped flowers with grey vine shaped foliage. Height to 4m/13ft. There is a clone with slightly flatter flowers called 'Tennant's White' which is very beautiful and flowers over a longer period than most. This is more attractive than *A. vitifolium album* which also has hollyhock shaped white flowers.

A. 'Veronica Tennant'. Rich pinky mauve saucer shaped flowers. H 3.6m/ 12ft.

ACACIA (*Leguminosae*)

A vast genus, commonly known in Europe as mimosa. Most have yellow flowers. Not entirely hardy but will tolerate some frost. Many prefer acid soil but those which do not can be grafted onto *A. retinoides* which does well in alkaline soil. *Origin*: S. Australia except where otherwise shown. *Temperature*: Zone A. *Water*: Type 1. *Pruning*: None except to cut out dead or damaged wood. *Propagation*: By seed, soaked overnight, in a temperature of not less than 18°C/65°F. Some people believe in heating the seed in a frying pan to simulate a bush fire and certainly this appears to give excellent results. *Pests*: Aphids.

A. *arabica*. *Origin*: Arabian Peninsula. H 5m/16ft. Grown only because it is very salt and wind tolerant. Needs constant trimming to keep a good shape. Has the usual fine, pinnate foliage and very large thorns. The yellow spring flowers are among the smallest of the genus.

A. *baileyana*. The Coottamunda wattle. H 5–7m/16–22ft. Yellow flowers in late winter.

A. *cyanophylla*. Australian blue leaf wattle. As its name suggests it has rather blue-green leaves and deep yellow flowers in spring. It is very salt tolerant and grows to around 5m/16ft in good conditions and about half that in the desert. Has a wide spread and is a good shade tree.

A. *dealbata*. H 15m/48ft. Silver wattle. Among the most commonly grown in the region. Pale yellow flowers in early spring. Parent of many varieties such as 'Le Gaulois', 'Mirandole' and 'Toison d'Or'.

A. *decurrens*. The green wattle is among the tallest mimosas, H 20m/65ft. Large light yellow flowers in immense panicles in March.

A. *farnesiana*. *Origin*: Sub-tropical America. This is a multi-trunk wide-headed acacia which grows to about 5m/16ft and has the usual yellow flowers in early spring. Very easy to propagate from seed and very salt tolerant.

A. × *hanburyana*. A hybrid of A. *dealbata* and A. *podalyrifolia* with unusual foliage though the flowers are similar to other mimosas, appearing in early spring. Not easily obtainable except in the S. of France and the Italian Riviera. H 3–5m/10–16ft.

A. *howitti*. Famous because of its variety 'Claire de Lune' which is probably the most beautiful but fragile mimosa of all. Yellow flowers in early spring. H 5m/16ft.

A. *longifolia*. The fastest growing mimosa, H 5m/16ft. Yellow flowers in March–April. Very wind resistant.

A. *mollissima*. The black wattle is sometimes considered a variety of A. *decurrens* but the leaves are softer and the flowers much bigger and a paler yellow, almost primrose, in April–May. Most attractive but needs to be grafted onto A. *retinoides* really to thrive.

A. *retinoides*. The most commonly grown in France and Italy for the cut flower market. Useful for grafting purposes as it tolerates alkaline soil. Flowers late February. Wind resistant.

ACAENA (*Rosaceae*)

The New Zealand burrs are evergreen trailing shrubs with small, neat leaves and tiny burr like 'flowers' which appear from May–September. Can be walked on. All are hardy to about 700m/2300ft and they prefer well drained soil and dappled shade. *Zone*: B. *Water*: 2. Their only require-

Acacia retinoides

ments are well drained soil and dappled shade. *Propagation*: By cuttings in summer with hormone rooting powder.

A. *adscendens*. Very prostrate carpeter with bronze foliage and purple flowers. There is a glaucous form.

A. *buchananii*. Prostrate carpeter with silver grey foliage and red burrs in August.

A. *microphylla*. Bronze/green foliage with long lasting red burrs in late summer and autumn.

ACANTHUS (*Acanthaceae*)

Marvellous large-leafed herbaceous perennials, drought and wind resistant. Flowers appear any time from May–July. In spring established clumps should be cut back in the warmer areas where foliage has become untidy and not died off. *Origin*: Mediterranean. *Zone*: B. Do not plant over 500m/1650ft. *Water*: 2. Half sun or dense shade. *Propagation*: Division of established clumps in early spring. In cooler parts root cuttings can be taken in autumn. *Pests and Diseases*: Usually free from insect attack but occasional mildew can occur.

    A. caroli-alexandri. White and rose flowers in spikes. H 30–40cm/12–16in.

    A. longifolius. Purple flowers. H 1.2m/4ft.

    A. mollis. Purple and white or purple and mauve flowering spikes. H 1–1.2m/3–4ft. Occurs in the wild all over Italy and the Adriatic region.

    A. spinosus. Very similar to above but will tolerate more drought and neglect.

Acanthus spinosus

ACHILLEA (*Compositae*)

Herbaceous plants with wide distribution – all those listed are European natives. *Zone*: B. *Water*: 2. *Propagation*: By division after flowering or by seed in early spring with minimum heat of 14°C/55°F. *Pests*: Occasional aphids but otherwise trouble free.

    A. chrysocoma. *Origin*: Greece. H 10cm/4in. Has a carpeting habit and each plant spreads to about 30cm/10in. Mustard yellow flowers from June–August. Leaves are grey green.

    A. ptarmica. Sneezewort. H 60–75cm/2–2.5ft, S 40cm/15in. Mid-green narrow leaves and small clusters of white flowers in mid summer. The best known variety is 'The Pearl'. Should be planted in large clumps and be well staked.

    A. tomentosa. Excellent ground cover plant – H 15–17cm/6–7in. Downy leaves with tightly packed yellow flower heads May–August or even September.

    A. × *wilczekii*. Another excellent ground cover or rockery plant with silver grey foliage and white flowers from July–September.

AEONIUM (*Crassulaceae*)

Whilst not a Mediterranean native, very commonly grown in the area and, provided you have no frost, one of the most dramatic and attractive succulent plants. *Origin*: Morocco and Canary Islands. *Zone*: A. *Water*: 1. *Propagation*:

Very easy by pulling off a small plant from the parent and planting in sandy compost. *Pests and Diseases*: No insect pests but can occasionally suffer from fungus problems and also damp which will kill the plant.

A. arboreum. This variety exists both in green and purple forms with thick, succulent leaves and yellow rosettes of flowers in August. The normal height is up to 2m/6ft but given perfect conditions they can be much taller.

A. canariensis. Bright apple green thick leaves sometimes with reddened tips in winter. Yellow flowers in rosettes in July.

AETHIONEMA (*Cruciferae*)

Dwarf sub-shrubs which are good for the rock garden. *Origin*: Mediterranean. *Zones*: All. *Water*: Type 1. *Pruning*: Although not necessary they benefit from being cut back occasionally in spring before new growth begins. *Propagation*: By seeds in spring and planted out the following year or by cuttings of non-flowering shoots, using hormone rooting powder, in a 50/50 mixture of peat and sand.

A. grandiflorum. The palest pink flowers in May–June, set against green oblong leaves. H 15cm/6in, S 45cm/18in.

A. iberideum. Same H as before but with smaller S. Medium white flowers May–July, slightly glaucous foliage.

A. thomasianum 'Warley Rose'. This variety has glaucous foliage and dark pink flowers in spikes. H 7–15cm/3–6in, S 30cm/12in. Flowers in late spring. Needs slightly more watering than the type.

AGAPANTHUS (*Liliacae*)

All mentioned below are hardy and start flowering in May and certain hybrids as late as September. *Origin*: Africa. H 60–75cm/2–2.5ft. *Zone*: A. *Water*: 2. *Propagation*: By dividing the fleshy roots in spring just when they come into growth again but will increase on their own. *Pests and Diseases*: No insect pests but occasionally a fungus can attack the roots and eventually kill the plant. Take out, throw away and disinfect the ground with a fungicide.

A. campanulatus. This species tends to die down in winter. It has very crowded umbels of rather pale blue flowers. The variety 'Isis' has darker almost lavender blue flowers which is an improvement on the type.

A. praecox. Evergreen in the Mediterranean. The flower heads are densely packed and come in blue, white and pink forms. There are many varieties (e.g. 'Sky Star', 'Torbay') which are nearly always more interesting than the type.

A. orientalis. Very similar to the above.

AGAVE (*Agavaceae*)

Succulent plants with sword shaped leaves and insignificant greenish flowers on a tall spike. Ideal for absentee gardeners. Will not tolerate temperatures below 10°C/50°F. *Origin*: Mexico and S.W. United States. *Zone*: A. *Water*: 1. *Propagation*: By offsets in 75/25 sand and loam kept fairly dry. *Pests and Diseases*: Agave weevil which is difficult to eradicate. Remove affected plants and do not plant succulents in same spot. Damp weather or over-watering can cause fungus disease.

A. americana. Better known as the century plant which flowers at around twenty-five years (flower spikes up to 10m/32ft) and then dies having left progeny to take over. There are several varieties, including *A. a.* 'Marginata' with rich yellow edges to the leaves; *A. a.* 'Mediopicta' with yellow central stripe to the leaves; *A. a.* 'Striata' with white or yellow stripes to the leaves; and *A. a.* 'Variegata' with very dark green and pale yellow twisted leaves.

A. atrovirens. Smaller than the above, H 2m/6ft and flowering spike up to 7m/22ft.

Agave americana 'Marginata'

A. horrida. Very fragile with large leaves 3m/10ft long and 65cm/2ft wide.

A. parviflora. A useful dwarf for rockeries from Arizona, H10cm/3–4in. Flower spike 2m/6ft.

AKEBIA (*Lardizabalaceae*)

Useful deciduous or semi-evergreen climbing shrubs for quick shade but can become invasive – do not give too rich soil. All have scented purple flowers in March–April followed by violet fruits which burst open to show black seeds in white flesh. *Origin*: Japan. *Zone*: B. *Water*: Type 2. *Pruning*: Try prevent seeding by cutting off seed heads in autumn. Shorten to keep within allotted space. *Propagation*: By seed which germinates all too easily. Cuttings in early autumn will have taken by the following spring.

A. quinata has leaves arranged in fives and will grow to 10m/32ft. Needs some support.

A. trifoliata. As above but leaves in threes.

ALBIZIA (*Leguminosae*)

Highly decorative, easy to grow decidous shrubs or trees with mimosa-like foliage and pink or yellow flowers in panicles. Ideal as shade cover for roses. Needs enriched soil and feeding twice a year to perform well. Allow six years to reach full height of 7–10m/22–32ft. *Zone*: A. *Water*: 2. *Pruning*: None except for removing damaged or dead wood. *Propagation*: By seed at any time providing the temperature is not below 18°C/70°F.

A. julibrissin. Origin: Sub-tropical Africa and Asia. The silk tree. Dark pink flowers in June–July. *A. j.* 'Rosea' has paler pink flowers.

A. lophantha. Origin: Australia and Asia. Has similar foliage to the above but yellow flowers in December–January. Often mistaken for mimosa.

Albizia julibrissin

ALOE (*Liliaceae*)

A vast family of succulent plants ideal for coastal regions and S. Mediterranean. Extremely drought resistant but will not tolerate frost. *Origin*: E. and S. Africa. *Zone*: A. *Water*: 1. *Propagation*: All aloes can be propagated by suckers, some of which occur slightly under ground. Seed can be used but germinates erratically.

A. abyssinica. Long prickly plain leaves 2m/6ft high with yellowy-orange flowers from February–April.

A. africana. As above but the leaves are in rosettes. Flowers are a darker orange in late winter or early spring.

A. arborescens. Magnificently tall, to 10m/32ft, with speckled leaves and rich purple-red flowers from December–March. Will take slightly lower temperatures than most.

A. candelabrum. As the name suggests the dark pink flowers are held high like candles, appearing in mid-late winter. Needs a certain amount of grooming to look at its best.

A. daviana. An attractive stemless plant with red spotted leaves and pale pink flowers appearing intermittently throughout the year.

A. variegata. The partridge breasted aloe. Well known as a houseplant in colder countries this is ideal in a dry garden. The leaves are pale green with darker mottling and the flowers are pink with undertones of green appearing from January–April.

ALSTROEMERIA (*Amaryllidaceae*).

The Peruvian lilies are ideal plants for the Mediterranean garden since they flower throughout the summer and, without being invasive, increase over time. Can be grown in pots where water is a problem. They need careful planting as the roots are very fragile and repay mulching and annual feeding. *Origin*: S. America. *Zone*: A. *Water*: 2. *Propagation*: By seed in deep pots to avoid root disturbance. Germination is erratic.

A. aurea (syn. *A. aurantiaca*). Large heads of yellow and red flowers. H to 1m/3ft.

A. a. lutea. As above but with all yellow flowers.

A. chilensis. Dark pink flowers.

A. Ligtu hybrids. H to 60cm/2ft with pink, lilac or white flowers, some striped. Very attractive. The Ligtu hybrids are the most commonly available in mixed varieties but it is possible, occasionally, to get these in individual colours.

A. pelegrina. Larger flowers than the type up to 5cm/2in across on 60cm/2ft stems. Lilac or spotted reddish/purple.

A. p. alba. The pure white form of the above.

Alstroemeria Ligtu hybrid

ANEMONE (*Ranunculaceae*)

In the Mediterranean it is best to grow only winter flowering anemones since the fierce heat will not allow the later flowering types to thrive. *Origin*: European native. *Zone*: B and C. *Water*: 2. *Propagation*: They seed themselves and increase over the years.

A. blanda. H 10–15cm/4–6in. Difficult to eradicate once established but an absolute joy when massed, particularly in its white form. There are several excellent cultivars including the white 'Bridesmaid', 'Blue Pearl,' and deep rose pink 'Charmer'. All prefer slight shade and slightly humid soil at flowering time in April–May.

A. coronaria. H 30–40cm/12–16in. The florists' anemone. This is usually found in its De Caen or St Brigid forms. Flowers around March–April in the N. Mediterranean. Needs rather more shade than *A. blanda*. One of the best cultivars is the violet 'Sylphide'.

ANTHEMIS (*Compositae*)

Useful grey-leaved low-growing plants relishing dry conditions. It is best to cut all anthemis hard back in autumn. *Origin*: European natives. *Zone*: B and C. *Water*: 2. *Propagation*: By basal stem cuttings in very sandy soil from late spring to autumn. The rooted cuttings can be planted out in autumn or spring.

A. frutescens (syn. *Argyranthemum frutescens*). The plant which is known throughout the Mediterranean region by this name will be found under *Argyranthemum* below.

A. nobilis 'Flora Pleno' (syn. *Chamaemelum nobilis*). Double flowered camomile. Flat carpet plant with small green centred daisies in summer.

A. punctata cupaniana. Useful for rock garden work this plant is 45cm/18in tall with silver grey finely cut foliage in summer and white daisy like flowers. The foliage becomes rich green in winter.

ARAUCARIA (*Araucariaceae*)

With the exception of the monkey puzzle (see below) all species need a minimum winter temperature of 5°C/40°F and plenty of water in winter and early spring. It essential to be sure of a perfect climate for the particular araucaria you wish to grow. If the tree is frosted and recovers it does so in a most unattractive way losing its symmetry, with small tufts of growth which never grow properly again. They are for the N. Mediterranean only unless water is available. *Zone*: A and B. *Water*: 2. *Pruning*: None is needed except to remove lower branches if considered necessary. This should be done in winter. *Propagation*: Although most araucarias produce either yellow catkins (male) or globular cones (female) they do not often give viable seeds. It is best to take 7–10cm/3–4in cuttings of vertical growth in early spring in sandy soil with hormone rooting compound. Allow three years before planting out in pots and another five to plant in open ground. Thereafter, growth is about 30cm/12in a year. *Pests and Diseases*: Honey fungus has been known to kill araucarias in N. France and the U.K. but so far it has not been found in the Mediterranean region.

A. araucana (syn. *A. imbricata*). *Origin*: Chile and Argentina. The monkey puzzle. H 10m/32ft. Needs a large space to grow well but gives plenty of useful shade. Can be pruned when older to form an umbrella shape though do not try to do this with forms whose branches sweep to the ground. Very spiny, dark green leaves.

A. bidwillii. Origin: Queensland. Bunya-bunya tree. Very high in the wild, up to 45m/150ft, this tree needs a minimum winter temperature of 15°C/55°F to do really well but it is happy by the sea. Branches have a tendency to slope slightly upwards and are often tufted – and partly bare.

A. cunninghamii. Origin: E. Australia and New Guinea. Moreton Bay pine. As tall but rather more fragile than the above and far more horizontally tiered in shape. A most spectacular specimen tree for the large garden. There is also a silver leafed form *A. c. glauca* but this is difficult to find.

A. heterophylla. Origin: Norfolk Island, Australia. Norfolk Island pine. H to 40m/130ft (much more in the wild). Commonly grown throughout the Mediterranean. A most beautiful, symmetrical tree with short horizontal slightly ascending branches.

ARCTOTIS (*Compositae*)

Invaluable sun loving, drought resistant daisy-like plants which flower throughout the summer in the Mediterranean. *Origin*: S. Africa. *Zone*: A and B. *Water*: 1. *Pruning*: Cut back half the growth in late autumn. *Propagation*: By seed, flowers in the first year.

A. acaulis. Bright orange flowers with dark centres. H 15cm/6in. Needs protection from cold.

A. grandis. White petals with dark blue reverse. H 45cm/18in. Spreads rapidly.

A. × hybrida. Large flowered hybrids in a wide colour range – yellow, reds, purples and whites. H 45cm/18in.

ARGYRANTHEMUM (*Compositae*)

Valuable sun-loving daisy flowered shrubs. *Origin*: Canary Islands. *Zone*: 1. Will tolerate no temperatures below about 10°C/50°F so should be given some winter protection. *Water*: 2 for open ground, 3 for pots. *Pruning*: Cut back each year to prevent plants becoming leggy. Sometimes wind or cold damaged plants will respond to being cut back hard into the old wood. Wait at least two months before throwing out as dead. *Propagation*: 5–7.5cm/2–3in cuttings of basal shoots in early spring in a 50/50 mixture of sand and loam with some hormone rooting compound. Plant out once the 7.5cm/3in pot is full of roots. *Pests and Diseases*: Black fly. Occasionally a rust can attack these plants and is virtually impossible to eradicate. Pull up and throw away the plants.

A. frutescens. This is commonly known throughout the Mediterranean region as *Anthemis frutescens* or as marguerite. No Mediterranean garden should be without it. May easily be bought in 7.5cm/3in pots from which it grows rapidly to 45cm/18in and more. It comes, nameless, as the more usual white daisy with yellow centre, or the less common yellow daisy type. There are named varieties but only two are common in the region: 'Double Yellow' and 'Chelsea Princess' and they will sold under *Anthemis*. There is also an Italian variety 'Albenga' which is a more compact plant about 40cm/15in high.

ATRIPLEX (*Chenopodiaceae*).

Salt bush. Extremely useful shrubs in dry locations where little else will grow. Ideal as ground or bank cover in S. Mediterranean or desert areas. Although all will tolerate drought they prefer long, deep and well spaced watering. *Zone*: A. *Water*: 1. *Pruning*: None necessary except to remove dead wood and keep within allotted space. *Propagation*: By seed which germinates all too easily.

A. canascens. Origin: S. United States and Mexico. Evergreen. H 1–2m/

3–6ft, S 2m/6ft. Can be clipped to shape if a little water is available. Deep yellow fruit.

A. lentiformis. Origin: Arizona. White thistle or quail bush. Deciduous. Very decorative yellow fruit in late spring against holly type foliage. H to 4m/13ft and can spread the same amount.

A. semibaccata. Australian salt bush. The most adaptable atriplex of all. Semi-prostrate, H 25cm/10in, S 2m/6ft; ideal as ground cover throughout S. Mediterranean. Stands some frost.

AZALEA (*Ericaceae*)

N. Mediterranean only. As long as you can provide shade and plenty of water in summer azaleas in pots can be very rewarding. *Zone*: B and C. *Water*: 3. You will need to add Sequestrene 138 Fe once or twice a year and grow them in bought-in acid soil or leaf mould. Deep shade in summer is essential with good air ciculation. Both the Japanese evergreen and the deciduous Mollis azaleas do well along the southern coasts of France, the Costa Brava and the western coasts of Italy. There is no point in giving named varieties as you can only purchase what is available. *Pruning*: None needed except to cut out dead or damaged wood. *Propagation*: Mediterranean outdoor conditions are too dry to permit satisfactory vegetative propagation.

BALLOTA (*Labiatae*)

A very attractive Mediterranean native and a most useful ground cover plant. *Zone*: A. *Water*: 2. *Pruning*: Cut back hard in late autumn or early spring to promote richer, greener growth. In colder parts the cut stems can be used as a protection. *Propagation*: By division in late autumn or early spring. Seeds are difficult to germinate.

B. pseudodictamnus. Evergreen, with tiny two-lipped flowers in summer, this grows throughout the area and has pale green heart shaped woolly leaves.
H 30–45cm/12–18in. It is often confused with the very similar *B. acetabulosa* which is leggier.

BANKSIA (*Proteaceae*)

If you have enough water and can provide acid soil these evergreen shrubs (trees in their native land) are most rewarding grown in large tubs or raised beds. They need protection from the wind and must have acid soil. All flower June–August depending on the species. *Origin*: Australia. *Zone*: A. *Water*: 3. *Pruning*: None needed. *Propagation*: By

Ballota pseudodictamnus

15cm/6in woody cuttings in July–August with hormone rooting compound. Wait until a good root system has developed before planting out.

B. coccinea. Bright red spikes of flowers. H 4m/13ft.

B. integrifolia. Same height as the above but with yellow/brown flowers.

B. quercifolia. Reddish brown flowers. H 1.6m/5ft.

B. speciosa. Spikes of yellow flowers. H 2m/6ft.

BAPTISIA (*Cruciferae*)

False indigo. A most useful lupin-like herbaceous plant which tolerates drought and poor soil. Needs protection from wind and must have good drainage. *Origin*: N. America. *Zone*: A, B and C. *Water*: 1. *Propagation*: Seed in autumn or early spring or by division in Mar.

B. australis. Spikes of blue flowers to 1.6m/5ft in May–June.

B. bractea. The shortest of the family at only 60cm/24in, cream flowers in May–June.

BAUHINIA (*Leguminosae*)

Orchid tree. A large family of tropical evergreen shrubs, climbers and trees. Only a few are grown in the Mediterranean. In their first few years they must have added protection as low temperatures will kill them when young. They flower on the previous season's wood. Any amount of extra care is worthwhile for the fabulous flowering and handsome foliage. Established trees will recover from cold damage but do not expect flowers. Will tolerate alkaline soil but should receive a yearly treatment against iron chlorosis of Sequestrene 138 Fe. Feed with a general fertilizer every three months. *Pruning*: Not necessary except to remove damaged wood. Be very careful about cutting into living wood and always apply a mastic or disinfectant on pruning cuts. *Zone*: B. *Water*: 3 or 4.

B. candicans (syn. *B. forficata*). *Origin*: S. America. A small tree, H 7m/22ft, with a wide crown and white orchid-like flowers in late spring. Can be deciduous in colder weather and then does not flower. Hardier than most. The best bauhinia for the area.

B. galpinii. *Origin*: S. Africa. Although a shrub it is often used as a trained climber. It has red flowers in June–July and relishes direct sun.

B. purpurea. *Origin*: India. A small tree, H 3.5–5m/11–16ft, with purple or magenta orchid-like flowers in late winter-early spring. Very tender and very thirsty.

B. variegata. *Origin*: India. This 10m/32ft tree comes with purple or magenta orchid-like flowers in late winter-early spring. Very tender and very thirsty.

BEGONIA (*Begoniaceae*)

All begonias are of tropical origin and as such will tolerate no frost. They need copious amounts of water. *Zone*: A for open ground work and B and C where plants are taken in during winter. *Water*: 3 or 4. That said they are, nevertheless, most useful plants in the Mediterranean garden and will flower all the year round in suitable climates. After twelve months it is best to cut back the foliage, dose with fertilizer and let them start into growth again. Alternatively, raise or buy new plants. Where begonias require winter protection bring in the tubers and store, well sprinkled with anti-fungus powder, in a dry, frost proof shed. Fibrous-rooted begonias are rather more tolerant of cool (but not cold) conditions and many of them can be used for winter bedding. These include *B. coccinea*, with deep pink flowers; *B. fuchsioides*, scarlet flowers; *B. incarnata*, rose flowers; and *B. socotrana* with pink flowers. With care the colourful leaved *B. rex* should last several years in the Mediterranean. The same goes for other ornamental leaved types such as *B.albo-picta*, *B. heracleifolia*, *B. imperialis*, *B. boeringiana*, *B. maculata*, *B. masoniana*, *B. olbia* and *B. sanguinea*. *Propagation*: Both fibrous and tuberous begonias can be raised from seed which is very fine and needs no covering. Very subject to damping off. *Pests and Diseases*: Slugs and snails. Fungus diseases for which the plants should be sprayed on a prevention basis.

B. semperflorens. Used all over the Mediterranean for bedding out schemes and really lives up to its name, flowering for as much as eight months. It will survive really mild winters in which case cut the plant back.

BELOPERONE (*Acanthaceae*)

The shrimp plant. *Zone*: A. *Water*: 3. Only two species of beloperone are available in the Mediterranean and both need a great deal of water so they should be confined to pots. They repay generous feeding. A winter temperature of 20°C/70°F is needed. *Propagation*: By 15cm/6in cuttings in sandy soil when night temperatures are at least 24°C/75°F.

B. atropurpurea. *Origin*: Brazil. Small purple bracts on a plant 1m/3ft high.

B. guttata. *Origin*: Mexico. More commonly seen. Deep pink bracts on a 60cm/2ft high plant. Flowers constantly once established.

BESCHORNERIA (*Agavaceae*)

A remarkably dramatic plant from Mexico which revels in sun and dry, poor soil. *Zone*: B. *Water*: 1. Once it has flowered the plant dies but this does not happen before there are other plants to take over. *Propagation*: By offsets which the plant will provide of its own accord. *Pests and Diseases*: Agave weevil (treat with lindane based powder) and occasional rot from too much water (for which there is no cure).

B. yuccoides. Large grey green strap shaped leaves. In late May bright coral tubular flowers appear on red stems 1.2–1.6m/4–5ft high. Should be planted in threes for the best effect.

BIGNONIA (*Bignoniaceae*)

Evergreen tendril climber which can become deciduous if temperature drops too low. *Origin*: S.E. United States. *Zone*: A and B. *Water*: 2. *Propagation*: By cuttings of side shoots in late spring with hormone rooting compound.

    B. capreolata. Climbs to at least 7m/22ft in the Mediterranean and needs strong support. Clusters of yellow trumpet flowers about 5cm/2in long in late summer. Plant in ordinary soil with the addition of some sand.

Beschorneria yuccoides

BILLARDIERA (*Pittosporaceae*)

Most attractive twining climbers grown for both their flowers and fruit. *Origin*: Australia and Tasmania. *Zone*: A. *Water*: 2. *Pruning*: Thin out weak growth and dead wood in spring. *Propagation*: By seed in sandy soil at a minimum temperature of 16°C/60°F. Keep soil damp but not wet and spray against damping off. Seed germinates erratically. Better by far are 10cm/4in cuttings in a 50/50 mixture of sand and loam or peat. *Pests*: Ants if you leave fruit to rot on vine.

    B. cymosa. Clusters of mauve flowers in May–June with magenta berries afterwards. H 1.6m/5ft.

    B. longiflora. The most commonly available. It has yellow bell shaped flowers in June which become purple with age. The fruit is a rich violet blue which is used for desserts and jams. H 2m/6ft.

    B. l. fructo-alba. Similar to above but with white fruit which may be more attractive for eating purposes but are less dramatic on the vine.

BOLUSANTHUS (*Leguminosae*)

Origin: S. and E. Africa. *Zone*: A and B. *Water*: 2. A really beautiful tree, *B. speciosus* is quite difficult to find but well worth growing even if it means ordering a small specimen from a nursery outside the Mediterranean. It resembles a wisteria in tree form having huge trails of violet blue flowers in late summer. *Propagation*: By seed in sandy loam with a minimum temperature of 16°C/60°F.

BOUGAINVILLEA (*Nyctaginaceae*)

Probably the most commonly used climber in the
Mediterranean and all too often in its
ugly magenta form. There are many
other colours ranging from white
through pale rose, coral, red and
purple. However, the magenta and
purple types are hardier than the
other colours. Evergreen but inclined to loose its leaves when temperature
drops below 5°C/40°F. It will reclothe in
spring and flower slightly later in the year.
Origin: Tropical and sub-tropical parts of S.
America. *Zone*: A and B. *Water*: 2 or 3 but will
survive, once established, with Type 1 treatment.
The tiny white flowers appear in the centre of
coloured bracts. Most bougainvilleas have thorns.
Pruning: Only when necessary to keep within limits.
Hard pruning can stimulate growth after plant has
been cut back by cold. *Propagation*: In autumn by
7.5cm/3in cuttings with a heel of old wood. If temperatures are on the low side give bottom heat.
However, bougainvilleas are relatively inexpensive
to buy compared with many climbers.

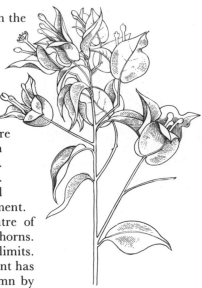

Bougainvillea glabra

    B. glabra. Very vigorous to 5m/16ft and free flowering with attractive pink
bracts throughout the summer. Fairly hardy. *B. g. sanderiana* is a smaller
form, to 1.2m/4ft, with violet-pink bracts, suitable for pots. Rather tender.
    B. spectabilis. The hardiest and most commonly seen. Very vigorous. Again
much hybridized but mostly seen as a dark-green leafed magenta bracted
plant. H 5–7m/16–22ft.

BRACHYGLOTTIS (*Compositae*)

What was *Senecio* 'Sunshine' is now called *Brachyglottis* 'Sunshine'. It is a silver
leaved plant which covers at least 1m sq/3ft sq and has small daisy-like yellow
flowers in summer. A most useful plant as it will grow virtually anywhere.
Origin: New Zealand. Quite difficult to find in the Mediterranean, more
common in France than in Italy or Spain. You may well have to order it
under the name senecio. *Zone*: A and B. *Water*: 2 when new; 1 when established.
Pruning: Cut back hard in autumn or spring if you have a cold winter to avoid
having a leggy plant. *Propagation*: In autumn by 7.5–10cm/3–4in cuttings in
sandy soil with hormone rooting compound.

BRUGMANSIA see DATURA

BRUNFELSIA (*Solanaceae*)

Beautiful, small shrubs which need hot, damp shade to flower more or less throughout the summer. Sometimes known as Yesterday, Today and Tomorrow because of the way they start violet, become mauve and then white before the petals drop. As all brunfelsias like rather acid soil it is best to grow them in pots. They need constant but weak feeding throughout the season. *Origin*: S. America. *Zone*: A with protection in winter or winter temperature of not less than 20°C/70°F otherwise it will become deciduous and flower poorly the following season. *Water*: 4 with occasional syringeing. *Pruning*: None except to cut out dead or damaged wood. *Propagation*: Difficult. 7.5–10cm/3–4in cuttings in a mixture of peat and sand and hormone rooting compound at any time when there is a minimum temperature of 20°C/70°F.

B. *calcyna*. The most commonly seen. Flowers in spring and again in late summer – purple five-petalled flowers, fading to violet then white. H 1m/3ft.

B. *latifolia*. Lavender flowers with white eye becoming white. Where temperatures are high will flower in late winter and early spring – otherwise in early summer.

CACTUS

There are many forms of cactus under various names which can be grown throughout the Mediterranean – less in the northern than in the southern part. Certain species will be found in this list under such names as *Carnegiea* and *Opuntia* but it is such a vast subject that those contemplating planting a garden of cacti and succulents would do well to consult both a specialist nursery and a specialist book.

CAESALPINIA (*Leguminosae*).

Deciduous shrubs, hardy in the Mediterranean, which have clusters of yellow flowers with long, bright red stamens. *Zone*: A. *Water*: 2 when newly planted, 1 when established. *Pruning*: It is best to remove pods as they form or you will get too many seedlings and the shrubs look untidy. Can be pruned hard if damaged by low temperature and will quickly recover when warm weather returns. *Propagation*: In spring or summer, from seed which germinates easily.

C. *gilliesii*. *Origin*: Argentina. Often called Mexican bird of paradise. A shrub to at least 2m/6ft with dramatic yellow flowers with bright red very long stamens which, if deadheaded, will appear throughout summer. Useful as a single plant in a courtyard or on a lawn or as a massed planting. However seeds are poisonous so it should not be planted where there are small children.

C. *pulcherrima*. *Origin*: Barbados. Even more dramatic than the above with bright orange flowers and richer green foliage which is fernier than that of the above but in other respects similar.

CALLISTEMON (*Myrtaceae*)

Drought resistant evergreen shrubs from Australian with interesting bottle-brush shaped flowers. *Zone*: A. *Water*: 1. Once established will survive in S. Mediterranean. *Pruning*: None except to remove dead wood and thin out top-heavy shrubs. All can be trained against a wall. *Propagation*: By 7.5–10cm/3–4in cuttings with heel of lateral growth and not too woody inserted in a 50/50 mixture of sand and peat with hormone rooting compound at any time when the night temperature is at least 21°C/70°F. Wait at least one year before planting out.

Callistemon citrinus

C. citrinus. Will reach 4m/13ft quite quickly and has spectacular red flowers in late spring. Does not like direct sun.

C. linearis. H 3m/10ft. This is the hardiest of the callistemons. Has red flowers in June.

C. pallidus. H 3m/10ft. Yellow bottle brush flowers in summer. Needs slight shade or only reflected sun to do well.

C. viminalis. H 3m/10ft. A narrow crowned tree to about 7m/22ft with bronze leaves when young and two or three flowerings (red) a year depending on the climate.

CALOTROPIS (*Asclepiadaceae*)

Useful, evergreen, drought resistant shrubs which are very salt tolerant. They hate damp conditions so soil must be very well draining. *Origin*: Middle East to N. India. *Zone*: A. *Water*: None. *Pruning*: Clip to keep in shape or remove damaged or dead wood. *Propagation*: By short, twiggy cuttings in a 75/25 sand and loam mixture with hormone rooting powder. Keep fairly dry or damping off will occur.

C. gigantea. Grows to a maximum of 4m/13ft. Has oval slightly spotted, two-tone green leaves which are rather leathery and felted underneath. The flowers are rose to purple small, bell shaped with a surrounded by ring of 'scales'. There is also a pale violet variety.

C. procera. Very similar to the above but the flowers are white with a large purple basal spot and star shaped. Although less attractive that *C. gigantea* this plant is even more drought resistant.

CAMELLIA (*Theaceae*)

This may seem an odd entry for the Mediterranean garden but so long as you can provide a certain amount of shade in the cool season and rather more in high summer there is no reason to deprive yourself of such valuable plants. *Origin*: Asia. *Zone*: All. *Water*: 2 and 3. They can seldom be grown in open ground in the region, though occasional acid soil outcrops do exist. They are best confined to large pots or tubs – preferably on wheels to move them out of direct sunlight. Camellias should be planted in lime-free soil incorporating plenty of leaf-mould which can be purchased in packets. Apart from ecological considerations, pure peat is not the best medium as it packs down too tightly and in the Mediterranean you should be very circumspect indeed about what sand, if any, you mix into your potting compost; it again be excessively sharp and/or alkaline. Again bought in, non-alkaline sand is best. Both lack of water and its alkalinity can be a problem but the second can be easily solved by using Sequestrene 138 Fe from Ciba-Geigy which is available everywhere. Dedicated camellia growers should buy it in one- or three-kilo packets which make it much cheaper in the long run. There is a temptation to suggest that camellia culture should be confined to the N. Mediterranean countries only but I have seen excellent specimens in Morocco, Egypt and in the mountains of the Lebanon. However, they do need constant attention and are not for the absentee gardener. Both *Gordonia* and *Stewartia*, near cousins of the camellia, can be grown equally easily. *Pruning*: None except to remove dead wood or keep within limits. *Propagation*: By layering in autumn or by stem-cuttings, about 10–15cm/4–6in in mid-February.

C. *japonica* and all its cultivars, and C. *reticulata* are best for the Mediterranean region. C. *sasanqua*, C. *taliensis* and C. × *vernalis* flowering in winter do not do nearly as well. Varieties of C. × *williamsii* can be quite spectacular.

CAMPANULA (*Campanulaceae*)

A vast family of some 300 species most of which can be grown successfully in the N. Mediterranean and some in the S part as well. All those listed below are herbaceous perennials. *Zone*: A and B. *Water*: Usually 2. *Propagation*: By root or clump division in autumn (every bit will take) or by seeds which germinate easily in autumn or spring. *Pests and Diseases*: Slugs and snails. Leaf spot fungus and rust.

Campanula isophylla

Campanulas most commonly have blue flowers but there are many white forms as well. They can be divided into two sorts: those with star-shaped blooms such as C. *arvatica*, C. *garganica*, C. *isophylla*, C. *persicifolia* and C. *porscharskyana*; and those with bell-shaped flowers such as C. *alliarifolia*, C. *aucheri*, C. *carpatica*, C. *cochleariifolia*, C. *glomerata*, C. *lactiflora*, C. *portenschlagiana* and C. *zoysii*. C. *isophylla* has been much hybridized and both F1 seeds and the ordinary sort are available all over the region. Certain members of the family are extremely invasive such as *C. carpatica, C. cochleariifolia, C. garganica, C. glomerata* and *C. portenschlagiana* but they provide good ground cover in a difficult terrain so one should not complain too much.

CAMPSIS (*Bignoniaceae*)

Useful, deciduous self-clinging climbers usually confused with bignonia. All flower from June to the end of September. *Zone*: A and B. *Water*: 2. *Pruning*: Cut hard back each year in February–March which will encourage basal growth. Non-pruned subjects tend to be leggy and flower only at the top. *Propagation*: In autumn by 10cm/4in cuttings in 50/50 sand and peat mix. *Pests*: Red spider, aphids and occasionally scale insects. Spray preventatively in any event. Occasional flower or bud drop because of lack of water.

C. grandis. Origin: China. H 10–13m/32–40ft. Large, trumpet shaped flowers in orange/red with mid-green pinnate leaves. Tender.

C. radicans. Origin: U.S.A. The most commonly found. Very similar to the above except that the flowers are tubular rather than trumpet shaped. Hardier.

C. × *tagliabuana*. A hybrid of the two foregoing and very similar. Usually sold in the variety 'Madame Gallen'. The flowers are a dark salmon red. Hardiest of all.

CANNA (*Cannaceae*)

Useful rhizomatous plants from S. America and Asia with large strap shaped leaves and the flowers are similar to gladiolus. Although there are over fifty species the most commonly available are *C. indica* (Indian shot) and its hybrids. These are approximately 1.2m/4ft tall with flowers in a large colour range from red, orange and yellow, purple and deep pink. There is a changing supply of several U.S. hybrids available in the U.K. which have more interesting colours than those available in the Mediterranean. They flower for months on end in summer but get a bit untidy after three or four months. *Zone*: A. *Water*: 2. *Propagation*: Division of rhizomes. *Pests and Diseases*: Slugs, snails, leatherjackets and wireworms. Sometimes affected by an orange rust on the leaves which a fungicide usually cures.

Canna indica hybrid

CAPPARIS (*Capparidaceae*)

Although not for the formal garden this is a useful plant for the top of walls (often self-seeded) and most decorative in flower in summer. The unripe flower buds supply the capers of commerce. Unfussy about soil except they require perfect drainage and a winter temperature of 10°C/50°F minimum. *Origin*: Mediterranean native. *Zone*: A. *Water*: 1. *Pruning*: None – it does not grow over 1–1.2m/3–4ft. If very untidy cut hard back.

C. *inermis*. Very little different from the following except that the white flowers are slightly tinged with dark pink and the stamens are marginally shorter.

C. *spinosa*. The common caper bush. A spiny deciduous shrub which has large white petalled flowers in June with dramatically prominent stamens.

CARDIOSPERMUM (*Sapindaceae*)

A trailing perennial vine with heart shaped leaves and white flowers followed by small balloon shaped fruit in early autumn. It climbs by tendril to about 3m/10ft. Needs a minimum night temperature of 70F (20C). *Origin*: Tropical Africa, India and Ceylon. *Water*: 3 or 4. *Propagation*: By autumn cuttings using 50/50 peat and sand mixture with hormone rooting compound.

C. *halicacabum* is the only species available in the Mediterranean. It needs full sun and should be given cold house protection in winter.

CARISSA (*Apocynaceae*)

Natal plum. Evergreen shrub or groundcover. *Origin*: S. Africa. *Zone*: A. *Water*: 2 or 3 but will tolerate some drought once established. *Pruning*: Not necessary but can be clipped to shape or to reduce size. *Propagation*: By layering. Do not sever until well rooted.

C. *macrocarpa*. Very fast growing shrub to about 2m/6ft with dark-green waxy leaves and bright white star-like flowers all summer which are followed by small dark red fruit which can be used raw or in jam. Needs sun to fruit well. There are several cultivars which are not always easy to get in the Mediterranean but worth seeking out. Of the prostrate sort for ground cover are C. *m*. 'Green Carpet' which is only 45cm/18in high and and spreads at least 1m/3ft and C. *m*. *nana tuttleii* which covers the same amount of space but which has smaller leaves. Of the shrubs C. *m*. 'Ruby Point' is one of the best and can be espaliered to make a good, impenetrable hedge. All this family have vicious thorns so wear gloves when picking fruit.

CARNEGIEA (*Cactaceae*)

A genus consisting of a single species of huge cactus. *Origin*: S.E. United States and Mexico. *Zone*: A. *Water*: None in N. Mediterranean. 1 in southern part. *Pruning*: None. *Propagation*: By seed which germinates readily but is very slow growing. *Pests*: Agave weevil. Susceptible to wind damage.

C. gigantea. In the wild this can grow to 12m/38ft but rarely reaches half that height in cultivation. A tall columnar cactus with two or three branches once it is 3–4m/10–13ft high. The stems are deeply ribbed and covered with spines. Fruit rarely forms in cultivated plants but is a red berry. Useful as a dramatic pot plant. Much used in the S. of France. Its siting should be very carefully considered as it is difficult to move later.

CARPENTERIA (*Hydrangeacae/Philadelphaceae*)

A genus of a single species. *Origin*: California. *Zone*: A (and with care B). *Water*: 2. *Pruning*: None except to remove dead or damaged wood. Not a long lived shrub. *Propagation*: By seed in summer which is difficult. Once germinated they should be wintered over in a frostproof greenhouse and planted out in the following early summer.

C. californica. A substantial shrub which grows to about 4m/13ft in the Mediterranean and about half as much across. It has large anemone shaped flowers with prominent yellow stamens from late May to July. You cannot give this plant too much protection and it should always be grown against a wall rather than in the open. It needs regular deep watering rather than a little daily. It does not like frost or wind, even when established.

CARPOBROTUS (*Aizoaceae*)

Common iceplant or Hottentot fig. Provided it is grown with care (and usually it is not) this is an invaluable ground cover plant for those who live in the S. Mediterranean since it will grow where little else will. *Origin*: S. Africa. *Zone*: A. *Water*: 1. *Pruning*: Remove woody, straggly bits since this presents a fire hazard. *Propagation*: Plant pieces from long trails and water once only. Most will take easily if this is done at the end of the summer. *Pests*: Rodents in autumn and wasps if fruit is left to rot on plants.

C. edulis. A prostrate plant with light green angular, three sided, succulent leaves. It trails about 1m/3ft and roots wherever it touches loose soil. Can be left to mound up to 45cm/18in high or can be trained (by pegging down) to spread neatly over the ground or bank to be covered. The flowers which are cream, yellow, pink or lavender are followed by edible but not enjoyable fruit.

C. chilensis. A native of the W. Coast of America from California to Chile. It has rich lavender flowers which are heavily scented from June onwards and occasionally earlier. Unlike *C. edulis* it will not tolerate any sort of cold weather.

CARYOPTERIS (*Verbenaceae*)

A most useful deciduous shrub since it flowers in late summer/early autumn when the garden can be a bit bare. *Origin*: Sub-tropical E. Asia. *Zone*: A. *Water*: 2 but will tolerate drought once established. *Pruning*: Cut back hard in early spring otherwise the plant will get leggy and flower poorly. *Propagation*: By cuttings of lateral shoots – 7.5–10cm/3–4in in a 50/50 mixture of peat and sand with hormone rooting compound. Best done immediately after flowering.

C. × *clandonensis* is the only species generally available in the Mediterranean region. It is not reliably hardy. Occasionally the variety 'Heavenly Blue' is available and is worth getting for the deeper blue flowers. H 1m/3ft and a similar spread.

CASSIA (*Leguminosae*)

Caryopteris × *clandonensis*

Only a few of this family are suitable for growing in the Mediterranean since many are natives of humid, tropical regions. All are evergreen. *Zone*: A. *Water*: 2. Drought tolerant once established and will tolerate cold but not frost. *Pruning*: C. *artemisioides* should be pruned to get a nicely rounded bush. Otherwise prune only to encourage new growth or to remove pods which form after flowers and can be unsightly in a formal garden. *Propagation*: In autumn from woody cuttings about 7.5–10cm/3–4in long in rich loam with hormone rooting compound and well watered. Seeds are slow to germinate but seedlings grow quickly.

C. *angustifolia*. *Origin*: Australia. This has needle-like green leaves and bright yellow pea-like flowers in June. Very decorative but needs supporting on a pillar or wall to be its best (and safest).

C. *artemisioides*. *Origin*: Australia. Sometimes known as silvery senna or feather cassia. Grows to about 2m/6ft and is covered with bright yellow flowers from February for several weeks which are most attractive against the grey-green foliage. Both these cassias should be planted in groups of at least three spaced about 1m/3ft apart to get the best effect.

CASUARINA (*Casuarinaceae*)

A large genus only three of which will grow adequately in the Mediterranean region. They are evergreen, drought resistant, and unfussy about soil though they grow better in rich, well prepared ground. Happy by the sea. *Origin*: Australia. *Zone*: A. *Water*: 1. *Pruning*: Branches should be trimmed from time to time to keep a balanced tree and to remove dead or damaged wood. Very easily damaged by wind. All these trees have the rather unnerving habit of shedding some of their lower branches from time to time.

Catalpa

C. cunninghamia. Australian pine. Has 'needles' rather like a pine which are in fact minute branchlets and the small fruit, on female trees only, is cone shaped. Grows to about 10m/32ft.

C. equisetifolia. Very similar to the above except that it is considerably taller to 30m/100ft or more with the 'needles' in whorls.

C. stricta. The Sheoak. A medium tree of 10–20m/32–65ft with very dense, rather drooping foliage. The 'cones' can be almost 5cm/2in long. Never becomes sparse looking as other casuarinas can.

CATALPA (*Bignoniaceae*)

The Indian bean tree is a fast growing deciduous tree to 13m/42ft which can be trained to an umbrella shape and is useful for shade. It is even later in coming into leaf than the lime tree and sometimes one has to wait until June. It has beautiful white, trumpet shaped flowers with brown markings in clusters above the foliage almost as soon as the tree has come into leaf. These are followed by decorative dark brown pods. *Origin*: Central United States. *Pruning*: Catalpas need annual pruning to keep in shape. The young wood is rather brittle and subject to wind damage. *Propagation*: In autumn by cuttings, with heel, in well draining compost, using hormone rooting compound. Wait at least three years before planting out in a nursery bed. *Pests and Diseases*: Red spider. Chlorosis can be a problem in very alkaline soils.

Catalpa bignonioides

C. bignonioides. H 7–10m/22–32ft with a similar spread when fully grown. Rich green heart shaped leaves and white foxglove type flowers in July. There is a golden leaved form *C. b.* 'Aurea'.

C. speciosa. H to 13m/42ft, S 7m/22ft or more. Slightly cold shy compared with the above. Flowers in June.

CEANOTHUS (Rhamnaceae).

Outstandingly beautiful shrubs, mostly from California, which are not planted often enough in the Mediterranean; indeed in parts of Italy they are hardly known, yet they are absolutely ideal drought resistant plants. They all have tiny star shaped, usually blue, flowers in umbels or panicles. *Zone*: A and B (C with winter protection). *Pruning*: The deciduous types should be cut back hard in March or April each year. The evergreen sort can be pruned in late March (or just before flower formation) if necessary. *Propagation*: 7.5–10cm/3–4in cuttings with heel in 50/50 peat and sand with hormone rooting compound. Pot on a year late and plant out in final position once pot bound. *Pests and Diseases*: Scale insects and occasionally red spider. Iron chlorosis can occur on very limey soil.

C. arboreus. Evergreen. Usually found in the variety 'Trewithen Blue' or 'Autumnal Blue' both are drought resistant once established. Height to 3.5m/11ft with blue flowers in panicles.

C. burfordiensis. Evergreen. Most attractive but the least successful in the Mediterranean as it needs more water than most.

C. 'Burkwoodii'. Bright green leaves felted grey underneath. Flowers in July and August.

C. 'Cascade'. Evergreen, H and S 3m/10ft. Narrow, oval, glossy green leaves. Blue flowers in panicles in May.

C. × delileanus 'Gloire de Versailles'. H 1.6m/5ft. Deciduous. One of the most popular varieties and rightly so. Pale blue flowers in panicles with light green foliage. Flowers in June and occasionally again in late autumn.

C. dentatus. Evergreen. Small low-growing shrub with dark green leaves and clusters of rich blue flowers in early May. Difficult to find.

C. impressus. Evergreen to 3.5m/12ft. Has tiny, very dark leaves crowded on the branches. Dark blue flowers in clusters in March–April.

C. 'Italian Skies' is probably the finest with rich, deep blue flowers in panicles during the summer months and occasionally in autumn. In spite of its name it is difficult to find in Italy!

C. × pallidus 'Marie Simon'. Deciduous. Very like 'Gloire de Versailles' but with pink flowers.

C. prostratus. Many ceanothus are sold under this name including *C. thyrsiflorus repens* (which is shorter). All do well as ground cover in full sun or on a large rockery.

C. thyrsiflorus. Evergreen. A very vigorous tree of over 3.5m/12ft in both height and width with small dark green leaves and bright blue flowers in May. Great care should be taken in choosing where to plant this tree since it can become very large indeed and as much as 4m/13ft wide. Needs support when very large.

CERATONIA (*Leguminosae*)

The carob tree, St.John's bread or locust bean. A large slow growing evergreen shade tree, native of the E. Mediterranean. It should not be planted near foundations but otherwise is an ideal tree for large patios. *Pruning*: None. *Propagation*: By seed with a little bottom heat if necessary in winter

C. siliqua. To about 13m/42ft but takes about ten years to reach half that height. Will tolerate cold but not frost and so young tree should be protected at below -5°C/25°F. Drought resistant once established but fares better on well spaced, deep irrigation. The carob beans which come in autumn and tend to remain on the tree are used as animal fodder and can often be bartered with the local population if you are in the country.

CERCIS (*Leguminosae*)

Spectacular spring flowering trees. Both species described are drought resistant when established and grow in more or less any well-drained soil. *Zone*:
All. *Water*: 1. *Pruning*: Can be espaliered to good effect when young. Improved
if bottom branches are removed to make umbrella effect. *Propagation*: By seed
in early summer which germinates at a temperature of 13–19°C/55–65°F in
well draining compost. Pot on to single pots and plant out at two years when
a good root system has developed.

C. canadensis. *Origin*: E. United States. H 10m/32ft.
The least commonly seen in the region but worth
growing in both pink ('Forest Pansy') and white
('Alba') varieties. Leaves turn bright yellow in
autumn.

C. siliquastrum. *Origin*: Mediterranean native.
H 10m/32ft. The Judas tree. Flowers, on bare
wood, before in its fourth year. As it gets older
flowers earlier – young plants can be as late as
May–June. There is a handsome white form *C. s. alba*.

Cercis siliquastrum

CESTRUM (*Solanacae*)

Very ornamental, fragrant wall shrubs mostly from S.
America. The flowers are tubular or pitcher shaped.
Give general fertilizer once a month. *Zone*: A. *Water*: 3.
Pruning: Cestrums tend to over-reach themselves and
get leggy in the process. It is best to cut back all laterals to about 15cm/6in
in February. At the same remove some of the old wood when you see new
shoots growing from the base. *Propagation*: 7.5–10cm/3–4in cuttings in rich,
well draining compost with a minimum temperature 24°C/75°F in July.

C. aurantiacum. *Origin*: Guatemala. H 2m/6ft. Bright orange flowers in late
autumn. Evergreen in the S. Mediterranean but loses it leaves on the Côte
d'Azur and Italian Riviera.

C. fasciculatum. *Origin*: Mexico. Evergreen shrub to about 3.5m/11ft with
salmon pink flowers in May.

C. parqui. *Origin*: Chile. A deciduous shrub which is hardier than the others
and has yellow flowers from July to September. Can reach 3.5m/10ft though
half that amount is commoner.

C. 'Purpureum' (syn. *C. elegans*). *Origin*: Mexico. Semi-evergreen shrub
grows to about 2m/6ft and has very bright carmine flowers in May.

C. roseum. *Origin*: Mexico. Evergreen shrub to 2m/6ft with flowers of a very
difficult bright pink from the end of March to the beginning of June.

CHAMAEROPS (*Palmae*)

C. humilis, the Mediterranean fan palm, is a native of the region and the only native European palm. *Zone* A. *Water*: 1. Will tolerate slight frost once established. It grows slowly – about 15cm/6in a year. Oddly for a palm it prefers rich, moist soils but will accept dry, alkaline conditions though it will remain smaller than the usual 5m/16ft achieved in good conditions. It is ideal for pots or for a small planting near a house entrance. Can be planted in full sun (in which case it will need rather more water) or under the shade of taller palms. *Pruning*: Little or none unless you do not want a branched trunk in which case you cut off the offending branch to make a single stem. Otherwise simply remove dried or cold-damaged leaves. *Propagation*: By seeds sown in September which germinate slowly and erratically or by removing suckers in autumn and planting in rich, moist soil. Keep in shade and pot on once roots have formed. Plant out one year later. *Pests and Diseases*: Ants. Occasionally a fungus attacks the heart of the palm – this is usually due to humid conditions in a rainy autumn.

CHIONANTHUS (*Oleacae*)

Zones: A and B. *Water*: 2. N. Mediterranean only. Only one of this genus is suitable for the region, *C. virginicus*, the Virginia fringe tree, which comes from the E. United States. It will tolerate drought once established but for the first few years water well in summer. Tolerant of frost. *Propagation*: By layering in summer. Wait until the following year before severing from parent plant.

C. virginicus. Deciduous. H 7m/22ft. Pure white flowers in open panicles throughout June looking rather like fringes. Very late to come into leaf. Golden leaves in autumn.

CHOISYA (*Rutaceae*)

Mexican orange blossom. A genus of one species only. *Origin*: Mexico. *Zone*: All. *Water*: 2 or 3 when newly planted. Thereafter, 1. Good seaside and excellent informal hedging plant. *Pruning*: Not needed except to keep within limits. *Propagation*: 7.5–10cm/3–4in cuttings any time when not flowering. Put in 7.5cm/3in pots in good well draining compost and some hormone rooting compound. Keep moist but not wet. If in doubt about your winter weather keep in a cold frost-proof greenhouse or on the window sill.

C. ternata. A rounded, very vigorous evergreen shrub up to 2m/6ft in height and as much across. Covered in white flowers rather like orange blossom (but more or less scentless) throughout May and sporadically throughout the rest of the year. *C. t.* 'Aztec Pearl' is a new variety with pink buds which become white flowers with the underneath flushed pink. Mid-green shiny leaves. *C. t.* 'Sundance' has bright yellow foliage but no second flowering and not so vigorous as the type. It also needs slight shade to do really well and will not tolerate much frost.

CIMICIFUGA (*Ranunculaceae*)

Useful, tall herbaceous plant for back of the border or infilling. *Zone*: all. *Water*: 1 once established. *Propagation*: Seed in the spring. Plant seedlings out in second year. By division in spring.

  C. americana. Origin: N. America. The most commonly seen in the Mediterranean with creamy white flowers in July and August. Slightly shorter than most at 1.2m/4ft.

  C. dahurica. Origin: N. China. Very similar to above. White flowers with slightly green reverse – in July.

  C. simplex. Origin: Siberia. Usually seen as the variety 'White Pearl' – creamy white flowers to 1.2m–1.6m/4–5ft in late summer.

CISTUS (*Cistacae*)

Mediterranean native. It is difficult to buy these plants in the region since most locals think of them as wild flowers which can be dug up in the wild nearby. Therefore, they have to be ordered from a specialist nursery. They are all evergreen and they all have papery petals. They flower from May to the end of July. They are not fussy about soil provided it is well drained and they require full sun. *Pruning*: Never – cutting into old wood causes death. *Propagation*: By seed in sandy soil in spring. They do not germinate easily. Keep frost free as seedlings although adult plants will tolerate frost and

Cistus ladanifer

snow in most cases (but not cold damp soils). Cuttings are difficult but a small percentage may take so it is worth the effort. Hormone rooting compound and very sandy soil both help. Colours include white, cream to yellow, lilac and pink. Among the choicest are – White: *C.* × *aguilari, C.* × *a.* 'Maculatus', *C. albidus, C. bourgeanus, C.* × *corbariensis, C.* × *cyprius, C.* × *florentinus, C.* × *glaucus, C. ladanifer, C.laurifolius, C.* × *laxus, C. loretii, C. palhinhae, C. populifolius, C. salviifolius, C.* × *verguinii.* Pink, Red or Lilac: *C.* × *canescens, C. crispus, C.* × *pulverulentus, C* × *purpureus, C.* × *skanbergii, C. symphytifolius, C. villosus.*

CLEMATIS (*Ranunculacae*)

An invaluable family of climbing plants. The large flowered, generally hybrid, clematis are not really suitable for the Mediterranean region and should be given slight shade or, like roses, their flowers will quickly bloom and fade within twenty-four hours. Those with striped flowers succumb quickest and the stripes scarcely show. However, the small flowered and species clematis do wonderfully well. All need some form of strong support unless being pegged down as ground cover. *Origin*: Very wide distribution in temperate areas, chiefly from the N. Hemisphere. *Pruning*: Only to keep within bounds. *C. montana* and *C. tangutica* should be cut back every year or they will get out of hand. Where space is limited remove flowering stems immediately after flowering. *Propagation*: In the Mediterranean it is best to raise clematis from seed which germinates all too easily. Alternatively softwood cuttings can be taken (approximately 15cm/6in long) and wintered over in a cold frame or in the greenhouse. *Pests and diseases*: Slugs and snails, aphids, earwigs and red spider. Clematis wilt due to a fungus can cause death. At present there is no cure. If near roses with mildew this can be transferred to the clematis.

C. alpina. *Origin*: S. and C. Europe. To 4m/13ft. Short and rather brittle growth which needs good support. Bell-like violet blue flowers. There are many cultivars available, one of the best being 'Frances Rivis'. There is also a white form *C. a. sibirica*.

C. armandii. *Origin*: China. To 6m/19ft. One of the best for the Mediterranean. Evergreen with shining dark green leaves and scented white flowers from April onwards. 'Snowdrift' has larger white flowers than the type.

C. chrysocoma. *Origin*: W. China. To 3.5m/11ft. Very like *C. montana* (see below) but without the excessive vigour.

C. fargesii. *Origin*: China. H 7m/22ft. Pure white six petalled saucer shaped flowers from June to September. Needs a little shade to do really well.

C. macropetala. *Origin*: Siberia. To 4m/13ft. Light and dark blue bell like flowers in April and May. The variety 'Maidwell Hall' has deep blue flowers and 'Markham's Pink' rich pink.

Clematis armandii

C. montana. *Origin*: Himalayas. Very vigorous climber to 10m/32ft. The type has 5cm/2in white flowers in March. 'Elizabeth' has pink flowers; 'Tetrarose', lilac pink; and 'Rubens Superba' pink flowers and bronze foliage. *C. m. wilsonii* blooms in July and has larger white flowers.

C. orientalis. *Origin*: N. China, Himalayas and Caucasus. To 7m/22ft. Very dissected ferny foliage in the palest of greens. The yellow flowers have dark brown centres and bloom from August until October.

C. tangutica. *Origin*: N. China. To 7m/22ft. Very similar to the above except that the leaves are grey green. Seeds everywhere.

C. texensis. *Origin*: N. America. To 3m/10ft. A rather tender species which dies back each year. Very drought resistant. Small, most attractive urn-shaped flowers in every shade of red appear from the end of May until August.

COBAEA (*Polemoniaceae*)

Cathedral bells. Useful climber which flowers late in summer. *Origin*: Mexico. *Zone*: all. *Water*: 2. *Propagation*: By seed as early in the year as possible. Needs a temperature of 18–20°C/65–70°F to germinate. *Pests*: Aphids, thrips, scale insects and red spider.

C. scandens. Climbs to 7m/22ft by tendrils so needs strong support. Dark green leaves. Flowers are purple and bell shaped with a light green calyx, from late summer to until temperatures drop. There is a white variety which is not nearly so attractive.

COMMELINA (*Commelinaceae*)

A large genus of herbaceous perennials of which only *C. coelestis* is commonly grown in the Mediterranean. It is 60cm/2ft high with long pointed leaves and attractive blue, lipped flowers in June. There is a white form *C. c. alba* which has in fact blue and white flowers. *Origin*: Mexico. *Zone*: A. *Water*: 2. Will not tolerate temperatures under about 5°C/45°F. *Propagation*: By seed in early spring.

CONVOLVULUS (*Convolvulaceae*)

There are three very attractive members of this family which warrant a place in a Mediterranean garden. All are hardy in the area to 400m/1300ft altitude. *Zone*: A. *Water*: 2 but 1 when established. All can be cut to the ground by cold winter weather but will come up again in spring.

C. althaeoides. Mediterranean native. A low growing twining sub-shrub to 60cm/2ft with very attractive silvery pink flowers throughout the summer.

C. cneorum. Mediterranean native. A small sub-shrub to about 1m/3ft with slender silvery leaves. The flowers are very pale pink to white typically bell shaped. It flowers in May and June and occasionally again in October.

C. sabatius (syn. *C. mauritanicus*). *Origin*: N. Africa. Moroccan glory vine. Ground morning glory. A low sub-shrub which is permanently in flower throughout the warm season. Where winters are mild you must cut it back hard *Convolvulus sabatius* to prevent leggy growth. The leaves are pale grey-green and the flowers a rich, pale blue. It can also be used as a hanging plant. Needs a little more water than the above but will survive quite severe drought.

COPROSMA (*Rubiaceae*)

A large genus of evergreen shrubs and sub-shrubs. Those in cultivation come from New Zealand. N. Mediterranean only. Coprosmas do not appear to fruit easily in the Mediterranean due, it is said, to lack of moisture. When they do it is in the form of a drupe varying in colour – yellow, red, brown or purple. *Zone*: A. *Water*: 3. Worth growing if you have no water problems. *Propagation*: By 7.5–10cm/3–4in cuttings in rich, moist loam with hormone rooting compound. Keep cuttings moist at all times.

C. acerosa. Sand dune coprosma. The only drought resistant coprosma but difficult to find in the Mediterranean. Forms a cushiony plant with needle-like leaves. H 50cm/18in.

C. repens variegata. The mirror plant. Shiny dark green and white leaves on a low plant about 75cm/2.5ft. The most commonly seen.

C. 'Coppershine'. Dark green foliage overlaid with coppery highlights. Good for edging and making formal parterres. H 1.2m/4ft by as much across.

CORDYLINE (*Liliaceae*)

Easily grown, drought resistant, very decorative plants. *Origin*: Australia and New Zealand. *Zone*: A. *Water*: 1. *Propagation*: By seed which germinates easily during late spring and early summer. Let grow to 60cm/2ft before planting in final position. They all like feeding approximately every two months in the growing season.

C. australis. An evergreen species with rich green sword shaped leaves attached directly to the trunk. When young it has a single stem which is clothed from ground level. Later it develops a broad head and becomes more palm-like. There are various cultivars with purple, variegated or triple coloured (white, crimson and green) leaves. Very rarely flowers in Europe. Provided the ground or potting compost has been well-prepared and care has been taken in the plants' youth cordylines will tolerate quite serious drought but prefer periodic deep irrigation. Once established, these cordylines will also take a certain amount of frost.

CORTADERIA (*Gramineae*)

Pampas grass. *Origin*: S. America. *Zone*: A. *Water*: 1. All cortaderias need a certain amount of grooming (wear gloves and goggles when trimming the plants since they are both sharp edged and pointed) and occasional feeding to look their

Cordyline australis

best. Do not cut back too severely as they take a long time to recover. In hotter parts of the Mediterranean cortaderias can shelter snakes. *Propagation*: By division in the coolest season of the year. Do not plant pieces which measure less than 15x15cm/6x6in or you will wait a long time for results.

C. selloana is the most commonly available in the region, with narrow ribbon-like leaves with sharp edges. It grows quickly to 3m/10ft and over 2m/6ft wide. It is not for small gardens. Excellent as a windbreak where nothing else will grow. A variety called 'Gold Band' has a gold stripe in the leaf and there is one called 'Rosea' with pink plumes. Both can be obtained at proper nurseries as opposed to garden centres.

DASYLIRION (*Agavaceae*)

The desert spoon. Not always easy to acquire but well worth the search since these magnificently architectural plants are extremely drought resistant and hardy to around 300m/1000ft in the Mediterranean region. They are ideal for dry and desert locations in the S. Mediterranean. *Origin*: Mexico and S.W. United States. *Zones*: All. *Water*: 1. If the average rainfall is less than 30cm/12in a year you will need to give two or three well spaced waterings over the summer period. When very young they will need a little more. Tolerant of the most arid, alkaline soil but they respond to occasional feeding (not more than once a year). Their main disadvantage is that they will not tolerate any form of damp, even for a short period, so be sure your soil drains well. *Pruning*: Not necessary except to cut off dead leaves. *Propagation*: Difficult out of its native land as the moth required for pollination does not exist. Therefore, home-produced seed is not viable. Seed can be purchased from the United States quite easily and germinates readily from late spring to the end of summer.

D. glaucophyllum. Narrow blade-shaped glaucous leaves with a white flowering spike of some 3–4m/10–13ft in spring.

D. wheelerii. Grows to about 1.6m/5ft by as much wide with blade-shaped grey-green leaves which have toothed edges. Older plants can develop multiple trunks though this will take some years. A white to pale yellow flowering spike appears about May and the flowers continue until July or August. There are several varieties, all very similar of which very few are on sale out of America. It is a case of buy whatever is available and be grateful. Only *D. hookerii* is really different having a large tuber instead of the normal trunk and leaves springing from its surface. The flowers are purple.

Dasylirion wheelerii

DATURA (*Solanaceae*)

Some of these have been reclassified as *Brugmansia* but are not yet generally known under their new names in the Mediterranean. Although there are annual forms of datura it is the shrubby sort which is mostly seen in the Mediterranean garden. All parts of the datura are poisonous, particularly the seeds. Therefore, do not plant them if you have small children around. They flower throughout the summer. *Origin*: S. and C. America. *Zone*: A. *Water*: 3 until established then 1 with occasional well spaced waterings if the plant flags. *Pruning*: Should be pruned quite heavily after flowering to keep the shrub to a good shape. *Propagation*: By cuttings with a heel in a 50/50 peat and sand mixtures at any time once the temperature has reached 22°C/70°F at night. *Pests and Diseases*: Scale insects and capsid bugs. Occasional mildew on leaves. Use a systemic insecticide/fungicide.

D. *arborea*. The angel's trumpet has large, heavily scented white flowers 15–20cm/ 6–8in long on a 3m/10ft plant. Evergreen but cold can make it deciduous. Feed once a month with liquid fertilizer.

D. *knightii* (syn. D. *cornigera*). A tall shrub to 3m/10ft with violet, white lined trumpet flowers. One of the most beautiful daturas.

Datura knightii

D. *sanguinea*. A shorter shrub than the former and good for pot work. The leaves are rather hairy with wavy edges. Flowers have yellow trumpets ending in rich orange-red.

D. *suaveolens*. To 4m/13ft. Usually grown in its double form and the most commonly found. Very heavily scented white flowers are trumpet shaped, single or double.

D. *versicolor* 'Grand Marnier'. H to 3m/10ft. Rich orangey-yellow trumpet flowers with slightly darker edges. Excellent for pots. Rather more tender than others.

DAVIDIA (*Davidiaceae*)

One of the most beautiful trees grown for its large white bracts in April which form a hood over the rather insignificant flowers. For a few fortunate gardens in the N. Mediterranean only since it requires rich, well watered soil. It will not tolerate dry, alkaline conditions. *Origin*: China. *Pruning*: None. *Propagation*: By cuttings of short side shoots in a moist loam with hormone rooting compound. Alternatively by seeds which are not easy and which need a period of scarification before they will germinate.

D. *involucrata*. H 20m/64ft. The leaves are coarsely toothed and bright green and white underneath.

D. *i. vilmoriniana*. The most commonly available in France. Very similar to the above except that the leaves are glaucous underneath.

DIANTHUS (*Caryophyllaceae*)

Very many dianthus – pinks, carnations and sweet Williams – are Mediterranean natives and thus are particularly suitable for gardens in the area. There
are too many to mention here. The best guide to them is a Mediterranean flora.
Those that do not do well in the Mediterranean heat tend to be the N.
European species such as *D. arenarius* and *D. superbus*. Nor do the trailing
Tyrolean pinks thrive unless they are given plenty of water and a certain
amount of shade. Allwood's laced pinks (easily raised from seed) stand up
to a great deal of sunshine and drought in my rockery but do not increase at
nearly so fast a rate as in a cooler climate. *Propagation*: By cuttings after
flowering in almost pure sand with hormone rooting powder or liquid. With
more vigorous varieties, such as 'Mrs Sinkins' smaller clumps may be divided.
Pests and Diseases: Frog hoppers. Carnation rust. Systemic fungicide prevention
is better than trying to cure.

DIOSPYROS (*Ebenaceae*)

The persimmon. Although there are over 200 species of diospyros only two
are commonly grown in the Mediterranean region, the first more than the
second. They are both deciduous and both grown for the beauty of their
orange red fruit on the bare trees in early winter. *Zone*: A. *Water*: 1 (but 2 when
young). Hardy in the Mediterranean. *Pruning*: Not necessary. *Propagation*: By
seed in spring – cuttings do not work.

    D. kaki. *Origin*: China and Japan. Round topped tree to about 10m/32ft
with bright orange fruit in late autumn/early winter. The taste is an acquired
one and the fruit somewhat acid. The most commonly grown for market is
D. k. costata or *D. k. mazelii*.

    D. virginiana. *Origin*: S. United States. Very dark green shining leaves on a
tree to about 15m/48ft with very rough bark. Fruit is less acid (and less
flavoursome) and smaller than *D. kaki*.

DIPLOPAPPUS (*Compositae*)

In the French and N. Italian region of the Mediterranean *D. fruticolosus*
appears to be the name used for *D. fruticosus*. Occasionally it is called *Cassinia*
but these shrubs are in fact much larger and have differently coloured flowers.
This is a small, trailing sub-shrub from S. Africa, 45cm/18in high with tiny
mauve flowers in late autumn and early winter. Depending on the temperature
these can continue for more than three months. It is ideal for rockeries and
low walls and brings a bright splash of colour to the garden at what is
often a dull moment. *Zone*: A. It will not tolerate frost. *Water*: 2. *Pruning*:
Dead-heading will help flowering to continue and cutting back hard after
flowering will keep the bush in shape and help flowering next season.
Propagation: Cuttings of non-flowering shoots in July in 50/50 peat and sand
with hormone rooting compound.

DODONAEA (*Sapindaceae*)

Useful plants for desert situations as they will tolerate drought and full sun. *Origin*: S.E. United States and Central America. *Zone*: A. *Water*: 1 or none. *Pruning*: None needed. *Propagation*: By cuttings in 75/25 sand/garden loam mix with hormone rooting powder. *Pests*: White fly and red spider.

D. *viscosa*. This shrub can reach 5m/16ft or more with as large a spread in rich soil with deep, well spaced watering. In desert situations it will reach about half that size. It has medium green leaves about 7.5–10cm/3–4in long on a rather irregular and angular bush. The flowers are insignificant but followed by attractive seed clusters. The plant flowers according to water available rather than the season. D. v. 'Purpurea' is similar to the above but with reddish purple foliage. It will not tolerate any frost at all. D. v. 'Saratoga' has deep purple foliage and is taller and narrower than the type.

DORYANTHES (*Amaryllidaceae*)

Origin: Australia. *Zone*: A. *Water*: 1. *Propagation*: By offsets in a 50/50 peat and sand mixture. *Pests and Diseases*: Fungus problems due to damp weather or too wet soil.

D. *palmerii*. The only species available in the Mediterranean. A very striking evergreen succulent plant about 2m/6ft high which has a flowering spike 3–5m/10–16ft high with brilliantly rich red flowers in a rosette in July–August. Flowers only on mature plants.

DOLICHOS (*Leguminosae*)

Origin: India and Tropical Africa. *Zone*: A. *Water*: 2 or 3. *Propagation*: Seed in very moist soil in early spring. *Pests*: Occasional black fly.

D. *lablab*. Hyacinth bean. H 3m/10ft. Useful, rampant climber which will quickly form a screen. The flowers are white and purple, from June to August. The beans when not too mature are edible. Successive sowings will ensure constant flowering.

ECHEVERIA (*Crassulaceae*)

Origin: Mexico and California. *Zone*: A. *Water*: 1. This is a very variable group and the only common denominator is that the fleshy leaves are always in rosettes and the flowers bell-shaped and slightly pinched at the open end. All work excellently in the Mediterranean garden so long as the temperature does not fall below 8°C/45°F – frost will kill most echeverias. *Propagation*: Easiest by offsets in the spring. But many echeverias hybridize between themselves and you can often get interesting results with your own seed. *Pests*: Aphids which should be treated with powder rather than sprays.

Echium

The most commonly obtainable in the region are: *E. agavoides* triangular sharply tipped leaves of very pale green and brown, and orange glowers; *E. australis*, one of the most tender with blue-green leaves in an open rosette and bright pink flowers; *E. candida*, loose rosettes of whitish furry leaves and white flowers; *E. cotyledon*, a dense rosette, wide at the base and narrowing towards the top of greyish leaves covered with white meal. Pale yellow flowers in racemes; *E. elegans*, almost white, thick leaves with pale green edges and pink flowers; *E. glauca* dense 8–10cm/3–4in rosettes of pale grey leaves with red edges. Many offsets quickly develop on the plants. Flowers vivid red with yellow edges; *E. pumila*, tiny rosettes of pale green foliage. Good for pots or troughs; *E. retusa hybrida*, bright green leaves, edges in red with a 60cm/2ft flowering spike in winter with crimson flowers; *E. viscida*, pale green rosettes with sticky leaves and pale pink flowers.

Echeveria gibbiflora metallica

ECHIUM (*Boraginaceae*)

Wonderfully dramatic spring and summer flowering plants which though not Mediterranean natives are thoroughly naturalized in the area. *Zones*: A and B. *Water* 1. The finest come from the Canaries and Madeira. All require a more or less frost free winters and make dramatic growth just before flowering. *Propagation*: By seed which germinates easily.

E. candicans. Pride of Madeira. A biennial around 1m/3ft high with long, narrow, prickly leaves. The flowers are in spikes of brilliant blue from May to July.

E. coeleste. *Origin*: Canaries. Very similar to above but flowers are paler with a white tube inside the blue flower. Flowers in late May.

C. fastuosum. *Origin*: Canaries. The most beautiful of all and a perennial. Rich dark blue flowers on a branched plant to 1.6m/5ft. Evergreen. Needs tidying up after flowering in May and June.

E. pininana. A monocarpic perennial which flowers in its second or third year, usually in May, on an unbranched stem. 4m/12ft high and very dramatic but the pale blue flowers are less beautiful than those of *E. fastuosum*.

E. wildpretii. Usually you get *E. pininana* under this name. The real *E. wildpretii* is difficult to find and has rather less attractive red flowers. H. 1.6m/5ft. Flowers late May.

ERIOBOTRYA (*Rosaceae*)

Loquat or Japanese medlar. A very handsome evergreen tree with the added bonus of attractive yellow fruit which is pleasant as ice-cream or jam. Will tolerate medium shade. *Zone*: A and B. *Water*: 1 when established, 2 when young. *Pruning*: Remove bottom branches as they appear in order to obtain an umbrella effect. If you want larger fruit development prune out thin branches to allow more light to penetrate. *Propagation*: By grafting on to quince or hawthorn stock. *Pests and Diseases*: Ants, aphids and red spider. Occasional mildew in humid weather.

E. japonica. *Origin*: East Asia. This tree grows to 6–7m/20–23ft and has large, leathery, heavily veined leaves which are bright green and glossy and felted underneath. Small white flowers develop in autumn and the rich yellow fruit in late April or early May. Ideal as a specimen or single tree in a large patio since it casts plenty of shade.

ERIOSTEMON (*Rutaceae*)

Australian Wax Flower. A genus of 30 evergreen species mostly from Australia of which only one at present is on sale in the Mediterranean. *Zone*: A. *Water*: 2 or even 3 in very hot, dry areas such as S. Spain and the E. Mediterranean. Prefers a winter temperature of 13–16°C/55–60°F but once established will tolerate slight frost on occasion. *Pruning*: None needed. *Propagation*: By cuttings in rich peaty loam with hormone rooting compound in early Spring.

E. myoporoides. Very beautiful shrubs about 1m/3ft tall by as much across with narrow, pointed leaves of light grey-green covered with pellucid dots with are in fact oil glands, fragrant when crushed. The whole shrub is covered in early spring with starry white flowers which have a slight waxen appearance. Occasional flowering at other times of the year. Appreciates a certain amount of shade and rich feeding. Not fussy about soil. *E. m.* 'Profusion'. As above but more so and with slightly larger flowers and leaves. A wonderful pot plant for a shady patio even when not in bloom.

ERYTHRINA (*Leguminosae*)

There are 100 species of erythrina of which only three are commonly grown in the Mediterranean. All have dramatic red flowers. *Zone*: A. *Water*: Best with 2 but will tolerate 1 once well established. *Pruning*: None needed except to remove dead and damaged wood but see under *E. coralloides*. *Propagation*: Very easy by taking small branches in spring and putting them into 50/50 peat and loam with hormone rooting powder and keeping moist. Plant out when pot is more or less rootbound – about 8–12 months. *Pests*: Scale insects and occasional red spider.

E. caffra. *Origin*: S. Africa. Deciduous in Mediterranean. A wonderful multi-trunked shade tree but slow growing to 12m/40ft or more. Brilliant, flame coloured spiky flowers – often before the leaves – in mid-Spring.

E. crista-galli. Coral or coxcomb tree. *Origin*: Brazil. This can be grown throughout the Mediterranean but will vary according to climate. In the warmer, frost free areas it can grow into a multi-trunked tree with rough bark up to 6m/20ft. In cooler areas or where there is some frost it can be treated like a perennial. The spring growth is prodigious, with brilliant red pea flowers in racemes in May or June on a smooth stemmed plant. Dead-heading and not allowing seed pods to form can encourage up to three flowerings a year. Good for pots in cooler areas.

E. coralloides. Origin: Mexico. One of the most beautiful flowering trees but it needs a great deal of careful pruning to keep a balanced shape. H 10m/30ft. Flowers once only after leaf fall in May and June. The flowers are coral red. Trees come into leaf again once pods have formed.

ESCALLONIA (*Escalloniaceae*)

Erythrina crista-galli

Useful shrubs since they are ideal for maritime sites and make excellent hedges in very windy situations. By no means all of the various hybrids are on sale in the Mediterranean region but in France, Italy and Spain there are several nurseries which carry a good selection. *Origin*: Most are from Chile. *Zone*: All. *Water*: 2. They will withstand considerable drought although they look better with plenty of moisture. In the south of France and N. Italy they are in flower for about nine months of the year. Unfussy about soil they will take full sun or partial shade and are hardy throughout the area. In the southern Mediterranean they should be given half shade if possible in order to avoid burn at mid-day. It is better to leave clipping as a hedge or pruning until the cooler months. Feed once a month with liquid fertilizer in the growing season. All escallonias are evergreen and the flower colour ranges from white through pink to bright pink and scarlet. Most are funnel shaped. Depending on the variety they flower from May to October. *Propagation*: By short heeled cuttings in late summer in a 50/50 peat sand mix with hormone rooting compound. Plant out 1 year later.

EUCALYPTUS (*Myrtaceae*)

There are over 500 species of eucalyptus, or gums, mostly from Australia. Most have small rounded juvenile foliage which elongates as the tree gets older. Many are used as shade trees or wind-breaks or are coppiced annually in late winter to encourage the rounded juvenile foliage. *E. globulus* and *E. gunnii* are cultivated on a large scale in Italy and France for the cut flower market. All the eucalpyts mentioned below are hardy in the Mediterranean to 700m/2300ft altitude. *Zone*: All. *Water*: 1. It is worth remembering that many plants refuse to grow in company with eucalpytus and it is as well to be prudent in the first instance. Roses and hydrangeas appear to hate their company in my garden. *Propagation*: By seed – which is minute – and which often needs a period of scarification depending on the variety. Plant in autumn and give heat if necessary to obtain 20C/68F. Cuttings do not work. *Pests and Diseases*:In very dry areas many eucalypts can suffer from iron chlorosis. Use as rich a planting mixture as possible and feed every six to eight weeks with liquid manure.

E. citriodora. The lemon-scented gum. Fast growing tree to about 25m/75ft which needs careful staking when young as it is subject to wind rock. Very graceful when adult and it has the habit of losing its bark annually.

E. ficifolia. One of the many red gums this has bright red flowers in July or August. Juvenile foliage is less rounded than most.

E. globulus. The blue gum. Juvenile foliage very rounded. Can be allowed to grow to full height of over 45m/120ft but better as stooled speciments. Excellent for bedding out.

E. gunnii. Another tree of over 30m/100ft which is rarely seen except as a stooled shrub. Very similar to the above. As a full-grown tree it has white flowers in umbels in late autumn/early winter. One of the fastest growing eucalypts.

E. microtheca. Coolibah tree. Ideal for the S. Mediterranean where it will tolerate poor soil, salt laden air, head, cold desert nights and still grow to over 12m/40ft. Needs firm staking when young to grow up straight.

E. sideroxylon. Pink ironbark. Tall tree to about 12m/40ft in the Mediterranean with black bark and attractive long pointed leaves to about 12.5cm/ 5in. Flowers in spring and has pale pink to crimson flowers. Excellent as a windscreen and the dark trunks make a dramatic driveway.

E. viminalis. Manna gum or weeping gum. The tallest of the eucalpyts though not in the Mediterranean. Has long pendulous branches on adult trees together with peeling bark which exposes shining white patches. Can be grown in large containers as small shrub when it has pale green, rounded foliage. Very tolerant of sudden changes of temperature.

EUPHORBIA (*Euphorbiaceae*)

A vast genus with several native Mediterranean species such as *E. biglandulosa* (syn. *E. rigida*), *E. biumbellata*, *E. characias*, *E. cyparissias*, *E. denroides*, *E. myrsinites* and *E. spinosa*. Some of these are excellent garden plants. Most countries have laws against digging up wild plants – but these are inexpensive to buy. *Zone*: see below. *Water*: 1 or none at all. *Propagation*: Mostly by division of roots except for *E. milii* where cuttings should be taken in early spring. Many people are allergic to the milk exuded by many species.

E. caput-medusae. Origin: Cape Province. A dwarf succulent species with long trailing stems which is ideal for a rockery. *Zone*: A. *Water*: 1

E. fulgens. Origin: Mexico. Long arching branches of scarlet flowers. *Zone*: A.

E. marginata. Origin: N. America. An 1m/3ft annual with white-edged green leaves – often called 'Snow in the Mountain'. *Zone*: A and B. *Propagation*: By seed in spring. Insignificant white flowers.

E. milii (syn. *E. splendens*). *Origin*: Madagascar. Short very prickly shrub, H. 1.6m/5ft, with bright scarlet flowers in summer. It does well in poor, stony soil. It is essential to have the ground weed-free before planting as it is impossible to weed afterwards. Very tender and will not tolerate temperatures below 18°C/65°F. Best to bring under cover in winter in N. Mediterranean.

FATSIA (*Araliaceae*)

Useful architectural plants with attractive leaves all year round, especially if they are regularly cut to produce new, juvenile growth. *Zone*: A and B. *Water*: 2. Ideal for pots and for using on terraces, against north walls, entrances and inner courtyards. Likes only reflected or early morning sun. Hardy throughout Mediterranean. *Propagation*: By cuttings in early summer from lateral shoots in a mixture of peat and loam which has been disinfected and treated with fungicide together with hormone rooting compound. *Pests and Diseases*: Slugs, snails, aphids and mealy bugs. Very liable to damping off when young.

F. japonica. Origin: Japan. Strikingly bold leaf creates a very dramatic silhouette against white or pale walls. Do not let the plant grow taller than 2m/6ft maximum. The leaves are dark green and glossy and fanlike in shape. Flowers appear in small balls and are a dirty white – I cut them off. Eventually the plant can reach 5–7m/15–20ft and will be multi-trunked.

FEIJOA (*Myrtaceae*)

A wonderful plant which is not planted often enough although virtually the whole of the Mediterranean is ideal for its culture. *Origin*: Brazil and Uruguay. *Zones*: A and B. Hardy to 500m/1650ft. *Water*: 1. Not fussy as to soil though prefers the richer sort. *Propagation*: By seed which is very slow or by cuttings in a 50/50 peat sand mixture with hormone rooting powder. Will not fruit for four to five years. *Pests*: Scale insects.

   F. sellowiana. Will grow to 5m/15ft though half that is more common. A medium, open, evergreen shrub with mid-green shining leaves and pale pink flowers with bright red stamens. The fruit is green and about 7.5cm/3in long and is ripe once it falls from the branch. It will keep for a week in the refrigerator. It is delicious in fruit salad (as are the petals) and in jam provided you use lemon-juice. The taste is said to be a cross between a pineapple and a banana. The shrub can be clipped into shape or trained as an espalier for formal use or left to grow high. Clipped it produces less leaf and fruit.

Feijoa sellowiana

FICUS (*Moraceae*)

A very large group mostly of tropical origin. Since much of the Mediterranean region is merely sub-tropical and subject to occasional rather low temperatures there are many species that cannot be grown. For instance *F. altissima* (the council tree), *F. benghalensis*, *F. nitida* and *F. religiosa* will all grow to tree proportions given the right conditions in the S. Mediterranean but will quickly succumb in the northern part. *Pests*: Mealy bugs and occasional scale insects.

   F. benjamina. *Origin*: Sudia. Evergreen. Well known as a houseplant and it never gets much further than this in the N. Mediterranean. Has 7.5cm/3in long wavy edged leaves and grows to about 3m/10ft in a pot. Prefers simi-shade and reflected sun. *Water*: 2. Drops its leaves about once a year in a most disconcerting manner but recovers in about six weeks with water and weak feeding.

   F. carica. Deciduous Mediterranean native – the common fruiting fig. Very decorative and a good shade tree if properly trained. Wood is very brittle so do not allow anyone to climb the tree. There are numerous good varieties of figs so you may as well plant a good one as a mere wild one. Never feed or you will get leaves instead of fruit. Needs occasional deep watering in a ultra-dry season. Pruning should be carried out only when the fruit gets out of reach and then in the dormant season.

   F. pumila. *Origin*: N. India and China. A marvellous evergreen wall coverer if you have the right climate. Will not normally tolerate temperature below freezing and

Ficus carica

needs some water in growing season (spring and summer). There is a variety which has even smaller leaves than the type, about 2.5/1in, *F. p.* 'Minima' and a variegated variety *F. p.* 'Variegata'. Needs tidying up from time to time.

F. retusa-nitida. Indian laurel or Chinese banyan. In the right conditions this can become a very pleasant shade tree with bright glossy green leaves. It comes from S.E. Asia so it will need more water than most but it is, strangely enough, tolerant of a certain amount of cold and slight frost – about −4°C/25°F. Full exposure to sun is no problem. It needs regular feeding particularly if it is going to be clipped. Do not plant too near buildings as roots can be a problem.

FREMONTODENDRON (*Sterculiaceae*)

Sometimes called *Fremontia.* Unusually beautiful shrubs from California with heart shaped leaves and saucer shaped flowers. *Zone*: A. *Water*: 1. Ideal for dry, sunny banks or desert locations. Prefers full sun, will not tolerate shade and damp. Its only demands are perfect drainage and above freezing temperatures. *Pruning*: None needed. *Propagation*: By seeds in mid-summer – early autumn.

F. californicum. Evergreen. H. 2.5m/7ft. Bright deep yellow flowers from spring until the end of summer.

Fremontodendron californicum

FUCHSIA (*Onagraceae*)

By and large fuchsias have a liking for cool summer temperatures, good winter drainage and adequate moisture. The Mediterranean, therefore, is not ideal for them. *Zones*: A and B. *Water*: 2. Nevertheless they can be grown on terraces, verandas or in shady corners with great success. There are several tropical fuchsias (from C. and S. America) on the market which will, providing you can supply the necessary watering, grow very well in the open such as *F. corymbiflora, F. fulgens* and *F. triphylla* together with their many, many hybrids. Those hybrids with *F. magellanica* in their background tend to be hardier than others. All fuchsias need feeding at regular intervals to perform well, particularly if they are in hanging baskets. There are so many named hybrids on the market, often carrying different names from one country to another, that it is impossible to give a list here. *Pruning*: Established, woody

Fuchsia fulgens

fuchsias can be trained to pyramid, conical, fan, pillar and espalier shapes and will need pruning to keep these shapes. Fuchsias cut down by frost should be given at least until May to start producing new growth. *Pests and Diseases*: Aphids, white fly, thrips, red spider - though not, mercifully, all at once. Fuchsias in the Mediterranean seem remarkably free of problems. Occasionally botrytis can occur after a cool, wet winter. Fuchsia rust is rare but if it does happen then try spraying with a proprietary fungicide. If this does not work then burn the affected plants and wait a few years before trying to grow fuchsias again.

GAZANIA (*Compositae*)

Evergreen, bright daisy like plants from S. Africa now seen only in hybrid forms of which there are hundreds. All have yellow, orange or occasionally maroon daisy flowers with dark green foliage. The plants hug the ground and bloom in late spring until early winter. Ideal as fillers and for rockeries, banks and similar situations. They become dormant if the heat becomes too intense. *Zones*: A and B. Hardy in Mediterranean. *Water*: 1. One of the best if *G. rigens leucolaena* which has bright yellow flowers on dark green trailing stems from June to October. They will not tolerate heavy clay soil which should be replaced with loose, well draining compost. Otherwise they have no special demands. *Propagation*: By seed in January at a minimum temp of 16C/61F. *Diseases*: Subject to damping off in poorly drained damp soil.

Gazania hybrid

GENISTA (*Leguminosae*)

Mediterranean native. A thoroughly drought resistant group which should have a place, in some form or other, in every Mediterranean garden. *Zone*: all. *Water*: 1. *Pruning*: Pinch out the growing points on young plants to encourage business – otherwise remove only dead wood. *Propagation*: By short cuttings in 75/25 sand and loam mix with hormone rooting powder. Take these in August and plant out rooted cuttings in the following March or April.

G. aetnensis. Mount Etna broom. A large shrub to 6.5m/21ft in good condition with rush like leaves and bright yellow flowers in terminal racemes in July and August.

G. hispanica. Good for a wild garden since it will grow anywhere – and does. Has masses of 2.5cm/1 inch flowers on leafless stems. There are better brooms for garden use. Grows to 2.50m/8ft.

G. lydia. A very drought resistant species from Syria which is virtually prostrate with a spread of 1m/3ft. Covered in yellow flowers in late May. Good for rockeries or tops of walls.

G. pilosa. Usually found as a leafless shrub about 45cm/18in high though there can be minute leaves on the underneath of the stems. Tiny yellow flowers appear over a six-week period from about mid-May to the end of June.

G. virgata. Origin: Madeira. One of the most beautiful – a magnificent large shrub of about 4m/12ft or more with grey green leaves of varying shape. The flowers are large, mid-yellow in terminal racemes and slightly scented and appear in late May and Early June. There is a variety 'Flore Pleno' with slightly larger flowers than the type.

GERBERA (*Compositae*)

Origin: S. Africa (Transvaal). *Zone*: A. *Water*: 2 or 3. Gerberas have been much hybridized and now come in yellow, orange, scarlet, maroon, cream, white, pink and purple. *Propagation*: By division – potting up the divided plants and planting out once they need potting on, usually in autumn. Remove faded stems at ground level. Gerbera stems are often weak and need support. *Pests and Diseases*: Aphids. Fungus diseases are not uncommon and there is a form of rootrot due to damp, cool ground. Use systemic insecticide/fungicide if you suspect such problems could occur.

G. jamesonii. H 30–40cm/12–18in, S 60cm/2ft. Large 7–10cm/3–4in daisy-like scarlet flowers throughout the summer.

GINKGO (*Ginkgoaceae*)

A genus with a single remarkable tree. *Origin*: China and Japan. For N. Mediterranean only since it does not thrive in tropical or very dry conditions. *Zone*: All. *Water*: 2. *Pruning*: None – and they resent it. *Propagation*: By seed (remove covering gently to speed things up) which germinates relative quickly and easily.

G. biloba. To H 30m/97ft but rarely as high. There are several cultivars including 'Autumn Gold', 'Saratoga', 'Tremonia' and 'Variegata'. Variable in shape, it can be columnar, multi-trunked or open branched. Male and female trees are needed to produce the fruit which has an unattractive smell and tastes even worse. The leaves are palest green in spring and darken to rich green in summer turning bright gold in autumn. They fall all at once. A most attractive tree and excellent as a lawn or patio centre piece.

GLORIOSA (*Liliaceae/Colchicaceae*)

These very showy bulbous climbers can be grown outside in the Mediterranean region provided you can guarantee a minimum temperature of 21°C/70°F – otherwise they must be given indoor protection during the colder period. *Origin*: Tropical Africa. *Zone*: A. *Water*: 3 with occasional syringeing in very dry climates. All gloriosas flower in succession over a long period – often three months in the Mediterranean. They need careful staking and occasional tying in and feeding at least once a month with a fertilizer not too high in nitrogen but rich in potassium – a tomato fertilizer is excellent. After flowering dry off corms, store in a well aired greenhouse and replant the following year. *Propagation*: By seed in spring. Allow four years for flowering. Alternatively offsets can be planted and these take a little less time. *Diseases*: Mildew and fungus can attack at anytime in the humid atmosphere required by these plants. Use a systemic fungicide as prevention.

Gloriosa superba

G. *rothschildiana*. H 2m/6ft. The 7.5cm/4in flowers are carried singly on long stalks. They are cup shaped and very striking – the crimson petals have yellow wavy edges somewhat resembling a martagon lily.

G. *superba*. Slightly more restrained than the above. The flowers are rich yellow with crimped edges and tend to become rich orange with age.

GRISELINIA (*Cornaceae*)

Most attractive rather slow growing plants much used for hedging in the N. Mediterranean. *Origin*: New Zealand. *Zone*: A and B. Will tolerate only very slight frost but is happy by the sea and in windy situations. *Water*: 2 but will manage on 1 when well established. All newly planted griselinias require protection by windbreaks or screens for at least two years. *Pruning*: Hedges should be trimmed once a year in May in the early morning or late evening – never in full sun. Otherwise prune off dead or damaged wood and straggly growth. *Propagation*: 10cm/4in cuttings in late spring, in a 50/50 peat and sand mix with hormone rooting compound. They are very slow to take and should not be potted on for at least eighteen months. *Diseases*: Subject to chlorosis.

G. littoralis. This will grow to over 7m/22ft but is more often seen at around 2.5m/8ft. The leaves are oblong, slightly oval, pale green, shining and rather leathery. Insignificant green flowers.

G. lucida. This has slightly larger and less leathery leaves than the above and is considerably more tender.

× HALIMIOCISTUS (*Cistaceae*)

A series of happy marriages between halimium and cistus – both Mediterranean natives – has given birth to a number of excellent hybrids which are not only beautiful but hardy and drought resistant. *Zone*: All. *Water*: 1. *Pruning*: Never, except to remove dead wood. *Propagation*: Seed does not come true. Cuttings of non-flowering stems in autumn, in very sandy soil with hormone rooting compound sometimes work but are difficult. The three most commonly available in the Mediterranean are:

× *H*. 'Ingwersenii'. A 60cm/2ft shrub with woolly foliage and 2.5cm/1in papery white flowers in summer.

× *H. sahucii*. H 45cm/18in. Slightly felted grey/green linear leaves and white papery flowers in clusters in summer. Probably the most attractive.

× *H. wintonensis*. The flowers are composed of a white, maroon and yellow basal ring all against rich green narrow leaves. Flowers all day in summer providing it is sunny.

HARDENBERGIA (*Leguminosae*)

Strikingly attractive climbing plants from Australia which are often still listed under *Kennedya* in the Mediterranean. They are evergreen in their native land but night temperatures below 18°C/65°F make them lose their leaves. *Zone*: A. *Water*: 2. They will tolerate semi-shade or reflected sun. If in doubt about winter temperatures winter over in a cold greenhouse. *Pruning*: None needed. *Propagation*: By cuttings in autumn in moist 50/50 peat and sand with hormone rooting powder.

H. comptonia. The most frequently seen and planted. Brilliant purple pea flowers in March–April in racemes with mid-green narrow pointed leaves. As it reaches less than 2.7m/9ft it can be grown as a shrub if properly trained and supported.

H. violacea. (syn. *Kennedya ovata*). A rather scrambling shrub to about 3m/10ft with pretty violet flowers with a small yellow spot at the base. Flowers a little later than the above.

Hebe

HEBE (*Scrophulariaceae*)

Although hebes will accept maritime salt-laden gales and
are not particularly hardy they do not like unremitting
dry heat. Therefore they are only suitable in the
coastal areas of France, N., N.E. and W.
Italy and the coast in Spain from the
French border down to about Valencia. *Zones*:
A and B. *Water*: 2 though well established
hebes will sometimes tolerate a certain
amount of drought. They prefer semi-shade
in the Mediterranean. *Pruning*: None needed
but dead head all hebes once flowering is
over. If shrubs get too leggy cut back hard
in late winter and new growth will break in
spring. *Propagation*: By autumn cuttings in 50/
50 peat and sand with hormone rooting compound. Keep pots cool but protected in winter. Plant
out following spring. Among the best for the area are:

Hebe 'Alicia Amherst'

H. armstrongii. A 'whipcord' hebe to a little
over 1m/3ft with tiny scale-like golden leaves. It
blooms in early summer and has small white flowers in terminal clusters.

H. 'Bowles Hybrid'. To about 60cm/2ft this hybrid is worth having as it
is permanently in flower throughout the summer. It has tiny lilac flowers in
terminal racemes.

H. brachysiphon. This can make a large bush up to 2m/6ft high or more and
about 90–120cm/3–4ft across. It has dark evergreen leaves and white flowers
in June. Can be pruned hard annually.

H. 'Carl Teschner'. Useful for rockeries where it hugs the ground, with a
spread of 45cm/18in. Absolutely covered with brilliant violet flowers in June
for about six weeks.

H. × *franciscana*. There are several varieties of this hebe all of which are
worthy of a place in the Mediterranean garden provided you can give the
right amount of water. H 1.2m/4ft and spread the same. 'Blue Gem' is one
of the loveliest and there is a variegated version ('Variegata') which is ideal
for pots and window boxes.

H. 'Great Orme'. Shiny, round pale green leaves with bright lavender
flowers in late Spring. Protect from direct sun and too much heat. Not hardy.

H. macrantha. One of the loveliest hebes with large 2cm/¾in white flowers
in racemes in early summer. H 60cm/2ft with similar spread. Hates direct
Mediterranean sun and cold wet winters.

H. speciosa. One of the best for the Mediterranean garden. Long, narrow,
dark evergreen leaves. There are several famous cultivars with *H. speciosa* in
their ancestry, among which are 'La Seduisante' with bright red flowers and
'Gloriosa' with bright pink flowers. The flower colour of the type is rich

blue-purple. Ideal for big pots. In the open ground it can reach 1.6m/5ft by about as much across. All flower from the end of May to early July.

HELICHRYSUM (*Compositae*)

Virtually all helichrysums on sale through nurseries and garden centres are worthy of a place in the Mediterranean garden where they will survive sun and drought. It should be remembered that in the intense Mediterranean sun almost all helichrysums give off an intense smell – unattractive to many – normally only associated with the 'curry plant' *E. italicum*. Among the most useful and elegant (and least smelly) is *H. petiolare* which is not at all easy to obtain in the area. If you do manage to acquire it at least take cuttings for the following year or for your friends. The type has rounded, grey, felted foliage which grows apace all summer. It has the advantage of never flowering. It is ideal for pots, window boxes, rockeries and acres of bare of earth one wants to cover with something more interesting than ivy or ajuga. It will spread to as much as 3–4m/10–13ft. There are three cultivars:- *H. p.* 'Aureum' with felted leaves in pale yellow; *H. p.* 'Limelight' with wonderful under rich pink or red flowers. It has bright, pale green rounded leaves and can light up a dark bed wonderfully. *H. p.* 'Variegatum' is the least successful cultivar with pale yellow-green and white felted leaves but can look good with strongly coloured other flowers.

HEMEROCALLIS (*Liliaceae*)

The day lilies are among the most useful spring-flowering plants for the Mediterranean garden. *Origin*: Japan and Siberia. *Zone*: All. *Water*: 1, or none when establish. *Propagation*: By seed – but allow four year before flowering. They are perennials with tuberous roots and come both evergreen and deciduous though the latter is more common. There are literally hundreds of cultivars. The orange, red and rust flowers last less long than the other colours of white, yellow and violet. The main problem is to find hemerocallis of one colour without having to buy new cultivars at an inflated price. All have broad grass-like leaves and lily-like flowers which last for a day or two only, hence the name. However, so many flowers are waiting to take their place that this disadvantage is scarcely noticed. They bloom in late spring and early summer. Their size ranges from a mere 30cm/1ft to over 1.6m/5ft. *Propagation*: By seed – allow four years between sowing and flowering.

Hemerocallis 'Pink Damask'

HIBISCUS (*Malvaceae*)

Very decorative flowering shrubs and herbaceous plants mainly from the tropics and sub-tropical areas. *Zone*: A and B. *Water*: 1. Although there is enough heat to grow the tropical hibiscus there is not enough moisture available either in the air or to water with and therefore the choice is usually confined to *H. sinosyriacus* and *H. syriacus*. *H. rosa-sinensis* (a tropical variety) grows quite well in the Mediterranean region where there is an ample supply of water all year round but other tropical hibiscus do not thrive. All need well-draining soil (the local clay will have to be changed) and dislike direct sunshine – semi-shade is ideal. *Pruning*: Clip established hedges back by a quarter in spring otherwise pruning is usually not necessary. *Propagation*: By cuttings in autumn – too often seed is not viable. Keep the soil permanent moist, not wet, spray with fungicide at fortnightly intervals and pot on once root bound. Plant out after it has outgrown its second pot. *Pests*: Aphids, scale insects and red spider.

H. rosa-sinensis. Chinese hibiscus, shoe flower or Bunga Raya. *Origin*: S.E. Asia. An evergreen shrub to about 2m/6ft in the right climate where it will make a good flowering hedge. Bright very showy flowers which bloom only in spring and autumn in the Mediterranean – the summer is too dry. The flowers are variously coloured but usually have five petals when not double. The most common colour is red but white, violet, yellow and pink are found.

H. schizopetalus. *Origin*: E. Africa. This deciduous shrub grows to about 3.75m/12ft and is among the most attractive. In mid-summer it has bright red pendulous flowers made up of dissected petals which turn back on themselves and the effect is of a coral red lantern. This needs daily syringeing in the Mediterranean and cutting back to half its height in spring. Well worth the trouble.

H. syriacus. *Origin*: Middle and Far East. H to 2.5m/7ft. Hardy in the Mediterranean. There are many cultivars in all the usual hibicus colours plus blue. Flowers are produced for about four or five weeks at any time between early July and the end of September. There are also double flowered cultivars which are marginally less hardy. The variety 'Blue Bird' makes an excellent hedge.

Hibiscus syriacus

HOHERIA (*Malvaceae*)

An attractive genus of five species of flowering shrubs from New Zealand which have white funnel shaped flowers. All are hardy in the Mediterranean. *Zone*: A and B. *Water*: 2. *Pruning*: None. *Propagation*: By layering in autumn and severing from the parent plant the following autumn.

147

H. glabrata. Height to 3.75m/12ft when fully adult. Deciduous with large jagged leaves and fragrant white flowers in July.

H. lyallii. As above but with grey leaves.

H. sexstylosa. This evergreen shrub has a stiffer habit than the two former – it can grow to 5m/15ft. There is a weeping form which is most attractive since the 2.5cm/1in white flowers, during July and August, are shown to their best advantage.

IOCHROMA (*Solanaceae*)

Origin: Tropical S. America. *Zone:* A. *Water:* 2, 3 when young. *Pruning:* None. *Propagation:* By 7.5–10cm/3–4in cuttings with a heel in mid-summer with hormone rooting compound. Keep well watered but watch for fungus diseases. *Pests and Diseases:* Iron chlorosis. Aphids, thrips, scale insects and red spider. Of the 20 or so species only one is worth growing for its rich purple flowers:

I. grandiflora. This medium sized shrub has large purple tubular flowers in tight pendulous bunches. Mid-green leaves, evergreen in its native habitat but deciduous in the Mediterranean. Needs rich, well fed moist soil and protection from wind which quickly shreds the leaves to ribbons. It starts flowering in July and continues to the end of the autumn.

IPOMOEA (*Convolvulaceae*)

The morning glory is an easily grown climber which is hardy, and perennial, in the Mediterranean. *Water:* 1. *Propagation:* By seed. *Pests:* Red spider. Only two are commonly grown:-

I. purpurea. Origin: Tropical S. America. *Zone:* A. Rich purple trumpet flowers from June to September and heart shaped mid-green leaves. Deciduous. Climbs at least 3.75m/12ft.

I. violacea (syn. *I. tricolor, I. rubro-caerulea*). *Origin:* Mexico. *Zone:* A and B. Paler trumpet flowers in shades of lilac and purply-blue. Occasionally they are rose coloured. H 4m/13ft or more – excellent for covering unsightly wire fences, ugly buildings and the like but they need some support.

IRESINE (*Amaranthaceae*)

A wonderful genus grown principally for its foliage which is bright wine red as are its stems. *Zone:* A. *Water:* 3. The plant is semi-succulent, very cold sensitive but easy to propagate and a marvellous subject for bedding out or filling in gaps. *Propagation:* By cuttings in August taken just below a node and put into 50/50 sand and peat and kept constantly moist. They take in about three weeks. It is best to take a number of cuttings for the following year as old plants become very leggy with age. *Pests:* Aphids. Red spider and occasional mealy bugs.

I. herbstii. Origin: Tropical S. America. The most commonly seen. To about

1m/3ft but it is better not to let the plants become too leggy. Rich carmine to wine red heart-shaped leaves with prominent dark veining. Often known as the beef-steak plant. The stems are the same colour and semi-transparent. Flowers are greenish-white and of no significance.

I. lindenii. Origin: Ecuador. This has darker leaves than *I. herbstii* and they are narrowly oval. A rather more compact plant but not always easy to find.

JACARANDA (*Bignoniaceae*)

This breathtakingly beautiful flowering tree is an absolute must for any Mediterranean garden where it will thrive. *Zone*: 1. *Water*: 2, with deep and well-spaced waterings, not more than every two weeks. *Pruning*: None, except to tidy. *Propagation*: By seed which germinates easily in the spring.

J. mimosifolia (syn. *J. ovalifolia*). *Origin*: Brazil. Will eventually grow to over 6m/20ft, by almost as much across. The flowers are blue-mauve and tubular, 5cm/2in long, in clusters. The flowering period ranges according to climate from April to late June. Some rarely seen cultivars have white or pink flowers but are not as floriferous as the type.

JASMINUM (*Oleaceae*)

Jasminum officinale

Evergreen or deciduous climbing plants. *J. officinale*, *J. nudiflorum* and *J. mesneyi* are familiar from colder climates and need no description here and all do well in the Mediterranean. Those described are less known and well worth a place in the garden. *Zone*: A. *Water*: 1 when established. *Pruning*: Cut out old and weak growth when necessary in order to stimulate new growth. *Propagation*: In early September take 7.5 10cm/3–4in cuttings of semi-ripe wood with a heel in a 50/50 mix of peat and sand with hormone rooting compound. Not always easy. Once well rooted pot on and plant out in early summer.

J. polyanthum. Origin: China. An evergreen climbing pink jasmine which can be used as ground cover. Very fragrant at night and with a long blooming period – often three-four months from March to June.

J. sambac. Origin: India. Arabian jasmine. A richly scented evergreen jasmine with white flowers which appear continuously provided the temperature is right. H 2m/6ft and ideal as a screen when properly trained. Very drought resistant but watering improves the scent. There is a famous double variety, 'Granduca di Toscana'.

J. × stephanense. A pink hybrid jasmine climbing to 5m/16ft and flowering in May and June. When established it is very vigorous and will tolerate a little frost.

KALANCHOE (*Crassulaceae*)

Much neglected succulent plants which can be the backbone of a garden in Greece or the S. Mediterranean. Normally seen as a houseplant (particularly *K. blossfeldiana*) there is no reason, except temperature, why they should not form part of a dry-garden design. Very easily grown and stand quite a bit of neglect so are ideal for the absentee gardener. *Zone*: A (not below 10°C/50°F). *Water*: 1. *Propagation*: Short stem cuttings at any time provided the temperature is above 21°C/70°F in fast draining soil with or without hormone rooting powder. It is best to dry off the cuttings for 48 hours to prevent fungus problems. *Pests*: Mealy bugs.

K. *blossfeldiana*. *Origin*: Madagascar. Most on the market are varieties from Germany and Switzerland. Large, fleshy leaves with scallopped edges all have clusters of tubular flowers 1–2.5cm/½–1in. The colours are white, yellow, pink or red and the last is the most common. In the open they bloom two months at a time, then have a two-month rest period and, provided the temperature is high enough, bloom for another two months and so on. H 30cm/1ft but occasionally more.

K. *marmorata*. *Origin*: Abyssinia. Unusual small shrub with stalkless leaves which are blue-green occasionally mottled with chocolate brown. The flowers are 7.5cm/3in long, white and produced about twice in a twelve month period. Very drought resistant.

K. *pumila*. *Origin*: Madagasgar. A most attractive slightly prostrate plant which has rich red leaves about 2.5cm/1in long. The whole plant is covered with a slight pinkish-white powder. Pale-pink flowers occasionally appear but it is for the foliage that this plant is grown so extensively.

LAGERSTROEMIA (*Lythraceae*)

The crape, or crepe, myrtles are most attractive shrubs when properly grown, with deep green glossy foliage and cone shaped panicles of flowers with crepe paper petals in white, pink, red or mauve. They bloom over a period of three months during mid-summer to mid-autumn. They need well drained, preferably neutral soil and occasional deep watering. *Origin*: China. *Zone*: A. *Water*: 2. Full sun or slight shade. *Pruning*: Only in dormant season. Cut back by about 45cm/18in to encourage flowering next season. Remove twiggy growth. *Propagation*: 10cm/4in cuttings in well drained loam with hormone rooting compound. Spray against mildew. *Pests and Diseases*: Mildew – avoid overhead or automatic irrigation. Spray with fungicide at regular intervals. Chlorosis.

L. *indica*. This is a large shrub or small tree to about 3m/10ft about 2m/6ft across. It has big clusters of bright pink flowers. There are many cultivars including: 'Near East', a small tree with shell pink flowers; 'Petite Embers', a dwarf bush with bronze foliage and rose coloured flowers; 'Petite Orchid', a dwarf shrub with orchid pink flowers; 'Petite Snow', a dwarf shrub with pure white flowers, the most compact of all to 1.5m/5ft.

LANTANA (*Verbenaceae*)

Useful drought resistant small shrubs which flower throughout the summer. *L. camara* can be clipped to shape though flowers can be lost. *Origin*: Tropical S. America. *Zone*: A. *Water*: 1. *Pruning*: None needed except to keep tidy or keep at required height. *Propagation*: *L. camara* by 10cm/4in cuttings taken in late autumn, in sandy loam with hormone rooting compound. *L. sellowiana* by division in cool season.

L. camara. A small shrub to about 1.2m/4ft with orange-red flowers which change to red, pink and even white. Leaves have toothed edges, are deeply veined and smell unpleasant when crushed. There are varieties in single colours.

L. sellowiana (syn. *L. montevidensis*). A trailing plant in constant flower provided it is given enough water – otherwise it will simply survive. Does well hanging over walls or parapets. The flowers are pale mauve and plentiful. Can be a bit invasive where water is plentiful.

LAPAGERIA (*Liliaceae*)

The Chilean bellflower. In the Mediterranean this must be grown in a large pot, in acid soil and given protection from the sun – on a verandah is ideal. *Origin*: Chile. *Zone*: A and B. *Water* 2. *Pruning*: Not needed though it can help to remove flowering stems when blooms fade and occasionally to pinch out growing shoots to encourage slight bushiness. *Propagation*: By seed in acid soil with a night temperature not below 20°C/68°F. Layering is said to be another way but I have never succeeded with this method. *Pests*: Slugs, snails, aphids.

L. rosea. Rich crimson waxy bell shaped flowers from June–October on a plant which grows to about 5m/16ft. It is evergreen with very dark green, leathery and slightly pointed leaves. There is a white form *L. a. albiflora* which I have found less vigorous than the type.

Lapageria rosea

LAVANDULA (*Labiatae*)

Mediterranean native. There are several lesser known lavenders which are well worth growing. Also in the S. Mediterranean the English varieties such as 'Grappenhall', 'Hidcote', 'Hidcote Blue', 'Munstead' and in particular 'Twickel Purple' seem not to thrive in the fierce sun. *Pruning*: It is essential to remove spent flower stems immediately after flowering and to cut back hard around March, but never into old wood. *Propagation*: By 15cm/6in cuttings taken in late summer in 75% sand and loam, with hormone rooting compound. Lavender cuttings appear to do best when crowded into a pot or box. Cuttings planted in situ do not do well in the Mediterranean. *Pests and Diseases*: Froghoppers. Fungus diseases such as grey mould and leaf spot. Honey fungus can kill the plant though this is rare in the Mediterranean.

L. angustifolia (syn. *L. spica*). H 1m/3ft. The least successful of the lavenders if grown in full sun. However, in slight shade an excellent proposition with bright mauve spikes from June to August or even September. Dutch Lavender is considered to be a shorter and more compact form of *L. a.*. There is always a great deal of argument about lavender names from country to country in the Mediterranean.

L. dentata. H 1m/3ft. One of the best with soft green dentate leaves. Often wrongly called *lavande anglaise* by the French. It blooms all the year round and has rich purple flowers.

L. lanata. Another excellent lavender for the Mediterranean. It has soft, woolly leaves which are decorative in their own right even without the pale mauve flowers in mid-summer.

L. stoechas. French lavender. H 60cm/2ft. This has the normal lavender mauve flowers with a darker bract on top which remains after the flowers have faded. Does well in full sun.

Lavandula angustifolia

L. pedunculata. H to 75cm/2ft6in. This has rich purple flowers in mid-summer, held high above the foliage and topped by a large purple bract.

LEPTOSPERMUM (*Myrtaceae*)

Manuka or tea tree. Evergreen. The height varies between 30cm/1ft to over 8m/25ft though the latter is uncommon in the Mediterranean. Tolerates a large variety of climates and thrives by the sea and in the mountains. In the S. Mediterranean region prefers not to be in direct midday sun. *Origin*: New Zealand and Australia. *Zone*: A and B. *Water*: 2.*Pruning*: Cut back hard after flowering to keep plants compact. Occasional pinching produces bushier plants. *Propagation*: By 8cm/3in cuttings in June, in well draining soil with hormone rooting compound. These are slow to root and you should wait two years before planting out. *Pests*: Scale insects which mani-
fest themselves by black sooty stickiness on stems and branches.

Leptospermum rupestre

There are single and double flowered varieties but the former is not only hardier but tolerates sun better. Single varieties have five petals around a dark, small central cone. It is difficult to find anything but *L. scoparium* and its cultivars in the Mediterranean region. This has needle-like leaves, usually dark green but occasionally bronze. The flower colour ranges from white through pink and rose to deep crimson. Very occasionally one can find two others:-

L. rotundifolium. *Origin*: Australia. This has a weeping habit and grows to about 1.5m/5ft with round leaves and large 2.5cm/1in pale mauve flowers in June. It is quite unlike New Zealand leptospermums. It takes time to get established but will tolerate full Mediterranean sun and quite a bit of drought.

L. rupestre (syn. *L. humifusum*, *L. prostratum*). This is prostrate and has single white flowers in June on red, wiry stems.

LEUCOPHYLLUM (*Scrophulariaceae*)

Attractive and useful shrubs for desert or very dry locations. *Origin*: S.E. United States. *Zone*: A and B. *Water*: 1 or none. Sometimes called the barometer bush because its foliage plumps out when water is available and virtually disappears after three months without. Detests being over-watered. *Pruning*: Can be clipped to shape but otherwise no pruning is necessary. *Propagation*: By tip cuttings in spring with minimal water in a 75/25 sand and peat mix, with hormone rooting powder. Only 50% take – many die of damping off fungus.

L. texanum. H 2m/6ft. This has dense grey-green foliage in spring and early summer when a certain amount of water is available. The flowers lavender and bell-shaped. Flowering depends on hot weather and normally occurs in early summer but sporadic flowering can occur anytime from May to October.

It should be planted in well draining soil otherwise heavy autumn or spring rains can kill it.

LOTUS (*Leguminosae*)

Coral gem. *Origin*: Canary Islands. *Zone*: A. *Water*: 1. *Pruning*: Cut back hard in early winter and protect if necessary with a mulch. *Propagation*: By seed in spring or autumn which germinates erratically.

L. berthelotii. A low, trailing perennial which has the appearance of a pale silver shawl when properly grown. In summer it has hundreds of pea-shaped scarlet flowers. It is ideal for hanging baskets, parapets and ground cover. Very drought resistant.

MAHONIA (*Berberidaceae*)

This plant is said to have the most beautiful of all leaf shapes. It is a native of the American Pacific N. W. and E. Asia and therefore unsuitable for the S. Mediterranean. In the northern part of the area, however, and at altitude it is an ideal shrub provided it is planted in shade and has enough moisture. *Zone*: all. *Water*: 2 or 3 depending on situation. *Pruning*: None except for *M. aquifolium* which needs cutting hard back around March or April. *Propagation*: *M. aquifolium* by seed which is slow to germinate and establish. Never let compost dry out. Use tip cuttings for other varieties in early winter. Pot on once rooted and plant out a year later. *Pests and Diseases*: Caterpillars which go for the new growth. Mildew and rust. Use a systemic fungicide on a prevention basis.

M. aquifolium. Oregon Grape. H to 1.5m/5ft. A wonderful ground cover, particularly under trees it has deeply cut, dark green foliage, yellow flowers in summer followed by dark blue-purple grape-like berries in clusters.

M. japonica. *Origin*: East Asia. This is a large shrub of about 3m/10ft by as much across. Racemes of lemon-yellow flowers are borne in early spring. However, it is worth growing for the leaves alone.

M. lomariifolia. *Origin*: China. H 3m/10ft, S 2m/6ft. Rather tender shrub very similar to the above but with deeper yellow flowers. There is a particularly beautiful cultivar called 'Charity' which has scented, deep yellow flowers from about Christmas until early March.

Mahonia japonica

MANDEVILLA (*Apocynaceae*)

Chilean jasmine. An evergreen (semi-evergreen in the Mediterranean) twining climber, native of Argentina and Chile. *Zone*: A. *Water*: 2. Will not tolerate low temperatures. *Pruning*: None except to keep within bounds. *Propagation*: By cuttings of side shoots in August, in a mixture of sand and peat with hormone rooting compound. Keep moist at all times. Not easy to propagate.

M. suaveolens. Rapid climber to 6–7m/19–22ft with heart shaped glossy leaves with pointed tips and downy underneath. The flowers, which bloom throughout the summer, are pure white, in clusters, and like flaring trumpets. Has a slight gardenia scent which you either love or hate.

MELIA (*Meliaceae*)

An easily grown canopy tree which is useful for quick shade. Its main disadvantage is that it seeds plentifully, virtually all germinate and the berries have an unpleasant smell whilst ripening. Therefore, it is not a tree for near the house but ideal for drives and the end of the garden. Also branches are brittle and can break in the wind. *Zone*: A. *Water*: 1. *Pruning*: Prune to keep tree properly balanced to prevent wind rock and to get a good 'umbrella' shape for maximum shade. *Propagation*: By seed dig up self-sown seedlings.

M. azedarach. *Origin*: E. Indies. Grows to around 10m/33ft with an equal spread. Lavender flowers appear in spring followed by yellow berries which remain until the following spring. The dark green foliage becomes bright yellow in autumn.

M. azadirachta (syn. *Azadirachta indica*). *Origin*: E. Indies. This is the famous Neem tree every bit of which is used in native medicine. H to about 15m/48ft and in summer produces creamy white very fragrant flowers in panicles 25cm/10in long, followed by purple berries.

METROSIDEROS (*Myrtaceae*)

New Zealand Christmas tree. For N. Mediterranean only and preferably in coastal districts or at altitude. *Zone*: A. *Water*: 2. Very wind tolerant. Prefers semi-shade. Will not tolerate frost. *Pruning*: Only to keep in shape. Lower branches can be trimmed off mature trees to get a less dense shrub. *Pests*: Leaf miners and caterpillars on new foliage.

M. excelsa. A very desirable large shrub to about 5m/16ft by about 3m/10ft across. The deep green leathery leaves are white felted underneath. In mid-summer the whole tree is covered with flowers with prominent stamens bursting from powdery buds. The colour can vary from scarlet to deep crimson depending on the variety – usually they are crimson. Not easy to find.

MIRABILIS (*Nyctoginaceae*)

Marvel of Peru. Not grown often enough and yet it will flower throughout the summer until the temperature drops below 20°C/68°F. *Zone*: A. *Water*: 2. Needs full sun. *Propagation*: By seed in April which germinates easily. Can be grown as an annual. *Pests*: Aphids.

M. jalapa. A slender plant about 30cm/1ft high with trumpet shaped flowers in colours ranging from yellow and white to pink and crimson which bloom in full sun but close up in shade and cool weather. The flowers last only a day but are constantly replaced so the plant is always in bloom. The leaves are heart shaped and a rich green.

MUSA (*Musaceae*)

Banana. *Origin*: Tropical Africa and America. *Zone*: A. *Water*: 3. The possibility of growing a banana tree, which is in fact more like a shrub, seems to go to some peoples' heads. It should be remembered that they need a great deal of water; that once grown they are difficult to eradicate; that they encourage insects, particularly ants and mosquitoes; and that they look terrible after having been battered by wind. To have edible fruit (usually from *M. cavendishii* or *M. paradisiaca*) you need humid tropical conditions which exist nowhere in the Mediterranean. However, certain bananas can be very decorative. *Pruning*: Remove damaged leaves at once. Damaged trees can be cut down to ground level and they will spring up again. Use high nitrogen fertilizers at frequent intervals to get bright green, sappy growth.

Musa cavendishii

Propagation: No need – those mentioned are all stoloniferous and will increase on their own. *Pests*: Ants can enter fruit which is not picked. Water can collect in branch forks and act as a breeding ground for mosquitoes.

M. basjoo. H 3m/10ft. The most commonly grown for pure decoration, with large pale green leaves 2m/6ft long and 30–40cm/12–16in wide. It is grown for fibre in Japan. Produces no edible fruit.

M. cavendishii. The most commonly grown and used in the Canaries, Madeira and parts of the U.S. for fruit. To about 2m/6ft. Large, slightly glaucous leaves about 40cm/15in wide and deep aubergine bracts.

M. coccinea. This grows to about 1.5m/5ft and has bright green leaves and a yellowish inflorescence. Rarely sets fruit.

MYOPORUM (*Myoporaceae*)

Evergreen trees and shrubs almost over-used for hedging in Spain but hardly known in France and Italy. *Origin*: New Zealand and Australia. *Zone*: A. Will not tolerate temperatures below 16°C/60°F. *Water*: 1. Ideal seaside plants. *Pruning*: Must be hard-pruned each year to get tidy compact growth. *Propagation*: By cuttings about 10cm/4in in loose soil with hormone rooting compound. Plant out when good roots have formed.

M. laetum. Grows about 1m/3ft a year and is rather untidy if left unpruned. Has dark green glossy leaves with semi-transparent spots on them. White flowers flushed with lilac in summer which are not always produced out of its native New Zealand. Will eventually grow to about 4m/13ft by about 3m/10ft wide.

M. insulare. *Origin*: Tasmania. This has more pointed leaves than *M. laetum* and they are freckled with the usual myoporum 'spots' due to oil glands. It is also more drought resistant. Grows to the same size.

MYRTUS (*Myrtaceae*)

A large genus of evergreen shrubs and trees some of which are Mediterranean natives. *Zone*: All. *Water*: 1. *Pruning*: None needed except to keep shrub tidy. *Propagation*: By semi-ripe cuttings in summer or twigs in 50/50 sand and loam and hormone rooting compound.

M. communis. *Origin*: Mediterranean. Hardy to about 600m/2000ft. A slow growing shrub which can reach 5m/16ft. Has tiny, dark green leaves and fragrant white flowers with prominent stamens in mid-summer, followed by black berries. *M. c. tarentina*. As above but with smaller leaves. There are several cultivars available both of *M. communis* and *M. c. tarentina* all of which are slightly more tender but have better leaf and flower forms.

M. ugni – see *Ugni molinae*.

Myrtus communis

NANDINA (*Nandinaceae*)

Origin: China. *Zone*: A. *Water*: 1 once established. *Pruning*: None needed except to remove dead or damaged wood. *Propagation*: By seeds in October which even when they germinate are not easy to keep going. Alternatively by 10cm/4in with hormone rooting compound in moist loam. They should be at least 45cm/18in tall before planting out into their final positions.

N. domestica. An evergreen shrub of 1.2–2m/4–6ft with pinnate leaves on bamboo-like canes. Small panicles of white flowers in mid-summer. The leaves become reddish-purple in autumn. In very cold weather can become deciduous but will leaf up again in spring. It is an ideal pot plant where it can be seen to best advantage. There are several cultivars available whose names vary confusingly from country to country. Some are extra dwarf and good for rockeries, others have larger leaves and flowers than the type.

NERIUM (*Apocynaceae*)

Mediterranean native. Tall, evergreen shrubs with narrow, pointed leaves and terminal clusters of usually single flowers from mid-summer to autumn. *Zones*: A and B. *Water*: 1. They will tolerate a great deal of dry cold and wind but do not like much frost or snow though once established will usually survive any weather the Mediterranean region has to offer. *Pruning*: It is best to trim off seed pods if and when they appear as well as dead flower heads. Otherwise little pruning is needed. *Propagation*: By twigs, about 15cm/6in long pulled off a branch, placed in water overnight and then planted in sandy soil with hormone rooting compound. Taken any time between July and early September they will grow roots within two or three weeks. This can also be done in a glass of water with hormone rooting compound. *Pests and Diseases*: Mealy bugs and scale insects. Discoloration of leaves due to an unknown physiological disorder. Remove all fallen foliage. Usually recovers by the following spring.

N. oleander. Oleander. Grows to about 3m/10ft in good conditions and can have single or double flowers any time between June and October. Colours include white, yellow, pink, peach, apricot, rose pink and crimson. Yellow, peach and apricot are more easily damaged by frost. Standard shrubs grafted on to a tall trunk are often on sale in France, Italy and Spain but, while useful as 'instant' trees, are considerably more expensive than the ordinary shrubs. All parts of the oleander are poisonous so do not plant where there are children. Also do not put twigs or leaves on a bonfire as smoke is poisonous.

Nerium oleander

OENOTHERA (*Onagraceae*)

Useful perennials for the dry garden which give late spring and summer colour. They spread by underground roots and can be difficult to eradicate. As they are not particularly attractive in winter it is best to cut them back and have an early bulb planting to take over. *Zone*: All. *Water*: 1. *Propagation*: By seed in spring or division of roots in autumn.

O. *berlandieri*. Mexican primrose. *Origin*: Texas and Mexico. Will be cut to ground by frost but re-appear next spring. H 15cm/6in, with narrow, pointed leaves and large cup-shaped flowers in white or pale pink.

O. *missouriensis*. *Origin*: S. Central United States. A wonderful perennial which will stand any sort of weather except constant wet. Bright yellow cup shaped flowers come from slightly red spotted yellow buds over a long period from the end of May.

Oenothera missouriensis

OPUNTIA (*Cactaceae*)

Prickly pear. *Origin*: The Americas. There is a tendency throughout the hotter parts of the Mediterranean to use this plant purely for hedging purposes. It gets planted and promptly neglected. This is a pity since well grown specimens against light coloured house or garden walls can be most attractive. They are dangerous near paths and entrances and should always be sited where they are difficult to reach. Those most commonly available have green pads with large spines. Some, such as the Barbary fig, *O. ficus-indica*, have edible fruit. One to avoid is *O. microdasys* which is really dangerous to touch and impossible to eradicate. Heights vary between 60cm/2ft to over 5m/15ft depending on the variety. The most beautiful of all is *O. violacea santa rita* which has bluish-purple blades and far less spines than others. Difficult to find except in those tiny pots of cactus collections sold widely in the Mediterranean region, but they can be grown on from these though you must be patient. *Propagation*: By seed sown at any time which does not germinate easily, or by taking a 7.5cm/3in piece, drying it off for twenty four hours and planting it in sandy soil with or without hormone rooting powder. *Pests*: New growth is much loved by rodents of all sorts – rats particularly in the S. Mediterranean.

Opuntia ficus-indica

OSTEOSPERMUM syn. DIMORPHOTHECA (*Compositae*)

All osteospermums are drought resistant and sun proof; indeed they do not thrive at all in the shade. Grown in pots they require a little more water than when in the open ground. I have seen only three of the seven species of this African daisy on sale in the Mediterranean. *Origin*: S. Africa. *Zone*: A and B. *Water*: 1. *Pruning*: Cut back season's growth by half on *O. aurantiaca* and *O. ecklonis* to encourage spreading and more flowers the next season. *Propagation*: By seed. Winter over in a cold frame if possible and plant out in final positions the following April or May.

O. aurantiaca. Star of the veldt or Cape marigold. 30–45 cm/12–18in high with bright orange daisy-like flowers with a dark brown centre. There are varieties of different colours such as 'Glistening White' which is shorter than the type and 'Las Vegas' which comes in a variety of pastel colours.

O. barberae. H 30cm/12in. Bright purple or magenta daisies with a dark central disc are produced from May until the frost. Flowers are darker purple underneath. Hardy virtually throughout the Mediterranean.

O. ecklonis. This is the most commonly seen in the region. A sub-shrub about 80cm/30in high by as much across with mid-green narrow pointed leaves. The flowers are brilliant white on top and purple underneath. The centre disc is navy blue. It flowers in April and will continue until the frost and should be given protection in the winter if the garden is at altitude. There is a prostrate form, *O. e. prostratum*.

PARAHEBE (*Scrophulariaceae*)

Closely allied to the hebes these wiry stemmed low growing evergreen shrubs are ideal for rockeries and borders. Only two species are available in the area. *Origin*: New Zealand. *Zone*: B. Although parahebes will tolerate some drought and occasional frost they then tend to lose their bottom leaves. These will re-appear in the following spring. *Water*: 2. N. Mediterranean only. *Pruning*: Tidy up and dead-head – nothing more. *Propagation*: By 5cm/2in cuttings in a mixture of peat and sand with hormone rooting powder. Keep moist at all times. They will root within two months or less. Pot on and winter over in a frost free place. Plant out in late spring. I have also divided plants and this has worked well.

P. catarractae. Only 15–22cm/6–9in high with tiny toothed leaves with pointed tips. The flowers are typical hebe spikes in white with magenta veining which open throughout the summer. The overall effect is pink rather than white.

P. lyallii is very similar to the above but more compact and has white, mauve or pink flowers. The white variety is best since the blue anthers show best against them.

PARKINSONIA (*Leguminosae*)

This is a very fast growing, deciduous S. American shrub which is so useful in desert situations that it has become acclimatized throughout N. Africa and the Middle East. *Zone*: A and it will tolerate slight frost to about -5°C/23°F and any amount of drought or torrential rains. *Water*: 1 or none. *Pruning*: None except to remove lower branches in order to get an 'umbrella' effect for shading. *Propagation*: By seed at anytime when the temperature is around 20°C/70°F. They germinate quickly and grow fast. Keep in pot until rootbound then pot on. Plant out a year later. Feed well when young otherwise give fertilizer only once in spring. *Pests*: Mealy bugs and red spider.

P. aculeata. Jerusalem thorn. In America this is known as the Mexico palo verde. H 5m/16ft with a similar crown spread. Growth is slower when older. Dangerously thorny. The vivid yellow flowers appear in May against bright green leaves with prominent midribs and the shrub is a splendid sight. In very hot weather and drought conditions the leaves drop. Irrigation quickly reverses this process.

PARROTIA (*Hamamelidaceae*)

Attractive slow growing shade tree with interesting peeling bark and amber and crimson autumn foliage. Very drought resistant once established. *Origin*: Iran. *Zone*: A. *Water*: 1. *Pruning*: None required. *Propagation*: By seed which is extremely slow and once germinated it takes at least five years before you have something big enough to plant in open ground.

P. persica. In the Mediterranean rarely reaches more than 3.6m/12ft by as much wide. There are petal-less flowers with bright red stamens in early spring just as the leaves are appearing.

PASSIFLORA (*Passifloraceae*)

A vast genus of some 500 species of climbers very few of which are available in the Mediterranean. Provided they have enough water and heat they will set fruit. With the exception of *P. caerulea* they will not tolerate frost. The are all semi-evergreen in the region. Being vigorous climbers they need strong trellis to support the annual growth. They all prefer protection from wind. *Origin*: S. America and W. Indies. *Zone*: A. *Water*: 2. *Pruning*: Severe pruning yearly in early spring to prevent leggy growth and promote flowers and fruit. Cut down by at least half and remove old and weakened stems. Feed well after pruning and again when the first flowers appear. *Propagation*: By seed kept at 21°C/70°F *all the time* until planting out well-grown seedlings in early summer when night temperatures are the same. 10cm/4in cuttings in sand and peat with a little hormone rooting compound work well. *Pests and Diseases*: Ants when rotting or fallen fruit has not been removed. Iron chlorosis can occasionally be a problem with very alkaline soil.

P. × alatocaerulea. This has very large 7.5–10cm/3–4in flowers, white flushed with pink. Used in Brazilian gardens as ground cover. Flowers in the summer for over four months.

P. caerulea. One of the most attractive, with 7.5cm/3in white flowers bearing a purple corona and prominent filaments. The fruit is yellow and oval. The variety 'Constance Elliott' is said to be even hardier than the type but it lacks the purple corona and does not set fruit.

P. edulis. Passion fruit. The flowers are very similar to *P. caerulea* but the greenish-white petals tend to hang down slightly from the lilac coloured corona. The fruit is purple and the skin quickly shrinks and becomes wrinkled. Used for ice-cream, mousses and iced drinks since the seeds are inseparable from the pulp except by sieving.

P. quadrangularis. The granadilla. If you are growing passiflora for fruit this has the best flavour. Large purple and white flowers have a deeper purple corona with prominent white and lilac filaments. A very dramatic climber. The fruits are orange/yellow, oval in shape and very sweet.

PAULOWNIA (*Scrophulariaceae*)

A genus of seventeen species of tree of which only one is on sale in the Mediterranean. Said to be hardy but many were lost in the two cold winters in the mid-1980s. *Origin*: China. *Zone*: A. *Water*: 2 but 1 when established. Best in the N. Mediterranean. Prefers slight shade in very hot gardens. *Pruning*: None needed unless stooled specimens required. *Propagation*: By 10cm/4in cuttings of lateral shoots in 50/50 peat and sand with hormone rooting compound. Alternatively pot up self-seeded seedlings. Seed sown with bottom heat also works well. Keep compost moist at all times. Very quick growing. *Pests and Diseases*: Occasional mealy bugs in late summer. Very subject to fungus problems in a wet or humid summer. Spray with systemic fungicide on a prevention basis.

Paulownia tomentosa

P. tomentosa. A quick growing tree to about 7m/22ft with large felted leaves which are mid-green and heart shaped. The flowers are purple, rather like a fox-glove, in loose panicles. This tree is frequently stooled each year to produce bedding plants with enormous leaves but no flowers.

PELARGONIUM (*Geraniaceae*)

One of the most commonly used garden plants throughout the Mediterranean. Fairly drought resistant but they do not particularly like seaside locations. There are some 400 species with at least double that number of varieties. Some are deciduous but those used in the Mediterranean are mostly ever-green. *Origin*: S. Africa. *Zone*: A. *Water*: 1. *Pruning*: Ivy-leaved geraniums can be pruned to keep tidy but the other sort should not be pruned after the second year but be discarded for new plants from cuttings. *Propagation*: Seed is best – particularly the new F.1 and F.2 hybrids. Tip cuttings about 10cm/4in long in September in a 50/50 sand and peat mixture should root within fourteen days. Pot on and protect until the outside night temperature is at least 18°C/70°F. *Pests and Diseases*: Whitefly, scale insects, red spider. Black leg (in cuttings) and other fungus diseases. Scrupulous hygiene is vital under cover. Use systemic fungicide to prevent this. The two most commonly planted are *P. peltatum* or Ivy-leaved geranium and Zonal Pelargoniums (syn. *P.* × *hortorum*). Ivy-leaved geraniums are best started with a circular support to make sure they will hang down nicely without crushing the growth underneath. People expect zonal pelargoniums to go on for ever when in fact they are fine in their first and second year but become leggy and leafless thereafter. It is best to take cuttings of a particularly loved plant in its second season. These zonal hybrids do better in slight shade in the Mediterranean giving richer coloured flowers and darker foliage marking. They will, however, produce flowers even in full sun. Excellent for pots. Geraniums do not like high nitrogen fertilizers so choose a specific proprietary fertilizer or use one suitable for tomatoes which is high in phosphorous and potassium. Deadhead at least once a week unless you want seed. Some of the zonal pelargoniums are worth growing for their foliage alone. Regal Pelargoniums have flowers of red, pink or mauve which are blotched with darker shades. They flower profusely over a period of about two or three months then suddenly stop. In cooler climes they may flower until October.

PEROVSKIA (*Labiatae*)

The Afghan sage is an ideal plant for the Mediterranean since it is hardy, drought resistant, untroubled by chalk and clay soil and is disease free. *Origin*: Afghanistan. *Zones*: All. *Water*: 1 or none. *Pruning*: Cut down to ground level in spring just before new growth begins. *Propagation*: By 7.5cm/3in cuttings in July in a 50/50 peat and sand mixture. Plant out the following spring.

P. atriplicifolia. H. 1.2–1.5m/4–5ft. A small shrub, with herbaceous incli-nations in severe winters, with grey-green highly toothed leaves which are aromatic. The rich mauve-blue flowers appear in late summer and last over two months. They are tubular and borne in 30cm/1ft panicles. 'Blue Spire' is the best variety with the richest coloured flowers. 'Blue Mist' appears too early and tends to burn in the sun.

PETREA (*Verbenaceae*)

Twining creepers and shrubs only three of which are available in the Mediterranean region. All are evergreen and dislike wind. They need good, friable soil and rich feeding. *Origin*: S. America and W. Indies. *Zone*: A. *Water*: 2. *Pruning*: None except to remove dead wood and keep tidy. Flowers on new season's growth. *Propagation*: Cuttings in 50/50 leaf mould and sand with a constant minimum temperature of 21°C/70°F. Seed can also be used and should be soaked for twenty-four hours before planting.

P. *arborea*. *Origin*: Caribbean. A small tree to about 5m/16ft with 10cm/4in elliptical leaves. Rich violet-blue tubular flowers in 15cm/6in racemes at the end of May–early June. There is a white variety that is much less attractive.

P. *racemosa*. *Origin*: Brazil. Purple wreath climber. The most commonly available in the area will grow to about 5m/16ft and will need support. Flowers are similar to P. *arborea* but in rather longer racemes.

P. *volubilis*. *Origin*: Caribbean. One of the most beautiful climbers and well worth seeking out. The tubular blue-violet flowers are held in long 30cm/12in racemes and have a heliotrope calyx which remains for a considerable time after the corollas have fallen away. With copious water this will flower twice a year in the S. Mediterranean – once in late April and again in September.

PHOENIX (*Palmae*)

Palms give an immediate tropical feeling to a garden but they involve not only considerable expense but a great deal of maintenance to look good and well cared for. *Origin*: Asia, Africa and Canary Islands. *Zone*: A. *Water*: 1 or 2 but prefer moist soil, particularly when young. Later they will stand considerable drought. *Pruning*: Annually, by a professional since it is dangerous to shin high up a tree with a pruning saw in one hand. A circle of about 1m/3ft deep should always be left on top of the trunk to support the palm fronds. *Propagation*: By offshoots which root fairly easily provided they are regularly watered and fed over a period of about three years.

P. *canariensis*. *Origin*: Canary Islands. This takes up a great deal of space but is a clean tree leaving no mess or litter so it is ideal for planting by a swimming pool. Produces no edible fruit. In the N. Mediterranean it will reach approximately 12–16m/38–51ft and has the typical feather duster palm top. By and large palms are naturally multi-trunked and have to be pruned to obtain a single straight trunk.

P. *dactylifera*. *Origin*: N. Africa and Asia. S. Mediterranean only. This palm will produce dates when it is about 10m/32ft tall. By that time the crown will be about 8m/25ft wide. Male and female trees are needed to produce fruit unless you are in a date producing area when you can purchase male pollen for pollination.

PHORMIUM *Liliaceae*

The New Zealand flaxes are valuable foliage plants with striking presence. *Origin*: New Zealand. *Zone*: All. Hardy throughout the Mediterranean. *Water*: 2 though they will survive drought conditions. They prefer to be well fed. *Pruning*: Cut out dead straps if necessary. *Propagation*: By seed which is slow and does not come true if hybrid seed is used. Alternatively division of large clumps can work well provided you nurse them through the early period.

P. cookianum. Very closely related to the following but the leaves are more arching as are the seedpods. Tall sword shaped leaves reach to approximately 2m/6ft and panicles of red flowers appear once the plant is four or five years old. There are many varieties.

P. tenax. The most commonly available, very similar to the above but straighter. The flowers are very slightly deeper red. There are purple, variegated and dwarf varieties which are more interesting than the type. Normally grows to about 3m/10ft by 1.6m/5ft across.

PHYGELIUS (*Scrophulariaceae*)

These are useful perennials for pots or borders and appear to be totally disease free. There are only two species of this S. African genus and both flower throughout the summer. *Zone*: A. *Water*: 2. *Propagation*: By division in early spring.

P. aequalis. A shrubby border plant to about 75cm/30in which has cream and orange flowers in small panicles of about 15cm/ 6in. P.a. 'Yellow Trumpets'. As above but with straw yellow flowers. Blooms profusely from June to the end of October.

P. capensis. The most commonly seen. A slightly shrubby border plant with light green leaves and brilliant scarlet tubular flowers in 30cm/12in panicles. In time it will reach over 2m/6ft.

Phygelius aequalis

PINUS (*Pinaceae*)

Evergreen coniferous trees some of which are native to the Mediterranean. Others, from elsewhere, adapt readily to a Mediterranean climate. *Origin*: N. Hemisphere. *Zone* and *Water* see individual entries. *Pruning*: None except to remove dead or damaged wood. *Propagation*: By seed which, depending on the species, germinates well or poorly. Seedlings should not be kept for more than two years before transplanting and the deformed and stunted should be thrown out. *Pests and Diseases*: Sawflies, bark beetles and pine weevils. It is a good idea to spray at least twice yearly (spring and autumn) against these pests. Various fungi attack pines though less so in the dry Mediterranean. Dieback of pine due to a fungus can be cured by removing the infected twigs or branches. Many pines have been killed or badly affected by a new bark beetle from Japan, *Mazococcus*, which enters the bark and eventually kills the tree. The disease started in France and has spread to N. Italy. Scrupulous hygiene and winter washing the bark with a tar wash or proprietary disinfectant can prevent the beetles entering. Slightly affected trees can sometimes be helped by bark-ringing and/or tree surgery which should be done only by a professional.

P. ayacahuite. *Origin*: Mexico. *Zone*: All. *Water*: 1. An attractive blue-needled pine which grows quickly to about 12m/38ft. Narrow sausage shaped cones are orange with white resin covering.

P. canariensis. *Origin*: Canary Islands. *Zone*: A. *Water*: 1 or none when established. A tall three-needled pine with 15–23cm/6–9in long cones of a vivid light brown.

P. eldarica (syn. *P. brutia eldarica* and *P. halepensis brutia*). The Quetta pine. *Origin*: S. Russia, Afghanistan and N. India. *Zone*: All. *Water*: 1 or none. *Pruning*: None. *Propagation*: By seed. New small plants are not expensive to buy. *Pests*: Aphids and bark Japanese bark beetle. One of the few pines that will grow in the S. Mediterranean basin. Similar to the Aleppo pine but it tolerates much colder weather down to -10°C/17°F. When subjected to extreme drought this pine is not an attractive sight but it is pleasant to know that with rain or artificial irrigation it will quickly recover.

P. halepensis. The Aleppo pine. *Origin*: Mediterranean. *Zone*: A and B. *Water*: 1 or none when established. A most attractive tree to about 20m/65ft with light green needles in pairs. The cones which remain on the branches for several years are about 10cm/4in long, whorled and yellowy brown. They tend to lean backwards on the branch.

P. mugo. *Origin*: C. and S. Europe. *Zone*: All. *Water*: 1. A most attractive short pine to about 5m/16ft maximum. It has grey-green needles in pairs and 5cm/2in long cones which remain on the tree for up to five years. Much seen in the dwarf varieties of which *P. m. rostata* 'Gnom' is the smallest.

P. nigra corsicana. The Corsican pine. *Origin*: Mediterranean. *Zone*: All. *Water*: 1. Attractive open branched tree to about 30m/97ft much grown in the area for timber. The dark green needles are in pairs and the cones 5–7.5cm/2–3in long end in a point.

P. pinaster. The maritime pine. *Origin*: Mediterranean. Very tall tree with wide crown. 20cm/8in needles in pairs are dark green. The solitary cones are about 15cm/6in long. Ideal to contain sandy areas. Needs properly staking in its youth.

P. pinea. The stone, or umbrella, pine. *Origin*: Mediterranean. A tall tree reaching 18m/58ft or more with a wide 'umbrella' head. Dark green needle leaves are in pairs and the cones which contain edible kernels the *pignons* or *pignoli* of commerce. Needs careful staking when young.

P. torreyana. The soledad pine. *Origin*: California and Mexico. *Zone*: A only. *Water*: 1. Drought and wind resistant. A medium sized tree to about 12m/ 38ft with attractive glaucous new growth. The needle leaves are in fives and the cones are 12cm/5in long. They mature in their third year and the kernel is edible. It is best to stake this pine well when young and feed it twice yearly.

PITTOSPORUM *Pittosporaceae*.

There are over 150 species in this genus of which only very few are available or used in the Mediterranean. All are evergreen and require slightly enriched garden soil. *Origin*: Australasia. *Zone*: A. *Water*: 2 when young, 1 once established. *Pruning*: Those species used for hedging should be clipped at least twice yearly. When used as a tree or shrub they needs little or no pruning. *Propagation*: 10cm/4in cuttings in a 50/50 mixture of sand and peat with hormone rooting compound. Shelter in winter and protect when young.

P. crassifolium. *Origin*: New Zealand. Tall shrubs, 5–7m/16–22ft, with oval, dark green leathery leaves which are felted underneath. The spring flowers are burgundy red in terminal clusters. Later there are white ovoid berries. There is a variegated variety, *P. c.* 'Variegatum', which is difficult to find.

P. 'Garnettii'. One of the most commonly seen varieties it has small, mid-green oval leaves deckle edged in white on a plant which grows to a maximum of 1.6m/5ft.

P. phillyreoides. Willow pittosporum. *Origin*: Australia. An ideal alternative to the bamboos since it needs much less water and is not at all invasive. Grows as a single trunk or multi-trunked tree at a moderate rate to about 5–7m/16–22ft. The willow-like grey-green leaves are about 10cm/4in long. Useful and unusual as a drive tree. Will tolerate a little frost.

P. tobira. *Origin*: China and Japan. Used as hedging, to the point of boredom, in the N. Mediterranean, this shrub will eventually reach 3m/10ft or more by half as much across. As a neglected and underfed hedging plant it rarely reaches half that height and breadth. It has dark green shining oval leaves and terminal clusters of pale cream flowers which are pleasantly scented. Properly grown it can be most attractive. There is a variegated form, *P. t.* 'Variegatum'.

PLUMBAGO (*Plumbaginaceae*)

Origin: Cape Province, S. Africa. *Zone*: A. *Water*: 2. Will not tolerate frost or low temperature unless very well established. *Pruning*: None needed unless used as hedging. *Propagation*: By seed which germinates easily and flowers in the first year. *Diseases*: Iron chlorosis.

P. auriculata (syn. *P. capensis*). H 1.2–2.5m/4–8ft. Beautiful climbing shrub which can be trained to hang down walls or cover pillars. It has clusters of celestial blue flowers about 1.8cm/¾in across. Ideal for softening the harsh magenta of bougainvillea. Needs fortnightly feeding with well balanced fertilizer. There is a white version which simply looks washed out compared with the blue. Produces the richest coloured flowers in reflected sun. It is frequently clipped and used as a hedge.

PROSOPIS (*Leguminosae*)

The mesquites are useful trees, many from the arid regions   *Plumbago auriculata*
of S. America but one is native to Asia. This is occasionally
for sale in the S. Mediterranean. Usually *P. juliflora* and *P. spicigera* are seen. *Zone*: A – will not tolerate any frost until fully grown but will take cold winds. *Water*: 1 or none. *Pruning*: Needs frequent trimming to get the shape you want. Wood makes excellent charcoal. *Propagation*: By seed which germinates and grows easily.

P. juliflora. *Origin*: Arizona and south to Chile. Grows to about 10m/32ft in the Mediterranean and has a wide crown of about 7m/22ft. The leaves are bipinnate and a brilliant emerald green when young becoming slightly blue with age. The flowers are yellow and hang in racemes followed by golden pods. Never plant near a building as the tap root can damage foundations in its search for water. Fast growing.

P. spicigera. *Origin*: Arabian Peninsula. The best mesquite for desert conditions as it puts down a tap root of over 25m/8oft to get water. Identical to the above except that it is taller at some 15–20m/48–65ft and has reddish-brown pods which are curved. It is rather slow growing.

PRUNUS (*Rosaceae*)

A very large genus of almost 200 species of shrubs and trees including the almond, apricot, cherry, plum, peach and Portugal laurel. Most are deciduous; very few are evergreen. All grow well in the N. Mediterranean but all, with the possible exception of the apricot, are very susceptible to peach leaf curl caused by the fungus *Taphrina deformans* and/or red spider. Otherwise they are more or less trouble free. Species from Europe and Asia tend to do rather better than those from N. America but this is a generalization that can easily be proved wrong since *P. maritima* grows extremely well in many Mediterranean gardens.

PUNICA (*Punicaceae*)

The pomegranate is much cultivated in the Mediterranean region for its brilliant flowers and attractive fruit. Needs a coldish winter to have good fruit. *Origin*: Middle East to Afghanistan. *Zone*: All. *Water*: 1 or none. *Pruning*: None unless used as hedging. *Propagation*: By 10cm/4in cuttings with a heel in 50/50 sand and peat mixture with hormone rooting compound in autumn. Keep at a winter temperature of at least 18°C/65°F.

P. granatum. A medium tree to about 3m/10ft with a spread of about 2m/6ft. The clusters of scarlet tubular flowers appear from April until July followed by yellow/orange fruits with a leathery skin. The inside pulp is rich crimson and full of seeds. *P. g. flora-pleno* is a form with red double flowers. Sets some fruit. *P. g. nana* is a dwarf version, 1m/3ft high, much used for hedging. It does not set fruit.

P. g. legrellii (syn. *P. g.* 'Madame Legrelle'). One of the most attractive pomegranates in cultivation this 4m/13ft shrub has coral red and white striped flowers which are slightly deeper coral in the bud. Flowers in June and July. It has no fruit but is very hardy.

Punica granatum

QUERCUS (*Fagaceae*)

The oak. Apart from the very widely grown oaks such as the Turkey oak (*Q. cerris*), the English oak (*Q. robur*) and the American red oak (*Q. rubra*) there are two Mediterranean natives especially worth growing.

Q. ilex. The holm oak. *Zone*: A and B. *Water*: 2 when young, 1 thereafter. Unfussy about soil or position. Normally seen as a shrub on waste land, properly grown this can make a beautiful, tall (20m/65ft) tree. The small, oval, evergreen leaves are 2.5–7.5/1–3in long, glossy dark green on top and pale and downy below. A small pyramid in youth the tree develops a fine crown in age. Pest and disease free.

Q. suber. Cork oak. *Zone*: A. *Water*: 2 when young, 1 when adult (i.e. when 7.5m/23ft high). Prefers spaced deep irrigation. Will tolerate occasional frost. Another evergreen oak with small, toothed dark green leaves, green on top and grey underneath. Very slow growing but well worth the wait. The bark, which produces the cork of commerce, is soft, deeply furrowed and greyish-brown. The site needs careful preparation as it will not tolerate chalk or over alkaline soil. Thereafter you need to add humus. *Pruning*: None. Pest and disease free.

QUISQUALIS (*Combretaceae*)

The Rangoon creeper is a most attractive semi-climbing shrub. *Origin*: S. India and tropical Asia. *Zone*: A. *Water*: 3 with occasional syringeing in very dry weather. *Pruning*: At the end of the season cut down by at least two-thirds. During the season the plant can be pinched out to encourage spread and flowering. *Propagation*: By short cuttings with a heel in a mixture of 75/25 peat and sand with bottom heat if necessary. In any event the heat should never drop below 21°C/70°F.

Q. indica. This is best grown in pots and allowed to weep over a circular support or to climb round a fountain or statue. It requires rich, peaty soil with fortnightly feeding. The flowers begin very pale pink and turn to rich crimson as they age. They come in clusters and have a very long calyx tube. The leaves are mid-green, slightly hairy and thin, long and entire. Except in the S. Mediterranean these plants should be given winter protection and not be put out before night temperatures are at least 21°C/70°F.

RAPHIOLEPIS (*Rosaceae*)

Useful evergreen shrubs with pale pink or white flowers usually in terminal racemes. *Origin*: China. *Zone*: A and B. *Water*: 2. *Pruning*: Only *R. umbellata* needs regular pruning to keep it tidy. *Propagation*: By 7.5cm/3in cuttings in late summer in 50/50 peat and sand with hormone rooting powder. They take about six months to root.

R. × delacourii. A 2m/6ft high French hybrid of the two following, and better than either. Usually, though not always, flowers in late May/early June but occasionally as early as March and as late as August. The leaves are thick, leathery about 7.5cm/3in long and the flowers are rich pink in erect, terminal panicles. In very alkaline conditions it is inclined to lose its lower leaves. Watering and feeding well should rectify this.

R. indica. Indian hawthorn. Rather shorter at 1m/3ft this shrub has similar but smaller leaves and flowers than the above. It is very tender and in the N. Mediterranean needs winter protection.

R. umbellata. A tall shrub, 2–3m/6–9ft, with the typical leathery leaves but white flowers. Hardy throughout the Mediterranean and the most drought resistant of the three.

RHODODENDRON (*Ericaceae*)

N. Mediterranean only. *Zone*: B and C. *Water*: 3. Although it is possible to grow the dwarf sort of rhododendron in pots it is not recommended for the beginner since it requires a great deal of time and care to achieve good results. Use only pure peat and purchased leaf mould which is available throughout the area in garden centres. Dose at regular intervals with Sequestrene 138 Fe unless you happen to have acid soil and non-alkaline water which is very unlikely. The following dwarf species which mostly come from China or Tibet as well as their cultivars will all do well in semi-shade in the summer but full or reflected sun at flowering time. Change the soil at least once a year – more often if salts appear round the rim of the pot – and feed with a balanced fertilizer once a month. All flower between March and May. *Pruning*: None. *Propagation*: Only layering works really well in the Mediterranean. Allow at least a year before severing the plant from its parent. *Pests and Diseases*: Whiteflies, caterpillars. Chlorosis.

    R. calostrotum keleticum. Origin: China. H 30cm/12in. Mauve-pink funnel shaped flowers.

    R. campylogynum. Origin: China and Tibet. H 30–60cm/1–2ft. Mauve bell flowers.

    R. forrestii. Origin: China. H 30cm/12in. Crimson bell flowers.

    R. impeditum. Origin: China. H 15–45cm/6–18in. Blue-purple funnel shaped flowers.

    R. leucaspis. Origin: China and Tibet. 30–60cm/12–24in. Shallow 5cm/2in wide white flowers. Very tender to spring frost.

    R. pemakoense. Origin: Tibet. H 30–60cm/12–24in. Rich mauve funnel shaped flowers.

    R. saluense. Origin: China. 45–60cm/18–24in. Wide funnel flowers in various shades of mauve and purple with darker blotches.

    R. tsangpoense. Origin: Tibet. H 30–60cm/12–24in. Pinkish purple bell flowers.

    R. yakushimanum. Origin: Japan. H 60cm/2ft. Pale pink funnel flowers. There are many cultivars of this species available though not always in the Mediterranean region itself. It is very hardy.

RHUS (*Anarcardiaceae*)

Useful quick growing drought resistant trees. *Origin*: Africa and United States. *Zones*: All. *Water*: 1. *Pruning*: R. typhina can be pruned to the ground in January or February if very large (45cm/18in) and decorative leaves are wanted. Otherwise just cut back by a maximum of one third. *Propagation*: By suckers which are plentifully produced. Alternatively half ripe 10cm/4in cuttings can be taken and put in a 50/50 peat and sand mixture with hormone rooting powder, in July or August, and kept in the shade until late October. They should root by the following season. Keep plants at around 18°C/65°F. *Diseases*: Fungus diseases like the soft new growth. Spray for prevention.

    R. lancea. African sumach. A wonderful evergreen shade tree which will grow virtually anywhere in the Mediterranean though it may be deciduous in the northern part. Grows to about 7m/22ft but has a huge 10m/32ft canopy. The 7.5cm/3in leaves are three-lobed narrow and pointed.

    R. typhina. Stag's horn sumach. Height 3–5m/10–16ft with a spread of about 5m/16ft if allowed to grow to maximum height. The leaves are dark green and pinnate. Small pink flowers in cones are followed by crimson fruits. *R. l. laciniata* is very similar but with deeper cut leaves and richer autumn colouring.

ROBINIA (*Leguminosae*)

Useful deciduous drought resistant trees with attractive foliage. *Origin*: United States. *Zone*: All. *Water*: 1. *Pruning*: None except to keep to desired shape or height. *Propagation*: By seed which germinates and grows easily. Plant out when a year old. *Pests*: Red spider and scale insects.

R. hispida. Rose acacia. A relatively short shrub of some 2–2.5m/6–8ft which has dark green pinnate leaves and bright pink flowers in pendent racemes in April and May.

R. kelseyi. Similar to the above but has sharp spines at leaf nodes. Usually seen as a trained standard. The pink flowers are slightly darker and appear in June.

R. pseudoacacia. Common or false acacia. This is a tall tree, to 25m/80ft, with very brittle wood so it should be staked until it is at least five years old. Pale green pinnate leaves and vicious thorns. The flowers are rich cream in 15cm/6in racemes. Useful as it is very quick growing. *R. p.* 'Frisia' has early foliage which is bright yellow becoming yellow-green with age. *R. p.* 'Umbraculifera', the mophead acacia, has no flowers or thorns. Useful formal tree.

ROMNEYA (*Papaveraceae*)

The Californian tree-poppy. *Origin*: California. *Zone*: A and B. *Water*: 1. *Propagation*. By seeds sown in early spring at a minimum heat of 16°C/60°F. Continue in the pot for one year and plant in final positions in the following late spring.

R. coulteri. A charming plant, usually cut down in winter, with grey-green deeply lobed leaves and white poppy-like flowers with vivid yellow centres. Flowers from the end of May to September. They can be very invasive in good soil but resent root disturbance and transplanting usually spells death unless the root-ball is absolutely intact. They like full sun and well fertilized soil. *R. c.* 'White Cloud' is a slightly larger and hardier version of the above.

ROSMARINUS (*Labiatae*)

The rosemaries are attractive, evergreen shrubs which are very drought resistant. Useful for low hedges. *Origin*: Mediterranean. *Zone*: All. *Water*: 1 or none. *Pruning*: None unless to keep tidy or as hedge. *Propagation*: Rosemaries self-seed easily and these can be transplanted during winter. Alternatively 10cm/4in cuttings taken in late summer with a heel in 50/50 sand and peat with hormone rooting powder should root within twelve weeks. Plant in final positions in late autumn.

R. × *lavandulaceus.* A prostrate mat-forming shrub with a spread of 2m/6ft. The linear-oblong leaves are lighter green than the ordinary rosemary but the flowers are the same mauve and produced in profusion from April to June.

R. officinalis. Common rosemary. This can become a tall shrub to 2.5m/8ft if allowed but can be clipped. Dark green leaves and bright mauve flowers in late spring. *R. o. alba* is a white-flowered form. There are many varieties of rosemary which are all rather similar whose names vary from country to country.

RUSSELLIA (*Scrophulariaceae*)

Only two species of this attractive genus are grown in the Mediterranean. They have tubular flowers and revel in full sunshine. They need regular grooming to look good. *Origin*: Mexico. *Zone*: A. Will not tolerate temperatures under about 21°C/70°F. *Water*: 2. *Pruning*: Dead head frequently and cut hard back in September/October to encourage strong new growth next season. *Propagation*: Short cuttings with a heel in late summer in very sandy soil with hormone rooting compound. Keep in semi-shade until rooted – about six weeks. *Pests and Diseases*: Red spider, scale insects. Iron chlorosis.

Rosmarinus officinalis

R. juncea. The most commonly seen russelia which has fine grass like foliage and scarlet tubular flowers, from May onwards, on a plant less than 1m/3ft tall. For best effect, it should always be planted where it can hang down.

R. sarmentosa. An uncommon leafy shrub about 1.2–1.8m/4–6ft high with vivid pink flowers in June, quite different from the above.

Russellia juncea

RUTA (*Rutaceae*)

For the Mediterranean region only two varieties of
rue can be recommended as really garden worthy.
They both have attractive divided leaves
and tubular violet flowers in June. *Origin*: Mediterranean. *Zone*: All. *Water*:
1. Grow in half-shade. *Pruning*: Clip
each year and pinch out new
shoots to encourage bushiness.
Propagation: By seeds in early
spring which should give plants
for setting out in September.

R. *graveolens* 'Jackman's Blue'. A small sub-
shrub about 45cm/18in tall with deeply divided
blue grey foliage. R. *g*. 'Variegata' has green and
white foliage and tends to flower sparsely which
can be an advantage.

Ruta graveolens

SCHINUS (*Anarcardiaceae*)

False pepper tree. Highly decorative trees of
weeping or canopy habit with finely cut ferny
foliage and small yellow flowers in spring. Fe-
male trees have coral red berries which can be used as a form of pepper.
Origin: S. America. *Zone*: A and B. *Water*: 1. Drought resistant once established.
Pruning: None. These trees have very brittle wood when young and are subject
to wind rock. Damaged wood should be removed. *Propagation*: By seed (inside
very ripe peppers) which germinates erratically.

S. *molle*. A small tree to about 6.5m/20ft with very pinnate foliage and
brilliant red peppers on the female trees which are the only sort usually on
sale. Useful as a lining tree for driveways or as a shade tree for a small patio
or courtyard.

S. *terebinthifolius*. Brazilian pepper tree. Similar to the above but shorter (to
5m/16ft) and with smaller, pinnate leaves. Makes a larger canopy than S.
molle so can used in larger spaces as shade tree. More easily damaged by
cold.

SCHIZANTHUS (*Solanaceae*)

These annuals are much used in Mediterranean gardens and are all varieties
of either S. *grahamii* or S. *pinnatus*. Seed should be sown in autumn to ensure
a spring flowering and should be kept at a constant temperature of 10°C/
50°F though higher temperatures will not harm. Do not aim for summer
flowering since the intense heat will ensure a shorter flowering period. It is

174

best to stake the plants since spring is a windy season. They are excellent for pots. *Origin*: Chile. *Zone*: A. *Water*: 2. *Propagation*: By seed. *Diseases*: Very subject to fungus problems.

The main colours of the flowers which are more or less tubular with a medium-long calyx and are in racemes on 45cm/18in plants are pink, red, mauve, purple and white. They are readily available in pots throughout the spring flowering period for those who would like to try them without going to the trouble of growing them from seed.

SCHIZOSTYLIS (*Iridaceae*)

Dramatic red-flowered plants which are hardy throughout the Mediterranean. *Origin*: S. Africa. *Zone*: All. *Water*: 1. *Propagation*: By division of the rhizomatous clumps which will quickly form if good soil is provided. *Diseases*: Inclined to fungus problems.

S. coccinea. The Kaffir lily or crimson flag is the only species commonly found in the Mediterranean. Just over 1m/3ft tall with sword shaped leaves, bearing twelve to fifteen brilliantly scarlet flowers in late autumn. Excellent for pots but needs some support. Flowers are quickly ruined by rainy weather but will happily grow on a warm, sunny veranda. There is a pink variety also.

SESBANIA (*Leguminosae*)

Properly grown this can be a most attractive and rapidly achieved plant with yellow or orange flowers which are often fried and eaten in the Middle East and India. Extremely tolerant of salt laden soil and often used as green manure. *Origin*: Middle East. *Zone*: A. Will not tolerate low temperatures or frost. *Water*: 1. *Pruning*: None. *Propagation*: By seed which germinates rapidly.

S. aegyptica. H 4m/13ft. Attractive pale yellow pea-type flowers from March to May onwards depending on temperature. Grows very rapidly and provides a quick screen. Seeds profusely.

SETCREASEA (*Commelinaceae*)

This plant is grown purely for its decorative foliage and weeping habit. *Origin*: Mexico. *Zone*: A. Will not tolerate frost or temperatures below 10°C/50°F. *Water*: 1. *Pruning*: This plant constantly produces offsets and can get leggy so should be cut back from time to time to keep a tidy effect. *Propagation*: By planting offsets in a 50/50 mixture of peat and sandy. They will root within a fortnight. *Pests and Diseases*: Mealy bugs. Occasional fungus diseases due to humid weather.

S. purpurea (syn. *S. pallida*). Purple heart. 15cm/6in long leaves of a rich aubergine purple. They are narrow and pointed and have fine silky hairs on both sides. The stems are long and trailing. Ideal for planting on top of walls to hang down or as ground cover. Flowers are insignificant and should not be allowed to form on properly tended plants.

S. striata. Slightly shorter trailing stems and much shorter pointed oval leaves, about 4cm/1½in long. These are striped green and yellow above and are slightly purple underneath. A most attractive plant but less sturdy than *S. purpurea.*

SISYRINCHIUM (*Iridaceae*)

Herbaceous perennials which are ideal for rock gardens, wild gardens and pots. *Zone*: All. *Water*: 1. *Propagation*. By seed which germinates easily. Plant in final position one year later. Self-sown seedlings abound. These can be transplanted. Established clumps can be divided and replanted during the dormant season.

S. bermudiana. Origin: Bermuda and E. United States. H 10–15cm/8–12in. An ideal plant for the rock garden it has sword shaped leaves and mid-blue starry flowers in May. Loves poor soil and full sun.

S. brachypus. Origin: S. America. A tiny 15cm/6in plant with iris like pale green leaves and brilliant yellow flowers which stand away from the plant. These are borne in succession from May to the end of September.

S. striatum. Origin: Peru and Chile. The most commonly seen in the Mediterranean, has strap shaped leaves and pale yellow flowers with a darker yellow centre, covering half the stem. The height is about 30–40cm/12–16in depending on the soil. Most attractive when in flower but it should be dead headed promptly.

SOLANUM (*Solanaceae*)

A vast genus of well over 1000 species which include edible plants such as the potato, aubergine and tomato, and others that are deadly poisonous. Those mentioned here are all decorative plants and all from S. America. *Zone*: A and occasionally B where evergreens may become deciduous. *Water*: 1 and 2. *Pruning*: Cut *S. jasminoides* and *S. pensile* almost to the ground at the end of the flowering season. The shrubs need pruning only to keep within bounds. *Propagation*: By 10cm/4in cuttings in 50/50 sand and rich loam kept constantly moist. Hormone rooting powder helps but is not essential. Let plenty of roots form before planting out in final position. They will not flower until two or three seasons later. *Diseases*: Although solanums are supposed to be subject to many fungus diseases as well as tobacco ringspot virus (Nicotiana virus) I have never seen any touched by disease in the Mediterranean nor has any nurseryman I know. Presumably we are very fortunate since fungus problems can be legion in the area. There is no cure for Nicotiana virus but the fungus diseases can be cured by careful and constant spraying.

S. crispum. Origin: Chile. A scrambling deciduous sub-shrub of about 5m/

Stephanotis

16ft in both directions. It has light purple flowers in corymbs non-stop from early summer to late autumn. *S. c.* 'Glasnevin', although an Irish cultivar, is ideal for altitude in the Mediterranean region. Identical to the above except that the flowers are a richer colour.

S. jasminoides. Origin: S. America. The potato vine. As its name suggests it has white potato like flowers and climbs like a jasmine. Two varieties exist which are more attractive than the type; *S. j. floribundum* has more flowers and *S. j. grandiflorum* has larger racemes.

S. pensile. Origin: Guyana. Rather more attractive than *S. jasminoides*, with slightly darker 7.5cm/3in leaves and amethyst flowers with a white star in the centre. Fruit occasionally forms in the Mediterranean after the climber has become established and this is an interesting pale violet as opposed to the normal yellow. They are about the size of a small damson.

S. rantonneti. Origin: Paraguay. A wonderful small shrub to about 1.6m/5ft with rich dark green slightly glabrous leaves which are furry underneath. The flowers are vivid violet with yellow centres and produced from May to October. Absolutely trouble free and one of the most attractive garden shrubs.

S. wendlandii. Origin: Costa Rica. This is only for the fortunate gardener with an unfailing source of water. It needs copious irrigation, rich balanced feeding and occasional syringeing. Climbs to over 7m/22ft has a mixture of pinnate and lobed leaves which are very bright green and between 15–22.5cm/6–10in long. 15cm/6in panicles of lilac flowers weigh down the branches in late summer. One of the most beautiful solanums but very, very tender.

STEPHANOTIS (*Asclepiadaceae*)

A very decorative climber to about 5m/16ft with dark shining leathery leaves and white waxy flowers. Plant in rich neutral or slightly acid loam. There are those who find the smell overpowering to the point of giving a headache rather as with gardenias. *Origin*: Madagascar. *Zone*: A. Will not tolerate even slight frost and needs a winter temperature of 10°C/50°F. *Water*: 3 to look good but will survive on weekly waterings. *Pruning*: At the end of January remove all weak, straggly growth and clip back leading shoots by half – they will quickly grow again. *Propagation*: By 10cm/4in cuttings in rich, well draining loam with hormone rooting compound. These should be taken from non-flowering shoots in early spring when the temperature is at least 18°C/65°F. It is common for 50% of the cuttings not to form roots. *Pests and Diseases*: Stephanotis seems to be plagued by virtually every pest in the Mediterranean from whitefly to scale as well as root mealy bugs which inhibit growth. The best prevention is a systemic insecticide at fourteen day intervals or more often if necessary. Occasional chlorosis can be a problem where irrigation water is very alkaline.

S. floribunda. Climbs to rather more than 3m/10ft and has rich green broadly oval leaves. The 4cm/1½in long tubular flowers come in groups of six to eight in panicles. They are heavily scented.

STRELITZIA (*Strelitziaceae*)

Very showy herbaceous plants which are also useful for pots. They should be grown in slight shade and never in direct sun which scorches the leaves. Both the species described below flower once the temperature reaches 21°C/70°C with approximately a four-month rest between periods of flowering. *Origin*: S. Africa. *Zone*: A. *Water*: 2. *Propagation*: By offsets which should be rooted at the time of detaching. Alternatively by seed kept at a constant temperature of 21°C/70°F or slightly more.

S. parviflora (syn. *S. juncea*). The flowers are blue and yellow in the shape of a crested bird's head and the leaves are very narrow bladed. The whole plant is rather more attractive than the more common *S. reginae*. Unless you are very lucky and find a plant you will have to raise this from seed but it is worth the trouble.

S. reginae. Bird of paradise flower, crane flower. Vivid orange, blue and white flowers in the shape of a crested bird's head on a 6ocm/2ft stalk with large banana like leaves.

STREPTOSOLEN (*Solanaceae*)

A genus consisting of one most attractive evergreen flowering shrub. *Origin*: Colombia. *Zone*: A and B. Will tolerate slight frost once established but should be mulched in colder areas. May lose its leaves. *Water*: 2. Needs fortnightly weak feeding. *Pruning*: The shrubs can get leggy with age and should be cut down to within 30cm/1ft of the ground. They will then regenerate. Otherwise confine pruning to cutting outdead and damaged wood. *Propagation*: 10cm/4in cuttings of lateral non-flowering shoots in well draining compost. Keep at a constant temperature around 18°C/65°F. They need to be potted on at least twice before planting out in the open.

Strelitzia reginae

S. jamesonii. To about 1.8m/6ft high and wide with mid-green ovate leaves about 5cm/2in long. The brilliant orange tubular flowers are produced in terminal panicles from the beginning of May to the end of July.

TAMARIX (*Tamaricaceae*)

Very useful, deciduous wind-resistant shrubs for informal planting. Salt tolerant but they do not like very alkaline soil. *Origin*: Both species mentioned are Mediterranean natives. *Zone*: All. *Water*: 1 or none. *Pruning*: To keep plants bush remove at least half if not two-thirds of the previous season's growth. *Propagation*: 22.5cm/9in hardwood cuttings in a 75/25 sand and soil mixture. Grow in the open. When rooted transplant to a nursery bed and grow on for a year before planting out in final position.

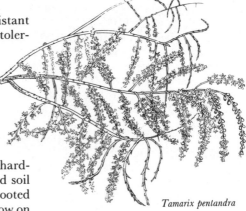

Tamarix pentandra

T. pentandra. Slightly glaucous foliage, reaches about 4m/13ft in height and wide, with long feathery racemes of tiny pale pink flowers in July. Ideal hedging plant.

T. tetrandra. Slightly shorter than the former and flowers in late April/early May on the previous season's wood so it should be pruned immediately after flowering. The foliage is also slightly paler than that of *T. pentandra*.

TECOMA (*Bignoniaceae*)

A genus which has contracted considerably in recent times having lost many of its species to *Tecomaria*, *Bignonia* and *Pandorea*. Only one remains which is commonly planted in the warmer parts of the Mediterranean. Should be given weak liquid fertilizer every two weeks. *Origin*: Caribbean and Mexico to Peru. *Zone*: A. Needs a minimum winter temperature of 10°C/50°F. *Water*: 1. *Pruning*: Cut back the previous season's growth by about a half; the laterals can be reduced to about 10cm/4in in January. *Propagation*: By short cuttings of non-flowering shoots in April. Use a 50/50 sand and peat potting mix with hormone rooting compound. Once a root system has established pinch out the new growth to make a bushy plant. Plant in final position in autumn.

T. stans. A climber to about 4m/13ft by about 3m/9ft wide. The leaves pale green and pinnate and it has yellow funnel shaped flowers borne in 20cm/8in racemes from the beginning of June until September. Very attractive and easier to accommodate than orange or magenta climbers.

THUNBERGIA (*Acanthaceae*)

Attractive, vigorous climbers which are all rather tender. Excellent in pots. *Pruning*: Only to tidy up since too heavy pruning leads to loss of flowers. *Propagation*: By seeds except for *T. grandiflora* from which you should take short stem cuttings and place them in a 50/50 peat and sand mixture with hormone rooting powder. Keep at a constant temperature of 21°C/70°F until rooted, then either pot on or put into final position.

T. alata. Origin: S. Africa. Black-eyed Susan. An easily grown annual to about 3m/10ft, which has dark centred, bright orange flowers backed by a purple tube. Flowers throughout the summer.

T. coccinea. Origin: N. India. Rich red flowers in racemes throughout early winter. Does not like full sun and needs protection from wind. In good conditions grows to almost 7m/22ft.

T. grandiflora. Origin: N. India. The most beautiful of the genus with violet blue tubular flowers and handsome evergreen leaves. H 6.5m/20ft. Flowers from late May until beginning of August, occasionally later.

T. gregorii (syn. *T. gibsonii*). *Origin*: S. and E. Africa. Very similar to *T. alata* but has triangular deep green leaves and richer coloured orange flowers. Can be grown as an annual.

TIBOUCHINA (*Melastomataceae*)

Although the genus has more than 200 species only one is generally grown. It is excellent for pots but tender and needs some shade in high summer. *Origin*: Brazil. *Zone*: A. *Water*: 3. *Pruning*: Plants should be cut back hard in January or early February. If grown in a border the plants can be cut back by about half and the lateral shoots to the second set of two leaves. *Propagation*: Take short cuttings of lateral growth in March. Root them in a 50/50 sand and peat mixture with hormone rooting compound. Pot on once roots have formed and put in final position (or pots) once the laterals are about 10cm/4in long. Keep pinching to encourage bushy growth.

T. urvilleana (syn. *T. semidecandra*). This can grow to over 5m/16ft in perfect conditions but it is more usually seen half that height. The leaves are deep green, veined and velvety often becoming bright red. The deep velvety purple saucer shaped flowers are 10cm/4in across. Should be fed once a fortnight from just before flowering in May until September. Thereafter, keep the soil just moist. Protect from the wind.

TRACHELOSPERMUM (*Apocynaceae*)

Attractive, evergreen climbers and hardy throughout the Mediterranean. They are all self-clinging. All need neutral to acid soil so dig out a large planting hole and fill with

Tibouchina urvilleana

a peat based compost. Top dress annually with peat or leafmould. Give occasional Sequestrene 138 Fe to be on the safe side. *Origin*: E. Asia. *Zone*: All. *Water*: 2, 1 once established. *Pruning*: None needed unless you wish to restrict growth. *Propagation*: Layering is the only thing which works in the Mediterranean and this should be done in late October, early November. Wait one year before severing from parent plant. *Pests and Diseases*: Aphids like young spring growth. Iron chlorosis.

T. asiaticum. H 6m/20ft and similar spread. Deep green narrow ovate leaves and 2.5cm/1in white, fragrant flowers in cymes are produced in June–August. The flowers become dark cream with age.

T. jasminoides. Known as Madagascar jasmine in France. The most commonly planted of this genus. Rather slow to start. Although the flowers are virtually identical to *T. asiaticum* it is shorter and the leaves are paler green and often slightly hairy. Slightly less vigorous and shorter than the above.

T. majus. The hardiest of the genus. Grows to over 7m/22ft and has very dark green foliage which becomes rich red in late autumn. The pure white flowers are unscented. This will cover vast expanses of bare wall.

TRACHYCARPUS (*Palmae*)

Chusan fan palm. Very decorative low-growing palms which are hardy throughout the Mediterranean. They are usefully planted where other palms would be a doubtful proposition. *Origin*: China. *Zone*: All. *Water*: 1. *Pruning*: None needed except to remove damaged growth. *Propagation*: Remove basal suckers and plant them in a mixture of sand and good garden loam. Wait for at least two years before potting on or planting out.

T. fortunei. This will reach 3m/10ft but normally it is seen at around 2m/6ft by as much across. In absolutely perfect conditions it can reach 10m/32ft after thirty years, but this is rare. The mid-green leaves are pleated into a fan shape and the stalks are very prickly. On older specimens panicles of yellow flowers appear in May. Very occasionally these flowers are followed by round black fruits (not edible). Any well drained soil will do but Chusan palms become straw coloured when damaged by wind. When young they are good for pots but later the root system is too big to accommodate in anything but open ground.

UGNI (*Myrtaceae*)

Chilean guava. This is still called *Myrtus ugni* throughout the Mediterranean. *Origin*: Chile. *Zone*: All. *Water*: 1. *Pruning*: None needed except to remove dead or damaged wood. *Propagation*: By short lateral, non-flowering shoots in a 50/50 peat and sand mixture with hormone rooting compound. Keep minimum temperature about 10°C/50°F. Pot on when rooted and plant out a year later.

U. molinae (syn. *Myrtus ugni*). This evergreen shrub has rather a stiff, erect habit and grows, slowly, to about 2m/6ft. Dark leathery leaves and waxy pink bell shaped flowers in late April–early May. Small berries, about the size of a pea, form and when ripe are a rich mahogany and taste delicious.

VIBURNUM (*Caprifoliaceae*)

A large genus of over 200 species of woody plants both deciduous and evergreen. Many come from Chile and Japan which often means they can only be grown in the N. Mediterranean due to lack of moist, rich soil. In any event it is best not to plant them in full sun or in thin, dry soil. Protect from wind and sun after early morning frost which can damage new growth. *Zone*: All. Hardy throughout the Mediterranean. *Pruning*: The winter flowering species should be pruned more or less immediately after flowering and the summer flowering species in June. *Propagation*: Layering is best and this should be done in September, severing the following year. This works particularly well with the horizontal types such as *V. carlesii*, *V. davidii* and *V. plicatum*.

V. betulifolium. Origin: China. H 3m/10ft and spread the same. Deciduous, with white flowers in 7.5cm/3in corymbs in April–May which should be followed by berries but seldom are.

V. × burkwoodii. Origin: China. An evergreen hybrid, to about 3m/10ft with a similar spread. Attractive pink buds open to scented white flowers early March–May. It is worth trying to obtain the English 'Park Farm Hybrid' since the habit is slightly less stiff and the flowers are larger.

V. carlesii. Origin: Korea. H and S 1.6m/5ft. Best to buy some of the named varieties such as 'Aurora' (or the similar 'Charis') with red buds and pink flowers or 'Diana' with paler pink flowers. All are richly scented.

V. davidii. Origin: China. A most attractive low-growing evergreen shrub but suitable only for raised beds or pot work since it needs shade and neutral to acid soil. H 90cm/3ft, S 1.8m/6ft. Flat heads of white flowers in June followed, if you have both male and female plants, by turquoise berries in early winter.

V. opulus. Origin: Europe and N. America. Deciduous with flat heads of richly scented white flowers in early summer. The variety 'Sterile' is known as the snowball bush. *V. o.* 'Xanthocarpum' flowers in the same way but has brilliant yellow berries in autumn.

V. plicatum. Origin: China and Japan. Attractive tiered, horizontal habit, up to 3m/9ft, with good autumn colouring. 7.5cm/3in white flowers in May. Allow at least 4m/12ft planting distance.

V. tinus. Origin: Mediterranean. Evergreen shrub to 3m/10ft, occasionally much taller. White flowers in small flat heads November–Christmas, followed by gunmetal blue berries. Many cultivars including a golden variegated one. An undemanding, trouble-free shrub.

VIRGILIA (*Leguminosae*)

Bloom tree. Although not generally available in commerce it is extremely easy to grow this tree from seed and have it in flower within three or four years. It needs light, well draining soil so when planting add plenty of leafmould and sand to the planting hole. Wood is brittle in youth. *Origin*: Cape Province, S. Africa. *Zone*: A. Will not stand frost. *Water*: 2. *Pruning*: None needed except to remove damaged wood. *Propagation*: Seed.

V. capensis. A tree up to 10m/32ft in its native habitat but probably half that in the Mediterranean area. The leaves are pinnate, about 15cm/6in long with many leaflets which appear ferny in a breeze. Clusters of pea-flowers in 15cm/6in in racemes in May. Although the overall effect is pale pinky mauve in fact the flowers are white, pink or purple.

WASHINGTONIA (*Palmaceae*)

Tall fan palms one of which is ideal for mixing with the shorter chamaerops or trachycarpus to give variety. However, it becomes very large when adult so is only for spacious gardens. *Origin*: California. *Zone*: A. *Water*: 1. *Pruning*: Once fully grown annual pruning to remove 'thatch' is for a professional. When young – they stay small for a long time – the dead thatch should be removed. To a degree washingtonias are self-pruning i.e. their old fronds drop off. However, as they grow older they appear to get lazier and need help. Always remove fruit when dry – it is not edible. *Propagation*: By seed which germinates in about two months. Small palms in pots can be used as decoration for many years.

W. filifera. Although usually seen around 7–10m/22–32ft this palm can grow to 26m/84ft in time so choose its position carefully. Several grown in a grove in the distance can be most attractive in an area where water is short.

W. robusta. This Mexican native should not be planted since it will reach 30m/97ft quickly. It has a large canopy head which can easily touch electricity lines. The cost of professional pruning would be exorbitant.

WIGANDIA (*Hydrophyllaceae*)

For years I wondered why this beautiful mauve climber was not more commonly planted in the N. Mediterranean since it takes no more water than, for example, mandevilla. I then discovered that it is covered with stinging hairs and has to be handled with gloves. Otherwise it presents no problems. It can also be grown as a bedding plant, flowering at only 1m/3ft high. *Origin*: S. and C. America from Mexico to Colombia. *Zone*: A. Does not like temperatures below 10°C/50°F in winter. *Water*: 2. Restrict water in winter. *Pruning*: Deadhead at regular intervals. Remove about one third of the flowering growth in early spring. *Propagation*: By seed which germinates easily. Make sure you provide a constant temperature of 21°C/70°F to get well grown plants.

W. caracasana. Caracas creeper, Caracas bigleaf. A semi-evergreen really large leafed climber to about 4m/13ft which throws out long shoots at the top. The leaves measure 45cm/18in by 38cm/15in wide and are mid-green on top and slightly felted underneath, covered with stinging hairs. Rich mauve flowers with a white tube, in terminal clusters, usually in June–July. Ideal for a small pergola in full sun where it provides good shade.

WISTERIA (*Leguminosae*)

Among the most beautiful climbers in the world but not without problems. Some are so vigorous they can pull a house down and have done so. In the Mediterranean, planting should be limited to the less vigorous species such as *W. floribunda*, *W. japonica* and *W. macrostachya*. *W. sinensis* which is always a bit of a gamble as to the eventual colour – I once waited six years for flowers which turned out to be dull grey-mauve – has the disadvantage of being far too vigorous. Never grow on wooden pergolas or supports since they will prove not strong enough. Try always to use a metal support. The pods and seeds of all wisterias are very poisonous. *Zone*: All but N. Mediterranean only. *Water*: 2 when young then 1. *Pruning*: Prune really hard back in late winter. It is also a good idea to shorten the leaf shoots in late summer. An old overgrown wisteria is difficult to deal with and ideally you should have someone knowledgeable to show you how to do it. *Propagation*: By layering shoots and severing them one year later.

W. floribunda. Origin: Japan. Deciduous, to over 10m/32ft with racemes of violet-blue flowers in June. Flowers open over a long period. *W. f. alba* is a white flowered form and needs a stone or dark background to look its best. *W. f.* 'Macrobotrys', probably the most dramatic, with racemes of rich lilac flowers often 1.5m/5ft long which look best grown on a high pergola.

W. × formosa. A very beautiful American hybrid which climbs to 10m/32ft, with light violet flowers 30cm/12in racemes in May/June. Very hardy.

W. japonica. Origin: Japan. White or cream flowers in 30cm/12in panicles in May.

W. macrostachya. Origin: United States. To a maximum of 10m/32ft but more usually around 7m/22ft with attractive 20–30cm/8–12in racemes of tiny lilac purple flowers in May.

YUCCA (*Agavaceae*)

Although yuccas will tolerate long periods of drought they look very much nicer with regular, widely spaced watering. However, if you are an absentee gardener it is pleasant to know that you can leave them for months at a time without water, come back, tidy them up, water them and have a totally different looking plant in a matter of two or three weeks. They all have dangerous spikes and should be planted away from frequented areas. Do not plant near anything that requires annual pruning or cleaning up. *Origin*: Mexico, S.E. United States. *Zone*: All. Unless mentioned most yuccas are hardy throughout the Mediterranean. With the exception of *Y. recurvifolia* they will all tolerate full sun. *Water*: 1. *Pruning*: None except to remove dead leaves. *Propagation*: By offsets or 5cm/2in root cuttings. Seeds are rarely viable as they require the intervention of a special moth which does not exist outside the Americas. *Pests and Diseases*: Agave weevil which, like nematodes, is difficult to eradicate. Do not plant susceptible plants where this pest has been a problem. Fungus diseases from wet weather or over-watering.

   Y. aloeifolia. Spanish bayonet. Has the sharpest spikes of all yuccas. Grows as a multi-trunked shrub to 3m/10ft with narrow bladed dark green leaves. Each head has one stalk of white lily type flowers in June. *Y. a. marginata* is a form with a yellow striped margin.

   Y. elata. This has a mass of thick grass like leaves at the base. In June the 3m/10ft flowering stalk has clusters of very white flowers.

   Y. filamentosa. Adam's needle. The most commonly grown is stemless with 60cm/2ft long 7.5cm/3in wide leaves. The edges are covered in thin filaments. White pendulous flowers in June. Wide, flat leaves tend to invite grafitti!

   Y. gloriosa. The most fragile of the yuccas – does not tolerate frost or south/west exposures in full sun. This is a multi trunked shrub which grows to 3m/10ft and is often sold as a small houseplant. It has a slightly palmate look and is attractive planted against house or garden walls. Palest blush pink flowers on rather short spikes. Not so prickly as most.

   Y. recurvifolia. This is a short pendulous yucca to about 2m/6ft. Thin blade like leaves bend over at about half their length. The flowers which appear in mid-summer are white on a 1.5m/5ft stalk. Prefers slight shade. *Y. r. marginata* is a form with yellow margins and *Y. r. variegata* has a yellow central stripe.

Yucca gloriosa

ZIZYPHUS (*Rhamnaceae*)

Useful evergreen and deciduous trees and shrubs for desert situations since they will tolerate extremes of heat, cold, drought, salt and alkaline conditions and still give deep green shade. *Origin*: E. Europe, Russia and N. China. *Zone*: All. *Water*: 1. *Pruning*: Can be clipped to shape – otherwise remove only dead or damaged wood. *Propagation*: By seed in late spring or by planting, during the rainy season, some of the many suckers. All zizyphus put down deep tap roots and are difficult to move once established. Looks good mixed with oleander, Jerusalem thorn and palms.

Z. jujuba. A very thorny shrub to about 10m/32ft with dark green leaves marked with white veins from the base. Light yellow flowers in early summer are followed by attractive russet berries which remain on the tree. There is a variety 'Inermis' which is thornless and well worth the slightly extra expense.

Z. spina-christi. A low growing shrub to about 3m/10ft which is very thorny and grows even more slowly than *Z. jujuba.* The berries are edible.

Index

Index

Index